The Limits of Human Nature

Essays based on a course of lectures
given at the Institute of Contemporary Arts, London

Edited with an introduction by Jonathan Benthall

ALLEN LANE

This book first published 1973

ISBN 0 7139 0598 0   cased edition

ISBN 0 7139 0668 5   paper edition

Printed in Great Britain by
Butler & Tanner Ltd, Frome and London

Editor's acknowledgements
The original idea for a project on these lines was suggested by Jonathan Miller of the I.C.A. Council. Thanks are also due to Philippa Scott, Diane Watts and Linda Lloyd Jones for their administrative services.

Contents

Acknowledgement for illustrations is made to the following people:
Dr Vernon Reynolds for plates 1–5; Professor Irenaus Eibl-Eibesfeldt
for plate 6; Dr Ewan Grant for plates 7–9; Radio Times Hulton Picture
Library for plate 10; Associated Press for plate 11; Donald McCullin
and the *Sunday Times Magazine* for plate 12; Dr Max Clowes for plates
13–15; Joseph Janni, the producer and John Schlesinger, the director,
for a still (plate 18) from the United Artists release *Sunday, Bloody
Sunday*; Dr Gerald Fisher for plate 19; Terry Winograd for plate 20.

Jonathan Benthall

Introduction

Each beast, each insect, happy in its own:
Is Heav'n unkind to man, and man alone?
Shall he alone, whom rational we call,
Be pleased with nothing, if not blessed with all?

> Alexander Pope, *An Essay on Man*, 1732

One knows, or one can know, the first point from where each of us departs to reach the common degree of understanding; but who is there who knows the other extreme? Everyone advances more or less according to his genius, his taste, his needs, his talents, his zeal, and the opportunities that he has to devote himself to them. I do not know of any philosopher who has yet been bold enough to say 'Here is the end which man can reach but which he can never pass.'

> Jean-Jacques Rousseau, *Émile*, 1762

Origins of this book

'The Limits of Human Nature' was the title of the Institute of Contemporary Arts' winter lecture-series for 1971–72, on which this book is based. In the prospectus, I explained the objects of the series:

The Limits of Human Nature aims to ask what are the irreducible foundations of human nature on which culture builds, and whether there are limits within which human nature develops or evolves.

The course will inquire:

in what sense it is meaningful to talk of 'constraints' or 'limits' on human nature

what limits have been defined in the past

what such limits could be suggested in the light of modern science

what are the ideological implications of differing theories about human nature.

Some of the lectures will be devoted to the straightforward presentation by authorities in their respective fields of scientific facts and theories with a bearing on 'human nature'. The remaining lectures will examine the problem from a yet broader interdisciplinary perspective. Even if science were to provide – which it does not – clear evidence as to what is irreducible human 'nature' and what is cultural artefact, the broad question would not be answered. The object is to gain insight by what might be called 'creative interference' between numerous disciplines . . . Integration of all the lectures will, we hope, be completed by the audience rather than the organizers.

No claim was made to cover the subject-matter comprehensively. Some disciplines with an important bearing on the topic – notably social anthropology, psychoanalysis and linguistics – were touched on only cursorily. On the other hand, we devoted two lectures each to two relatively new disciplines animal ethology (behaviour studies) and artificial intelligence research – which may offer new insights into the old problem of human nature, but which have both in the recent past suffered from the more sensational kind of popularization.

Some readers of this book may be disappointed that none of our contributors are preoccupied by the topic of Race; this is touched on by three contributors,[1] but the lack of emphasis on Race certainly corresponds to editorial policy, rather than to negligence.

General introductory remarks

I sit down to write this Introduction having just read the page proofs of the book. It is like writing an introduction to an Atlas whose pages had been jumbled, where one might find now a set of diagrams explaining the various systems of cartographic projection, now an analysis of the earth's geology, or a panoramic view of the solar system; now a facsimile of some illuminated medieval map, now a stern warning to the reader that maps are tools of economic exploitation.

But all these would indeed be features of a really complete Atlas, designed to encourage understanding rather than merely enable the reader to get from A to B. So, surely, a book that proposes to inquire into the Limits of Human Nature – where the information for a complete survey is missing – must give a taste of the wide diversity of mappings and speculations that this *terra incognita* has provoked.

There can be no more important topic than the specific qualities of man – even if we come to accept Robert M. Young's view that the topic needs 'demystifying'; for assumptions about such qualities underlie all cultural systems and all political positions, and hence bear strongly on many burning debates about society and politics. If any scholar lived today who had mastered all the ground covered in these fourteen essays, then indeed it might be preferable to read his linear exposition rather than to progress by the tacks and gybes that this book demands. But it is very unlikely that such a single scholar exists. We can only hope that the reader will feel exhilarated rather than sea-sick from the trajectory that is in store for him.

Before explaining the structure of the book, I shall offer one or two general suggestions about the richness and subtlety of the problem of Human Nature. The closing essay by Robert M. Young reflects back onto many of the earlier contributions as a challenging criticism. Indeed, he criticizes as ideologically loaded the I.C.A.'s very project of investigating theories of human nature (p. 238). Young's critique carries with it the weight of Marx himself, and of some important modern interpreters of Marx, whose views Young summarizes; indeed, it could be said to depend substantially on Marx.

Without questioning the validity of Young's arguments, it must be pointed out that the question 'What are the specific qualities of man?' was one asked and deliberated by Marx. It is true that Marx's conclusion was in effect that there are no limits on human nature, as the following quotation from his *Grundrisse* illustrates:

When the narrow bourgeois form has been peeled away, what is wealth, if not the universality of needs, capacities, enjoyments, productive powers etc. of individuals, produced in universal exchange? What, if not the full development of human control over the forces of nature – those of his own nature as well as those of so-called 'nature'? What, if not the absolute elaboration of his creative dispositions, without any preconditions other than antecedent historical evolution which makes the totality of this evolution – i.e. the evolution of all human powers as such unmeasured by any *previously established* yardstick – an end in itself? What is this, if not a situation where man does not reproduce himself in any determined form, but produces his totality?

Marx's view may be summed up more briefly as the view of man as *l'homme de l'homme* rather than *l'homme de la nature*.[2]

However, one of the symptoms of man's 'alienation' in capitalist society is (according to the early Marx) that he ceases to have consciousness of himself as a 'species being' (*Gattungswesen*), a being that is consciously aware of the species to which it belongs. Marx complicates this notion by asserting that man's unique specificity consists in its unique universality (as opposed to the limited partiality of all the other beings of nature).

It is a matter of controversy how far Marx discarded the notion of Alienation in his later work.[3] The older Marx was certainly more preoccupied with social institutions and power relations than with the question of man's specific nature. But no understanding of this uniquely influential thinker – for we live in a Marxian era in the same sense as we live in a Christian era – can be adequate, which ignores Marx's early interest in 'species being'.

Robert Young is right to warn us to be on our guard to see that political bias does not intrude into speculation about human 'universals', as they are sometimes called. But it does not follow that we should leave this field of speculation to people who have no such scruples. Should it ever be possible to define a formal restrictive patterning, transmitted by the genetic code, which structures human thought and learning, it certainly does not follow that such a discovery would be restricting in an ethical or cultural sense.

One French social anthropologist whose work I only came across after the I.C.A. series, Dan Sperber, specializes in the problem of human universals – in a discipline dominated at present by cultural relativism.[4] Sperber believes that so far we have no certain, detailed knowledge of any universals, except a few relatively unimportant behavioural examples such as the eyebrow-flash;[5] whereas it is theoretically possible to conceive of some genetic universals which are still latent, yet to be elicited by some level of technology that society has not yet reached. Sperber questions Lévi-Strauss's detailed formulations of the restrictive patterning inherent in human thought, but hails Lévi-Strauss's *project* as the true task of anthropology. This project is explored in the present book by Jean-Marie Benoist.

Structure of this book

The fourteen essays that make up this book have been grouped into three parts. Part One, 'Advocacy', consists of essays each of which aims primarily at arguing a case. Part Two 'Evidence', consists of essays which aim primarily at marshalling and analysing available data. Part Three, 'Criticism', consists of a single essay which questions the assumptions under which the previous essays were written, and the assumptions under which our project called The Limits of Human Nature was devised.

This structuring is a matter of emphasis. Obviously, advocates always summon evidence to support their case, just as all expert witnesses' presentation of data is coloured to some extent by personal convictions and assumptions. There are in fact many thematic interconnections between the essays, such as mechanical models for human behaviour, and man's relationship with the animals.

Alan Ryan was invited to open the series with his lucid discussion of Hobbes and Rousseau; for both philosophers have been very influential, and together they set most of the interesting problems inherent in the concept of 'human nature'.

Hobbes was a secular utilitarian, a materialist and a mechanist. Ryan shows how this view of human nature has triumphed since Hobbes's day, in fields as diverse as experimental psychology and strategic studies. He also distinguishes two possible roles for the state (Leviathan) that Hobbes seems to offer as alternatives. Rousseau, 'that ambivalent and alarming man' according to Ryan, inherited many of Hobbes's ideas but his intellectual descendants are quite different – ranging from existentialists to revisionist Marxists, though he rejected the idea of historical progress. Ryan summarizes some central concepts of Rousseau's which are often misunderstood.

From the 'clerk of Oxenford' to 'Frenssh of Parys'. **Jean-Marie Benoist** ambitiously maps onto each other the two, very different, transformational systems proposed as determining the human mind by the anthropologist Claude Lévi-Strauss and the grammarian Noam Chomsky. Benoist puts this in the context of what he sees as the central problem of Western metaphysics, the relationship of culture to nature; and ends by criticizing each master in turn for appearing to revert to an 'essentialized' notion of human nature. I shall not attempt here an inventory of the cornucopia of ideas that Benoist presents, but it is worth noting the continuity between Ryan's discussion of Rousseau and the use which Benoist makes of Rousseau to illuminate Lévi-Strauss's distrust of the myth of history.

Benoist's essay is called 'Classicism Revisited' because it argues that Lévi-Strauss recapitulates certain ruptures made by Rousseau with the conventional wisdom of his time, as Chomsky in his fight against empiricism and behaviourism recapitulates a comparable rupture made by Kant in epistemology. In his final pages, Benoist suggests that the concepts of 'structural mobile networks' of the mind introduced by Lévi-Strauss and Chomsky must be articulated with other current research – in biology and in psychoanalysis.

Next **Arthur Koestler,** the distinguished writer (author of at least one classic, *Darkness at Noon*), contributes a pungent reminder of the dismal record of our species in managing its situation in nature. He believes this is due to many limitations, such as the poverty of our sensory equipment. He rejects the view that man is fundamentally aggressive or driven by a 'territorial imperative'; rather, man is given to excessive devotion to groups, beliefs and slogans. Language, too, has been a source of immense disruption. He closes with some more speculative ideas about a paranoid streak in man attributable to an evolutionary misfit between the neocortex and the brain-stem.

Cornelius Ernst, O.P., contributes a perspective from Roman Catholic theology – a discipline which has given sustained and systematic attention to the problems under scrutiny in this book, even though its axioms are today accepted by a minority only. Father Ernst's essay is clearly a counter-current in this otherwise secular volume. However, several thematic links with other contributions may be found in his subtle exposition. For instance, we may relate Blake's challenge to the old hierarchic view of the cosmos, where man was God's viceroy over nature (Ernst, pp. 63 and 70), with Wilhelm Reich's challenge to the bourgeois family where the father represents societal authority (Young, p. 258). Again, the theological doctrine of the Fall – a 'disfigurement' of human nature – seems to reappear implicitly in much social and political theory since Rousseau and Blake, and can even be read into early Marx.

John Casey proposes an alternative to the scientific study of human nature, which he sees as fraught with philosophical problems. This alternative is to extend and enrich, without departing from, the concepts 'that man naturally uses in picturing to himself his own activities'. From the basic situation of the Embodied Mind, Casey builds up the concepts of will, intention, desire and emotion, and then the concepts of rationality and the virtues. He then argues that it is meaningless to speak of animals as having virtues (for instance, being brave) since they are incapable of language and hence of reason, motive and choice. Casey sketches two important possible conclusions. First, he defends the traditional concept of the virtues as part of an 'unchanging human nature': the picture of the good man cannot change, whatever the moral and ideological fashions of the times. Second, it would follow that it is difficult to imagine human nature being different from what it is, and that it is impossible to *desire* such a change. Casey's essay is impressive as a theoretical analysis which deliberately excludes the social dimension, in a strategy that recalls Rousseau's.

A very different view is articulated by **David Bohm,** a theoretical physicist who has also worked on problems of language and thought. He has written elsewhere that 'all is art', because 'art' means simply making thought and language fit with perception. Bohm argues that man has always developed mental models of what the human being is or ought to be. We must now try and eliminate *all* mental models about human nature, by means of a thoroughgoing change in the processes of thought and language (which Casey would no doubt regard as inconceivable).

According to Bohm, models are desirable in other domains of human activity but not where the self is concerned. We must learn to pay attention to the 'universal formative movement' of life as a whole. His essay is followed by a résumé of the discussion that followed his original I.C.A. lecture; this gives him an opportunity to answer objections and clarify some misconceptions about his proposals.

The last essay in Part One is by **Raymond Williams** on Social Darwinism, that is, the application of evolutionary theory to social theory. This in fact might well have been paired with Robert M. Young's essay, since both writers approach the history of ideas from a committed socialist angle. Social Darwinism provides a classic case-study of the interaction between the natural sciences and society. The author of *Culture and Society* is uniquely equipped to lead us through this chapter in the history of ideas.

Part Two, 'Evidence', is more homogeneous in method. **John Maynard Smith** points out that geneticists use 'nature' in a technical sense, as opposed to 'nurture'. The genetic 'nature' of an individual once conceived cannot be changed, by definition. But can the frequency in the human population of individuals of different genetic constitutions be changed? His essay addresses this problem.

A pair of essays on ethology follows. **Vernon Reynolds,** without belittling the capacities such as symbolic thought and concept formation which are specific to man, thinks that we should also consider the capacities which we share with other species of primates, and offers a broad summary of the ethological evidence – including studies of postures, gestures and facial expressions, and relationships both friendly and hostile. He considers the period during which the genus *Homo* evolved, and argues that the few surviving 'hunter-gatherer' societies – though differing enormously in language, morality, technology and cosmology – are remarkably similar to one another in social organization, so that we may speak of this kind of social organization with some justification as being 'natural' to man. Reynolds goes on to describe some recent research in human ethology by Edward T. Hall, Eibl-Eibesfeldt and others. (Some of this ground has since been covered in the subsequent I.C.A. lecture-series, *The Body as a Medium of Expression*.)[6]

Michael Chance chooses a more specialized branch of animal ethology: forms of group cohesion among the higher primates. He distinguishes two modes of group cohesion: the *hedonic mode* based on 'display' as a means of gaining attention (hooting, waving sticks, kissing, etc.), and the *agonistic mode*, based on conflict and avoidance of attack from the dominant male. The hedonic mode characterizes chimpanzee and gorilla societies; the agonistic mode, macaque and baboon societies. In some species, an individual seems to be capable of both modes of behaviour. Dr Chance proposes more speculatively that these models can be applied to human non-verbal behaviour.

Liam Hudson concurs with some other contributors that we know very little about human limits in the sense of intellectual constraints. He criticizes much psychological and sociological research in this field for setting itself the wrong problems (for instance, mental measurement) which often bear a heavy ideological load before experimenting and testing have even begun (here Hudson's position links up with Young's).

The study of intelligence should focus on intelligence as it exists around us, which is closely tied to the emotions. Hudson closes by outlining some current research programmes he is involved with.

A pair of essays on Artificial Intelligence concludes Part Two.

Max Clowes starts by pointing out that though mechanistic models of man are accepted in most other branches of natural science bearing on human life, they are not yet accepted by our culture as far as human problem-solving is concerned. This is partly because our culture has an 'impoverished concept of mechanism', and partly because so many actual attempts to model intelligent behaviour mechanically are plainly crude. He reviews some recent research in Artificial Intelligence which may help towards genuine understanding of the mind; especially *scene analysis programmes* (which have now superseded pattern recognition techniques). Clowes explains the main weaknesses in current mathematical formalisms of visual perception (for instance, the immensely varied prior knowledge we have of the visible world), but he is confident enough in the future of Artificial Intelligence to add some final words on its social implications.

Terry Winograd is a leading critic of Chomsky (who maintains that human language can never be satisfactorily modelled by computational linguistics). Winograd attempts to give the lay reader some feeling for new ways in which the computer can get us to think about the dynamic interaction of language processes. In the 1950s, vast efforts were spent on the problems of 'automatic translation', which were abandoned some ten years ago. The reason for their failure was that syntax and meaning were handled by separate programmes. Winograd's new approach is to integrate syntax, semantics and also learnt information about the immediate situation that the system is 'modelling'. This is the same concept of *heterarchy* that Clowes uses – the facility for independent parts of a programme to communicate in a variety of ways.

The gist of **Robert M. Young's** contribution, which forms Part Three, has already been outlined at the start of this Introduction. His essay should, I believe, be taken very seriously by anyone involved in the 'human sciences' or in social theory.

1 Williams, p. 122; Maynard Smith, pp. 134–5; Hudson, pp. 176–82, 190–1.
2 The phrase *l'homme de l'homme* is borrowed from Jean Starobinski's introduction to Rousseau's *Discourse on the Origin of Inequality* (a work referred
  to in this book by both Ryan and Benoist) in Rousseau, *Œuvres complètes*,
  vol. iii, Bibliothèque de la Pléïade, Gallimard, Paris, 1964.
3 This discussion is indebted to István Mészáros, *Marx's Theory of Alienation*
  (Merlin Press, 1970), pp. 13 and 80–2. Louis Althusser is the best-known
  exponent of the view that in about 1845 Marx broke radically with any
  theories that would base history and politics on a view of 'human nature'
  (*Pour Marx*, Maspéro, Paris, 1965; English translation *For Marx*, Allen
  Lane The Penguin Press, 1970). The world of Marxian studies is split on
  this point.
4 Dan Sperber, 'Contre certains a priori anthropologiques', in *L'Unité de
  l'Homme*, proceedings of Royaumont symposium on 'Biological invariants
  and cultural universals', edited by Edgar Morin and Massimo Piattelli-
  Palmarini (Éditions du Seuil, Paris, 1973).
5 See in this book Reynolds, pp. 150–2 and Plate 10.
6 Jonathan Benthall and Ted Polhemus (ed.), *The Body as a Medium of
  Expression* (Allen Lane and Dutton, in press).

Part One

Advocacy

Alan Ryan

1 The Nature of Human Nature in Hobbes and Rousseau

Our images of human nature are centrally important ideological phenomena, for the evident reason that what distinguishes an ideology from a merely random string of moral and political imperatives is the way it incorporates the validating assumptions of those imperatives. The assumption that these imperatives – whether taken for granted, defended desperately, or pressed for the first time – have their roots in 'human nature' is one main condition of their very intelligibility. Philosophical theories of ethics which have analysed their subject-matter in formal, non-naturalistic terms – Kant's *Groundwork*[1] or Hare's *The Language of Morals*,[2] for instance – are unsatisfactory just because they cut themselves off from recognizable answers to the question: what is the *point* of acting in such and such a way? But if any viable ideological position implies the *possession* of an image of human nature, this is far from suggesting that most cultures have felt any great need to *articulate* that image. Indeed, it is arguable that this possession like many others is only noticed when it is lost. A society where the going rules are universally accepted, where conflicts of interest do not appear to be intense or deep, may well get along in the belief that how men ought to behave there is how men ought to *behave*, because how men are there is how they *are*. Whether there are many, or any, such societies is unclear; the old sociological image of 'primitive society' may simply be a myth which tells us less about the moral orderliness of savages than it does about the anxieties of our own social theorists. At any rate, what is clear is that an account of human nature is intrinsic to moral and political argument, and the need for an explicit account is the more urgent when moral and political argument becomes fiercer and gets more swiftly down to basics. Thus the discovery by the Greeks that their way of life was so different from that of many of their neighbours provoked at once the question of how convention was, or was not, rooted in nature. Was there one justice, as fire burned in Athens and Persia alike; or was there nothing coherent to be said about the relative merits of different social arrangements?

The question to which students of human nature inevitably address themselves is: what are men *really* like? And it is important to stress that 'really', since it is at the heart of all sorts of problems. If we were to ask what men are like, we might invite a mere catalogue – men here have such and such beliefs, men there have such and such other beliefs. The tricky word 'really' tells us that this won't do. When we add 'really' we always mean to rule out some possible deceptive factor – is she really a blonde or does she dye her hair; is that really a Great Dane, or will it turn out to be a rug when I put my spectacles on? Now, we have to ask what 'really' rules out when it appears in this context. What kind of tampering or deception are we ruling out? Plainly the tampering is that stemming from social conventions, moral, religious or political brainwashing. The point of asking what human nature is like is to see through – or behind – what men locally believe, want, approve, and abhor, to uncover the substratum beneath man as he locally appears. But this presents us with a problem to which no wholly compelling answer has been given, certainly a problem which Hobbes and Rousseau set for us rather than solve. Men always live in society; so far as we can see, all the more complex forms of behaviour which we regard as characteristically human are ones we learn slowly through social interaction. But if our evidence of human capacities comes from socialized man, what can we infer about non-socialized man's resources for good and evil? Even to ask the question shows up more problems. It is, in the first place, not clear that anyone does want to know what men would as a matter of fact be like without socialization. Rousseau explicitly denied that this was his concern, and neither he nor Hobbes would have gained much moral purchase from the occasional feral child. In the second place, if we hope to get at human nature by 'stripping away' the effects of socialization, it looks as if we must already know what the effects of social life are. To then explain the effects of social life by reference to an under-lying human nature looks very like arguing in a circle. No wonder, then, that practically the first remark that Rousseau makes is *'écartons donc les faits'*; the concept of human nature is confessedly a theoretical construction. All the same, it is worth making one methodological point here; up to this point, nothing said about the difficulties of getting at human nature implies that these are different in kind from those involved in getting at the nature of non-human objects. To the seventeenth-century scientist – and to John Locke – a knowledge of the nature of lead was beyond us; for all we know of lead is what happens to samples of lead in various experimental situations – just as all we know of men is what happens to samples of humanity in those experiments which we call society. But a sufficiently dashing scientist would not stop here; he could reply that he had a good deal of elaborate chemical and physical theory about the internal structure and organization of lead, such that he was justified in believing that he knew the nature of lead, and knew why samples behaved as they did in experiments. No doubt the internal organization of men is imperfectly understood, and no doubt the variety of effects which environment exerts on that structure is far beyond our present knowledge. But there is, in principle, no more reason to despair of knowing the nature of man than there is to despair of knowing the nature of lead.

Such, anyway, would have had to be the reply of Thomas Hobbes (1588–1679), and there have been no more dashing or ambitious figures in English philosophy. The very blandness with which he announces that all the conclusions of *Leviathan* save the pre-excellence of monarchy are demonstrative truths is immensely appealing in view of the shock and outrage which those conclusions created. For a man who prided himself on his caution, even cowardice, in political matters, he was extraordinarily brave in intellectual fields. The ideological collapse which provoked Hobbes's response was, of course, an overt and very far-reaching one, and Hobbes was an acute observer of its near and remote causes. The disorder Hobbes most minded was literal civil war, the collapse of law and order. The source of disorder was men's inability to agree about the status and grounds of the rules which ought to maintain the legal and political system. Two particular causes of these disagreements were, in the first place, the conflict between the defenders of the traditional common law, who held, with Coke, that the fundamental rules were traditional, built-in, not open to change by royal say-so, and the defenders of royal prerogative, who held that law was what the sovereign said it was; and, in the second place, the multitude of religious prophets who preached doctrines of individual illumination which were in implication anarchic in the extreme. Now, it is easy to make two related errors about Hobbes's work. The first is to detach it too completely from its time – for Quentin Skinner[3] has certainly shown that *Leviathan* had immediate political implications which were perceived by Hobbes's contemporaries. They knew that his equation of *de facto* and *de jure* authority implied a duty to swear allegiance to the new Commonwealth. But the second error is to underestimate the oddity and originality of Hobbes's arguments in this context. He saw more plainly than his contemporaries that an entire picture of the natural order had been dealt a mortal blow. The old Christian-cum-Aristotelian metaphysics was simply played out; the usual inquiries about man's place in the natural hierarchy were therefore nonsensical. Attempts at a rational inquest into the good life for man as laid down by Nature or God were old-fashioned scholastic junk. To understand nature, human nature, and the imperatives of social life, it was essential to throw out this meaningless rubbish and begin on scientific foundations. No account which sees Hobbes as other than a secular, materialistic utilitarian is an account of Hobbes at all, which is why Leo Strauss's[4] attempt to present Hobbes's science as a mere tarting-up of old-fashioned conceptions of the state as a remedy for sin just misses the point. So equally do more recent attempts to present Hobbes's political system as a derivation from Christian theology.[5] Hobbes's own contemporaries knew better than more recent commentators: orthodox supporters of royal prerogative knew that this secular, calculating politics was a creed quite unlike a belief in the divinity of kings.

Hobbes's science of human nature is part of Hobbes's science of nature in general – a fact which instantly puts Hobbes on the 'hard' side of today's debates about the status of the human sciences. Hobbes's science of nature is the science of bodies in motion; what he is committed to is a universe in which there is nothing in the world except matter in motion. Hobbes's psychology is in principle reducible to physiology, and ultimately to physics. Again, this puts Hobbes into some thriving contemporary company – that of those philosophers who call themselves 'identity theorists' or 'central state materialists', on the strength of identifying psychological and physiological processes as the *same* processes. A good deal of (not very successful) ingenuity is devoted by Hobbes to trying to account for, e.g., memory in terms of 'interior motions': if present perception involves 'phantasms' caused by the physical interaction of the internal motions of our brains and the corpuscular emanations of bodies external to us, then memory is a weakened 'phantasm'. Which ignores all sorts of difficulties, the most obvious of which is that my now remembering having read a book last week is nothing like my now reading a book – either a neat or a dilute version of that event. Hobbes's physical analysis of human activity would no doubt have been more persuasive had his experience of 'machines' extended beyond the clocks and watches which were the common basis of seventeenth-century corpuscularian analogies and on to that twentieth-century source of analogy, the computer. Certainly what Hobbes wanted to tell the world was that human beings are self-regulating and self-maintaining mechanisms. That he was faced with the intractable difficulties we, too, face in explaining the 'emergent' properties of self-maintaining physical systems is only one more of the things he shares with us.

It is a consequence of Hobbes's mechanistic approach that he presents men as having two crucial properties. Firstly, their actions are wholly determined. There is no such thing as free-will; men are free in just the same sense that anything else in the world is free, and no more so. A stream runs downhill freely when nothing impedes its progress – though that progress is certainly caused. A man acts freely when there is no external impediment to his actions, but those actions have determinate causes. What men call the will is simply the last appetite in deliberation; willing is in no sense a voluntary act, as the nonsense of saying 'I will to will ...' shows. As we shall see, there are a good many hidden problems here. The second crucial quality is human selfishness. Not only are our actions determined, they are determined by our desire to maximize our own pleasure. The successful maintenance of the human organism is accompanied by pleasure – pleasure is, so to speak, the way that the maximization of vital motions appears to us, just as 'phantasms' are the way our sensory interactions with the external world appear to us. Thus, the self-maintaining mechanism pursues the maximum of pleasure for itself. Hobbes was quite aware that the assertion that we always try to pursue our own pleasure is fraught with danger. A friend saw him giving alms to a beggar, and raised the obvious question of how a believer in selfishness could act in this seemingly altruistic way. Hobbes's reply – absolutely correct in terms of his theory – was that the beggar's distress caused him distress and by relieving the beggar he relieved himself.[6] But the reply itself creates another puzzle, for it reveals an ambiguity in the concept of pleasure. If it is a necessary truth that every action is done to maximize the apparent pleasure of the actor, then it is certainly not necessarily true that men are selfish or pleasure-seeking in the usual sense of the terms. It is not true that the benevolent man is 'really selfish'; rather, the reason why we call him benevolent is that his gaining pleasure depends upon the pleasure of others. The difficulty for Hobbes is that if it is only in this rather formal sense that men are pleasure-seeking or selfish, this in itself offers no reason for thinking that they will be selfish in the usual sense. But only if they are selfish in the usual sense will they get themselves into the kind of trouble which Hobbes's state of nature describes, and out of which the Leviathan is supposed to rescue them.

Self-maintenance is clearly the major imperative facing the Hobbesian man. The organism is so to speak programmed to keep itself in existence. So clear is this to Hobbes that he regards suicide as proof of madness; and this imperative underlines his claim that the one thing we cannot promise to do is destroy ourselves even if our absolute ruler requires us to, for nothing would count as a genuine promise to do so, so contrary is it to our basic nature. Equally importantly, it explains Hobbes's claim, made in opposition to the Aristotelian tradition, that there is *no* natural *summum bonum* for men, although there is a *summum malum*. The open-ended imperative to survive means that we must do what looks like the survival-enhancing thing on each occasion. Felicity in this life is not attained in a condition of happy and tranquil rest, for all life is incessant motion and incessant change of desire; felicity can consist only in achieving the objects of our different desires one after another. But the absence of vital motion is an absolute evil; death, the cessation of all desire and activity, is the *summum malum*. Hence Hobbes's assumption that the great evil of ineffective government is the way it exposes us all to the danger of violent death; hence, too, his belief that it is our common interest in avoiding such risks that provides the securest foundation for the power of Leviathan.

Before leaving Hobbes's premisses about human nature for his conclusions about the plight it gets us into, it is worth summarizing the legacy he has left us. His belief that explanation in terms of matter in motion – mechanical, causal explanation – is the only satisfactory kind of explanation has been triumphant since his day. During this century, the goal of tough-minded scientists has been to reduce the psychological vocabulary of desire, purpose, intention, to something more akin to the austere vocabulary of mechanics. The efforts of psychologists of the persuasion of Hull or Watson has to a large extent been directed to the Hobbesian programme, though in a more empirical and inductive way, and one that is more cautious in hypothesizing interior mechanisms.[7] Crucially for our comparison, it is the suspicion of talk about mental entities which carries across the centuries, the fear that talk about the contents of consciousness verges on mysticism. Conversely, the problems which Hobbes found intractable remain intractable today for the same reason. Hobbes, for example, tries to graft an account of the conventional meaning of words on to a causal foundation in terms of words provoking ideas – a sort of stimulus–response backing. But he cannot manage it with any ease; to raise merely one problem, logical symbols such as 'if . . . then . . .' are utterly recalcitrant to a name–object analysis. And attempts to resolve the problem invariably wind up in circularity, since the only way of identifying the appropriate response to the word-stimulus depends on already knowing the meaning of the word which the response is meant to explain. Who, after reading Noam Chomsky's devastating attacks on B. F. Skinner's view of language, would not agree that Hobbes's difficulties are alive and unsolved and living in Harvard?[8] Again, all the phenomena of self-consciousness – except, perhaps, anxiety about the open future – receive a rough analysis from Hobbes. Is the process of trying to make up our minds only a matter of overhearing the decision-making machinery hunting through its routines – the conflict of one good reason with another a matter of the ebb and flow of motions until a decisive shift is made? Do we stand as spectators in our own bodies, such that what seems phenomeno-logically to be a choice is no more than a spasm when the machinery settles down? Like his successors in this tradition,

Hobbes found it hard to explain consciousness without thereby explaining it away.

The condition of hypothesized selfish, rational man is familiar today from another contemporary hypothetical science – strategic studies. Our natural condition is one of merciless competition. For rational, selfish creatures, competition has three sources – scarcity, fear and pride (or vainglory). Scarcity hardly needs elaboration, but the other two causes do. The effects of fear are, again, the commonplaces of deterrence theory. In a condition where there is no power sufficient to overawe us all – which is, by definition, the condition we are in without government – we know that another man can, by brute force, or by guile, do us any injury up to and including death. The ability to kill one another is the one basic equality which Hobbes assumes, and it gives us all an approximate equality of vulnerability. It also gives us all a powerful motive to strike first rather than be struck against. I know that any of my fellows sees me as a threat; he knows that my only certain defence against him is to eliminate him before he can eliminate me; he knows, too, that I know this, that I have, therefore, every reason to strike at once, and that knowledge gives him every reason to beat me to it. Where each of us has a lethal first-strike capacity, and none of us has any second-strike capacity at all, the strategic logic necessarily leads to a war of all against all – individually, it is irrational to forgo the pre-emptive strike, but individual rationality leads to destruction for all. This is not to say that men have any intrinsic lust for conquest, desire to dominate their fellows, or the like. That men seek restlessly for power after power throughout their lives is a result of their insecurity. Men, unlike animals, can fear tomorrow as much as today. We cannot enjoy the goods we have at the present moment, unless we have some certainty that we can enjoy them in future, and this means we must have some way of protecting them. But the demands of power are inexorable, for we must always protect the position from which we protect our goods – to eat the apple we grab the tree, to defend the tree we build a fence, to protect the fence we dig a ditch and so endlessly on. But as if this were not enough, Hobbes endows man with an urge to emulate, to outrun his fellows. Not that Hobbes moralizes about pride; he merely asserts that since men can recognize other men as essentially like themselves, they begin to compare their own success with that of other men, and having done so become dissatisfied with any position other than the best. We do not merely wish to survive, we wish to survive better than anyone else. And this introduces a kind of scarcity which nothing can cure, and a kind of competition to which there can be no end. Where we are all intent on occupying first place, and the evidence that it *is* the first place is the envy of the defeated, there is no possible way to create enough goods to go round. The state of nature is thus overdetermined.

Recent writers on deterrence have argued that the war of all against all can be averted by the creation of second-strike capacity. The urge to launch a pre-emptive strike disappears when it is obvious that it will only bring lethal retaliation in its train. In the nuclear field, doomsday machines or a belief in the human urge for revenge are enough to create the plausible threat. For Hobbes's system it is the Leviathan who provides second-strike capacity; if you murder me, I certainly cannot kill you in reply, but the state can, and this knowledge ought to powerfully reduce your enthusiasm for making the first move. In short, Hobbes applies the logic of the games theorist to human nature, and much like Rapaport[9] arguing that rational egoists will get into an irrational mess, Hobbes shows us that the state of nature is a state of universal war. And like his successors, Hobbes argues that some enforceable system must be found whereby it is made the interest of every party to pursue the common interest in peace.

But what does the Leviathan do when he creates order in this chaos? I have argued all along that the point of inquiring into human nature is to inquire into the underlying reasons why social order is both necessary and possible; it must also be to show what *kind* of order is required. And here Hobbes seems to offer two responses, which are worth distinguishing rather sharply. On one view, the sovereign creates a minimal order of peace and security. Men may do whatever they wish, within the limits of keeping the peace. The sovereign certainly judges, for example, what religious views may be put forward – but he does not judge their *truth*; all he does is ensure that ceremonies of praise and honour to a deity are agreed on and cause no dissension. Religion, as Hobbes insists, is law not philosophy – conventions, not truth. What men choose to believe in the privacy of their hearts concerning such contentious matters as the origin of the world is their own business. In other words, there is no legal limit on the sovereign's authority, and no theoretical limit on what he may find it necessary to regulate. But men being what they are, an effective government can be a very *laissez-faire* one. Much of what Hobbes says supports this view. It accords well with his jokes against original sin and his dislike of interfering clerical authority. And this side of Hobbes suggests that the association between liberalism and secular utilitarianism is more than a historical accident.

Yet there is another side to the story, less obvious, but well brought out in Professor Watkins's *Hobbes's System of Ideas*. On this view, the Leviathan is more than a mere contractual arrangement. It is, as Hobbes says, a real and perfect unity of them all. We become literally one body – though an artificial body, none the less a real one. The famous frontispiece to the first edition of *Leviathan* is to be taken quite literally. Now what this suggests is a much more radical jump from pre-political man to political man. The state is to take each of us and so mould us that we become elements of it. Yet the way in which this is to occur is not through coercion, but through teaching us the language of civility, a vocabulary in which treason becomes unsayable, hence unthinkable. Since the Leviathan is, although a body, a body whose sinews are conventions, its parts – the citizens – must have as little choice about keeping these conventions as have things in the natural world about obeying the laws governing them. Hence Hobbes makes it a primary task of the sovereign to lay down rules by which acts are to be named and judged. Common rules of right and wrong are to be established, and Hobbes appears to envisage these as being so established that it will appear self-contradictory to question them. The simplest example is Hobbes's claim that what the sovereign does is by definition just – 'just' means here 'in accordance with the sovereign's commands' – so that nobody can think himself unjustly treated by the sovereign. This is a profoundly totalitarian image, and one which speaks to our contemporary terrors. Orwell's 'newspeak' and Godard's dictionary-eating computer in *Alphaville* are powerful images of the ways in which vocabulary may shape the political possibilities. But Hobbes's state is still light-years away from the horrors of the twentieth-century totalitarian state. His successors in our century are fictional ones – the rulers of *Brave New World* and the planners of *Walden Two*. But the only moral which I want to draw is that – as the preceding account of a more liberal Hobbes shows – utilitarian, manipulative accounts of human nature are not *bound* to lead in this direction. The revolt against recent applications of a certain kind of Benthamite rationalism which several writers have documented – none more soberly or clearly than Stuart Hampshire[10] – is a revolt against possible rather than inevitable applications. But what is true is that once we have, with Hobbes, taken up this secular, mechanical, naturalistic approach to human nature, we are left with no absolutely forbidden actions, no intrinsically wicked behaviour. The limits of politics, even when pursued by the undeniably benevolent, are set by psychological technology rather than independent standards of human dignity or the like.

But if human nature is so manipulable, one of the functions of the notion of human nature is much impaired, for it plays a much-reduced role in setting a limit to political possibility. Unless something substantial, basic and important survives the process of socialization, and remains intact behind the social appearances, we are unable to say anything very profound about how well or how ill social arrangements satisfy human needs and aspirations. Hobbes begins by setting up social arrangements to cater for human needs, but ends by teaching us how to remake human beings to fit social arrangements. Certainly the friendly relativism of a lot of sociology owes what respectability it possesses to a similar emancipation of the social sciences from their psychological basis. Societies create their own raw material; they can therefore be coherent or incoherent in the way that they do it; if they are too incoherent, then they will grind to a standstill, but as between two equally coherent societies there seems nothing to choose – neither would satisfy the 'human nature' created in the other, but each satisfies the 'nature' it creates. But there is no question of a society coherently violating human nature. The suspicion that appeals to human nature were politically ineffectual in just this way was one of the many doubts that tormented Rousseau. I do not want to embroil us in a blow-by-blow account of the similarities and divergences between Hobbes and Rousseau, but I do want to show how this suspicion fits into a use of the concept of nature which is different from Hobbes's in important ways. If Hobbes's descendants are the 'tough-minded' behaviourists, then Rousseau's are a ragged collection ranging from revisionist Marxists through to the existentialists and beyond.

The disorder to which Rousseau responded most keenly was

psychological disorder. It was the chaotic condition of the individual self which distressed him, and although he insisted that this condition had social causes and social consequences, it was the fusion of the personal and the political which unified his essays, his novel, his autobiography. He described the disorder he saw as alienation: '*l'homme est devenu hors de lui-même*'. Men cannot live within themselves, they are not self-sufficient, either singly or together. This was both the cause and the effect of inequality and injustice. But where Hobbes is willing to accept the world's account of who wins and who loses in the social race, Rousseau says that everyone loses. One man thinks himself the master of many and yet remains a greater slave than they. Competition breeds greed, envy, servility, false conceit and false humility. It forces men to perform for the sake of public approval, and where they cannot or will not, it forces them to retire into themselves, to dream of revenge and pre-eminence founded on fear. Rousseau was a great admirer of his own talents as a painter of the human heart, and he excels himself at the end of the *Discourse on Inequality* with a description of the lonely crowd which encapsulates an entire tradition, pre-echoing Hegel and Freud, and looking back to Plato's account of the self-enslaving tyrant in Book x of the *Republic*.

But how had men got into this condition, where had they taken a wrong turning, and could they have done better? Rousseau provides no one answer, and his hopes for improving the human condition are minimal. But there are some illuminating suggestions. In the *Discourse* Rousseau claims that men without society must be mere isolated animals. For him natural man is *not* the noble savage, nor is he Hobbes's rational egoist. Both these conditions are social conditions and in an important sense non-natural. As an animal, man is neither moral nor immoral, but amoral; his conduct cannot sensibly be judged by moral standards, any more than that of animals can be. Such 'natural goodness' as man does possess, he possesses only in potentiality – and this potentiality is by no means certain to be realized. As an animal, natural man shares with animals an advantage denied to social, truly human, man. He is lacking in any sort of self-consciousness, and therefore he is lacking in any kind of anxiety. Animals are afraid in the presence of a terrifying thing which provokes their fear, but the haunting fear of extinction which pervades human life, the factitious anxieties about how we look in the eyes of others – these are fears the animal knows nothing of. That these anxieties are a central element in the *human* condition and are importantly non-natural is, of course, one respect in which Rousseau anticipates the central commonplaces of existentialism. But human nature contains seeds of a total transformation which animals cannot undergo – we alone are so educable that we change individually over an entire lifetime, and so adept at transmitting what we have learned that as a species we change as drastically. An animal is the same after a few months as during its whole life; the species is the same at the end of a thousand years as at the beginning. Only human beings can properly be said to have a history; but once we enter history, our former nature is irretrievably lost, and knowledge of it merely hypothetical. This capacity for indefinite transformation Rousseau terms *perfectibilité*, but it is by no means a capacity to make ourselves perfect – indeed, its chief effect is to put us quite at odds with ourselves. Our 'natural' condition, in the sense of our existence as mere isolated animals, is not an elevated condition – we eat, sleep, copulate at random and fight at necessity – but it is one where desires and their satisfaction are matched to one another. Dissatisfaction has not yet entered the world. And this matching of desire and attainment gives the state of nature a moral quality for Rousseau,[11] though not that of prescribing how we should behave in society. It is rather as an image of harmony, the opposite of the restless striving competitiveness of civilization, that it finds its moral role; but the critic with an ear attuned to Rousseau's pessimism catches the implication that such harmony is possible only where everything that is distinctively human – speech, self-consciousness, individual and social aspiration – is absent.

The arrival of language and society drastically transform the situation; they make morality possible – but they also make men depraved. '*L'homme qui pense est un animal méchant.*' The raw animal material of morality was the twin sentiments of self-love and sympathy; we shun by an instinctive reaction both pain to ourselves and pain to our fellows. The arrival of reason transforms these into principled benevolence and a proper, conscientious self-respect. We recognize other men as *entitled* to correct treatment, and we *claim* it from them in return. We also, more alarmingly, become able to grade men for their qualities, to rank them as

more and less estimable. And we can therefore desire to be
esteemed ourselves. At this point someone emerges who closely
resembles Hobbes's natural man – proud, selfish, competitive.
Rousseau draws attention to the fact, and goes on to draw
Hobbes's conclusion that this will be the prelude to the war of all
against all. But he is at pains to point out that the state of war
exists only *within* society and as a consequence of social dealings.
This claim is not, of course, a straightforwardly historical or
sociological one. Rather, it is a way of denying Hobbes's comparatively cheerful assumption that if this is how men are, then we had
better construct a social order which will accommodate them
without bloodshed. The perpetual motion of Hobbesian man
is not a neutral phenomenon, but a disease to be cured. And
Rousseau's concern for the damage done by the universal competition is not limited to fearing that we shall make war on one
another, that the fist, the knife or the gun will replace the market.
It is not the danger that we shall damage one another which agi-
tates Rousseau, it is the certainty that we are damaging ourselves.

Civilization is a condition in which we lose touch with ourselves.
We put on masks, we play particular social roles as if we were
actors in the theatre, or even puppets on a string. Rousseau was
fascinated and repelled by the theatre – it was both an allegory of
the falseness of social life and a celebration of that falseness. The
more society develops, the more elaborate its games become, then
the greater the temptations which beset the man who tries to be
himself, and to live within himself. Social distinctions are, of
course, merely conventional – but none the less real. It was quite
impossible for Rousseau to address his aristocratic patrons as if
they were his equals, just as it was impossible for him to pretend
that he thought their disparity in rank based on a like disparity
in merit. Once the conventions are set, they are as much an objective part of the world as anything else is. And if they give us no
chance to build up a liveable-with character, that, too, is a fact
about the nature of civilization. What haunted Rousseau was the
fear that there might be no real self behind the several masks we
wear; this emerges even in his *Confessions*, where he both promises
to reveal everything about himself and yet produces such a
variety of disparate revelations that we can only suppose that
even he was unable to find one single coherent story about a
single coherent self.

But where, we might ask, does Rousseau go from here? What escape is there, and how does the knowledge of human nature help? One thing only is certain, that he found the *status quo* quite intolerable. Moreover, he had enough of a sense of history to feel that our situation had to be explained genetically, that the present is unintelligible until related to its origins in the past. Unlike his historicist successors Hegel and Marx, he had no faith that the process would ultimately reveal itself as benign. The obvious similarities between his ideas and theirs make it the more necessary to insist on this difference – as Marshall Berman's otherwise excellent book[12] fails to do. But if there is no optimism about the benefits of history, there is no assumption that we can simply go back on our tracks. If the present is intolerable, the condition of natural man no longer charms us; and even Rousseau agrees that a refusal to embark on human history at all is no answer to the question of how to be both human and happy. Not that natural man is unimportant as a critic of civilized society – the mindless paradise of Adam and Eve testifies to the vitality of the image. But the pre-social state is not offered as a utopia to which we might aspire. And the simple lives which Rousseau does praise are at most *nearer* nature, and they are not exactly paradise either. The Caribs of the *Discourse* are already corrupted by vanity, they are cruel too; the shepherds of the Haut Valais are more attractive, but even they are clumsy and ignorant by the standards of civilization.

The question remains whether the things that are lacking in the simple life really are losses – are they goods which we have bought at too high a price, or are they not really goods anyway? It seems to me that Rousseau's answer is the former. Certainly it is more than mere rhetoric when Rousseau claims that the simple life is better than the life of Paris; but the *situation* is not simple. Maybe we are the better for suppressing our literary talents, but we are also the poorer; these are genuinely human talents we have suppressed. Harmony would involve the blending of our many and diverse skills; all we ever seem to achieve is discord; therefore we would do better to settle for unison. Still, all this is in a sense beside the point; for Rousseau's major claim is that even if we saw that the simple life was the better life, *we* could not choose it. Rousseau's propagandist motives are infinitely less direct than were Hobbes's. We would die of boredom in the Haut Valais and of disgust among the Caribs. And Judith Shklar[13] is more than persuasive when she claims that Rousseau's utopias set no positive goals – that they serve to point out the irremediably rotten condition of this society, not a perfection to be found in some other.

That the simple life of this kind is not intended by Rousseau to be a picture of the good life is suggested too by the most famous of all Rousseau's works, the *Social Contract*. For there Rousseau contrasts the condition of natural man with the condition of the man who is both free and virtuous – indeed, free only because he is virtuous. The life of impulse is a form of slavery, but obeying laws which we prescribe for ourselves is freedom. All this shows up one further important aspect of Rousseau's concern with human nature. Pre-social man's desires and satisfactions coincide; civilized man's desires and satisfactions are drastically at odds with one another. The depravity of society and the arbitrariness of social convention create an obsession with personal prestige that is utterly self-destructive. One of the insights which Durkheim extracted from Rousseau was the idea that nature could be recreated *inside* society; for this to happen, social rules must possess the same degree of impersonality, non-arbitrariness and externality to our desires which the descriptive laws of nature possess. This links up with some very characteristic ideas in both the *Social Contract* and in *Julie*. The legislator of the *Contract* has to know how to abolish human nature and create something new and socially adaptable. And Wolmar's talent is precisely that he can do this for his own charges – his wife, children and servants – by so arranging the environment of Clarens that the obvious (or natural) path is the path of virtue. But all this remains as ambiguous as everything else in Rousseau's work – the legislator of the *Social Contract* seems to end up with nothing more attractive than Sparta to his credit, which hardly suggests that Rousseau was the originator of totalitarian democracy. And Wolmar's Clarens is not the greatest success we can imagine – Julie remains in love with Saint-Preux, and the artificiality of the life at Clarens is eventually reflected in her unwillingness to go on living it. Something in her nature must surely have been mortally abused, and Wolmar is as much her murderer as her benefactor.[14]

The Rousseau whose views of human nature I have sketched so briefly and crudely is not, of course, the only Rousseau to be found in the writings of that ambivalent and alarming man. There is a good deal of straightforward Hobbes-like utilitarianism in the *Social Contract* – where Rousseau acknowledges with perfect calm that conflict of interests makes society necessary and shared interests make it possible. But what there is in Rousseau which possesses a curiously current interest is the fear that not enough of our nature is visible or recoverable to provide us with a clear guide to what viable self we can create. The anguish at having so many masks to wear, so many roles to act, so many choices with so few guides on how to make them, this is something which really does seem to have begun with Rousseau. It is all too easy to read Sartre, Hegel or Marx back into Rousseau and thereby blur the contributions of all of them. But even the most austere and historically cautious writer can hardly ignore that new tone of voice. To become as familiar as it has, it had to start a long tradition, one which has recently re-emerged in sociological theory, literary criticism, and philosophy. But if Rousseau's successors have added their own, original contributions, he ought, I think, to get the credit for starting the argument in these distinctively modern terms.

1 Immanuel Kant, *Groundwork of the Metaphysics of Morals*, ed. H. J. Patton (Hutchinson, 1952).

2 R. M. Hare, *The Language of Morals* (Oxford University Press, 1953).

3 Quentin Skinner, 'The Ideological Context of Hobbes's Political Theory', *Historical Journal*, 1966.

4 Leo Strauss, *The Political Philosophy of Hobbes* (Chicago University Press, 1952).

5 F. C. Hood, *The Divine Politics of Thomas Hobbes* (Oxford University Press, 1964).

6 *Aubrey's Brief Lives* (ed. Oliver Lawson Dick, Penguin English Library, 1961).

7 See D. E. Broadbent, *Behaviour* (Methuen, 1968).

8 'B. F. Skinner: *Verbal Behaviour*', *Language* 35, 1959.

9 For example, in his account of 'the prisoners' dilemma': A. Rapaport, *Fights, Games and Debates* (Ann Arbor 1957).

10 Stuart Hampshire, *Morality and Pessimism* (Cambridge University Press, 1972).

11 E. Durkheim, *Montesquieu and Rousseau* (Ann Arbor Paperbacks).

12 M. Berman, *The Politics of Authenticity* (Allen & Unwin).

13 J. Shklar, *Men and Citizens* (Cambridge University Press).

14 See the long chapter on *Julie* in Berman, op. cit.

2 Classicism Revisited: Human Nature and Structure in Lévi-Strauss and Chomsky

Culture and Nature

One of Plato's dialogues[1] rests on an essential debate between two characters, Cratylus and Hermogenes, whose positions are completely antagonistic to each other. The question at stake is the adequacy of nouns and names. Hermogenes, who speaks first, considers that names and nouns are the consequence of a convention, a treaty, a contract or a covenant: that they are artificial and arbitrary. Cratylus, on the contrary, holds the view that nouns and names are proper, that is to say they are mapped on the nature of things which they imitate, or to which they are linked according to a binding of causality: in any case, a natural relationship.

Hermogenes versus Cratylus, law versus nature, *nomos* versus *physis*, or culture versus natural necessity. Socrates is invited to take part in the debate. He declares himself incompetent, but ready to study the question with them. Against Hermogenes he will establish that nouns, words and names represent the essence of things; against Cratylus he will show that the relationship between names and things is anything but steady and that there is a mixture of motion and rest in the act of designation.

Unable to admit Cratylus's thesis that a god might have attributed names to things, he rather proposes the more modest image of a self-contradictory or intoxicated legislator.

This is one of the most exciting dialogues, for it is one which does not end in certainty but in *aporia*. And this *aporia*, this inconclusive outcome, this lack of ascertained answer, continues all through the twenty-five centuries of Western metaphysics and Western knowledge. Philosophy first, and then linguistics and the so-called human sciences, have given no satisfactory reply. The whole history of Western knowledge unwinds its way between the two poles set by Plato in the opposition between Hermogenes and Cratylus, caught up in the matrix of the opposition between nature and its antonyms, between *physis* and *nomos*, *physis* and technique, nature and culture. No wonder if we rediscover this pattern in the claim made by Ferdinand de Saussure according to which *the sign is arbitrary*,[2] and no wonder if D. L. Bolinger replies in a definitive paper: *The sign is not arbitrary.*[3]

To the eyes of a grammarian who wishes to study language as a self-regulating set of forms or structures, the sign is arbitrary; it is unmotivated; the words and the code do not bear any relation of likeness or necessity with the things they stand for. In that case, the whole of a language can be compared with a contract which was never signed but whose provisions would explain the relative status of signs towards one another.

But for the users of language, for those who speak, those who are within the limits of the contract, who denote and communicate, there must be some sort of link between the sign and its referent, or at least with its signified; there must be a minimal propriety of nouns, on which the users of the code agree and rely. Otherwise language would be nothing but a subset of Lewis Carroll's 'Jabberwocky', or a tale told by an idiot.

From the former point of view, linguistic or cultural *signs* are seen as self-regulated *symbols*; from the latter, they are *icons*, i.e. rooted in the thing they represent.

Western knowledge since the Greeks has always posed, and tried to solve, the question of relationship between culture and nature. Is culture rooted in nature, imitating it or emanating direct from it, or, on the contrary, is culture at variance with nature, absolutely set against it since its origin and involved in the process of always transforming nature? The matrix of this opposition between culture and nature is the very matrix of Western metaphysics. Metaphysics constitutes it, or, by way of a circular argument, whose name is history, is constituted by it.

Are we still bound to reply, as Socrates was tempted to do, that the legislator when he instituted language and culture must have been self-contradictory and even drunk, drunk to the point of playing sometimes the game of aping the world, and sometimes the more luxurious game of creating with words a world of their own, both at the same time?

But this myth of a drunk legislator risks blurring another question. Whether one considers that there is a split, a discontinuity between culture and nature, or on the contrary that they are linked by a relationship of continuity, one cannot avoid the problem: how is man and how is human nature related to culture and to nature? Is there a human nature that one has to consider as integrated with the nature of things, or has this concept of human nature a role to play as a connector, mediator or shifter between culture and nature? The position which is at stake here is that of man as a centre of the universe, as interpreting the world and ruling over it, as an absolute source of codes, languages, practices and meaning as a whole. Man, the meaning-giver? or on the contrary is not this concept of human nature an obstacle, a nuisance that epistemological purity would have to dismiss?

The work of Claude Lévi-Strauss and Noam Chomsky will help us to raise these points. Because they are not philosophers. but specialists – each engaged in a research connected with mankind without being obscured in his quest by humanist ideology – they both meet the question of the relationships between nature and culture at the very root: language and code. Not only do they touch this question technically, in the process of their researches as an ethnographer and as a linguist respectively; but also the philosophical question of their concept of human nature can be raised at the level of the epistemological claims they make. And there we shall notice a certain kinship with classical formulations, as if the breakthrough they had made in the field of their techniques were redeemed or compensated by their belonging to a classical universe of concepts.

The epistemological question that one is entitled to ask these two researchers runs as follows: is the concept of *human nature* as a stable essence the necessary corollary of their exploration of the borderline between nature and culture, and are they right to situate it where they do? Lévi-Strauss will indeed postulate under the name of *nature* a universal combinatory matrix whose local and particular cultures are only empirical products, ever destroyed and ever rebuilt by the motion we call history. Chomsky in his fight against empiricism and behaviourism will revert to a concept of innate structures which characterize the human mind, and which make it capable of building language.

Are these two concepts of human nature, which we shall

scrutinize, the inevitable and necessary results of their approaches? Or on the contrary do they bear arbitrary ideological connotations which will have to be examined and contested? In other terms, assuming that, in spite of the novelty of these thinkers, we have remained on a Platonic stage with the same scenery where Cratylus, Hermogenes and Socrates are performing the same hackneyed play, we may ask the following question. Is the only escape from the spectre of a drunk legislator to be found in an anthropocentric conception of the *gnōthi seauton*, know thyself, prescribed by Socrates?

Lévi-Strauss and Rousseau

Let us first consider how Lévi-Strauss fights against traditional metaphysical concepts of human nature; in this he will remind us of Rousseau and the difficulties Rousseau had with the thinkers of the Enlightenment. Then we shall be entitled to ask: what relationship between culture and nature does Lévi-Strauss provide for us?

Lévi-Strauss's approach to anthropology has now become common knowledge. It assumes that customs, myths, attitudes, behaviour that an external observer of a culture collects at random are not the accidental or fortuitous products of haphazard circumstances, but that they are the performances of an underlying logic which generates them from below and that this logic can be deciphered and formalized far beyond the awareness that the performers caught within a code have access to.

This system of rules, which articulates partial and isolated phenomena, constitutes a logical network which allows the building of a 'model' of how the social system works both at the level of denomination and at the level of attitudes. We shall take three examples of this structuralist method concerned with formal relationships between elements more than with the individual elements themselves, and see how they militate against traditional substantialist notions of human nature conceived in terms of individual subjectivity. These three instances are: structures of kinship; myths; and totemisms.

Lévi-Strauss's structuralist method has been built under the influence of Saussure's and Jakobson's linguistics, which deal with systems of formal oppositions that are, at the same time, tables of possible permutations between terms. An empirical phenomenon – for instance, the actual observable structure of kinship in a given group – will be only one example among all the possible combinatory permutations for that group. Moreover the marriage systems of different societies are treated as paradigmatic transformations of an underlying common logical structure. In his book *Structural Anthropology* (the section on language and kinship),[4] Lévi-Strauss produces a comprehensive table which shows how various communities, completely isolated from one another, in fact embody each in its turn a possible transformation of the whole combinatory system: the terms combined here are patrilineal–matrilineal filiations, relations of brother and sister, father and son, and relations governing the extent of affection or hostility, reserve or intimacy. If the question is 'What does the avuncular relationship consist of?', one can easily see that the uncle's relationship, to be understood, must be treated as a relation within a system. The first consequence of this structure is to produce a shift from any existentialist, or phenomenological, concept of human nature and human relations. The image of each individual as an independent subject, or source of meaning, is replaced by that of a term, an element interdependent with the others in a formal pattern. Within each structure, a type of kinship behaviour is prescribed to each of the performers by the rule of the code – which means he does not choose it, even in a primordial choice that existentialists would have called a project. And of these forces by which the kinship behaviour is programmed, the performers are not necessarily aware, although they are *sometimes* able to formulate it consciously: Lévi-Strauss resorts to a social *unconscious* which is at variance with the phenomenological concept of human nature as subjectivity and consciousness. Simple as this structure is (Lévi-Strauss calls it the unit of kinship), and given the fact that it is still at the level of field observation, it still allows us to measure how remote is Lévi-Strauss's approach to culture through kinship behaviour from any existentialist concept of conscious free subjectivity and especially from Sartre's in *Critique de la raison dialectique*.[5] It even helps us to show Sartre's treatise as part of an ethnocentric pattern restricted in its relevance to Western societies.

An important consequence of this is that Lévi-Strauss repudiates the idea that culture merely imitates nature: he writes in

Structural Anthropology: 'The system of kinship is a language.' And we can imagine that here he ranks with those who, after Saussure, have proclaimed the non-motivation of the symbolic function. The fact that the avuncular relation, which has no procreative foundation, is a key feature of the elementary structure indicates that Lévi-Strauss does not map his basic kinship structure on *biological* relations.

He is at variance with Radcliffe-Brown whom he quotes as follows in this book: 'The unit of structure from which a kinship is built up is the group which I call an "elementary family" consisting of a man and his wife and their child or children.'[6] Lévi-Strauss replies: 'The idea . . . according to which the biological family constitutes the point of departure from which every society elaborates its system of kinship does not belong only to the English master . . . but there is no more dangerous idea.'[7]

A system of kinship does not consist of objective links of filiation or consanguinity given among individuals: it exists only in men's consciousness; it is an arbitrary system of representations, not the spontaneous development of a factual situation. In a sort of Copernican revolution, comparable to that achieved by Kant in knowledge, Lévi-Strauss shows that biological filiation is not the basis of kinship structures but a parameter which has a limited and defined location in a wider unmotivated network. 'In order for a kinship structure to exist, three types of family relations must always be present: a relation of consanguinity, a relation of affinity and a relation of descent.'[8]

Hermogenes has evidently won the first round. Culture is different from nature and cut off from it. Lévi-Strauss indeed still speaks in this early quotation in terms of *conscious representations*; but, later in his work, he argues that conscious representations are only surface layers produced by a set of deep structures which can be deciphered through the combinatory process. Linguistics presents us with a totalizing dialectic external to or below the level of consciousness and will-power. As a non-reflective totalization, language is a human reason which has its reasons that man does not know. This universal logic is only implicit in the confrontation among the five patterns already mentioned. Trobriand, Siuai, Cherkess, Tonga, Kutubu; taken together they lead to the claim that there is a general matrix whose combinatory power, agent of all possible permutations, is the law of these empirical arrangements. We shall see later that this leads Lévi-Strauss, as in the example of totemism that I shall discuss later, to conceive of a deep source of these operations and combinations and that this deep structure might be called *nature*, because it roots culture back into natural laws.

But before we are invited by Lévi-Strauss to accomplish this *vaterlandische Umkehr* or repatriating detour (as Hölderlin puts it in his *Remarks on 'Antigone'*), before one is led to postulate a structural nature which would be the source and the substratum of these deep combinatory structures, we must note that Lévi-Strauss uses these confrontations and convergences among various patterns isolated from one another as heuristic instruments, i.e. he claims only that they build a network of probability for the finding of other family structures: like the Mendeleyev table of elements in chemistry. But the limit to formalization must here be carefully set. Even though the avuncular relationship is seen as part of a structure, first of all it is difficult to universalize the system in spite of the striking congruences among these isolated groups; and second, these surface structures do not exhaust the family reality, and one can easily find other types of relationship which are omitted by this pattern. For instance, an exchange between husband and wife can be compounded of affection and reserve together; and this is but one example of the complexity of relations which Lévi-Strauss admits he has tactically simplified. As in the field of dreams and the unconscious analysed by Freud, we are in the field of *overdetermination*: that is to say, a symptom or a sign is the crossroads for several threads of significance. And this articulation of overdetermined symptoms on the features of a combinatory matrix, far from being a repudiation of culture as a formalizable language, might be related to the harmony which in Leibniz's writings prevails between the formal network of the Monads and the semantico–syntactic display of a universal characteristic or theory of writing.

This is the first shift operated by Lévi-Strauss: human nature no longer rests in the field of consciousness, or of the universal substratum or subjectivity of man as centre of the world. Various cultures have to be considered as decipherable overdetermined patterns produced by a deep set of structures which, according to his argument, altogether constitutes a great combinatory power. Might we call such a power 'nature in a new key'? Human mind is not consciousness but concept. But the syntactic law of this linguistic pattern is the incest taboo, as we shall see later on. This assimilation of culture to a language is not new. Marcel Mauss in his remarkable essays on gift-giving and on magic[9] had already emphasized how the associations brought about in the universe of so-called primitive societies are comparable in their structure to a rhetorical *corpus*: the system of give-and-take, the sacrificial exchange of goods which characterizes potlatch, and the associations between signs and symbols operated by magic, have been analysed by Mauss as a world where *tropes*, that is symbolic and rhetorical structures, were at work. But Lévi-Strauss's approach represents a step further, for he succeeds in formalizing the field, getting the structures rid of their semantic remainder in favour of paradigmatic networks which lead to the fecundity of harmonic Leibnizian isomorphism. Marriage rules and kinship systems are

a sort of language, that is to say a set of operations designed to ensure, between individuals and groups, a certain type of communication. The fact that the 'message' would here be constituted by the *women of the group* who *circulate* between clans, lineages or families (and not, as in the case of language itself, by the *words of the group* circulating between individuals) in no way diminishes the fact that the phenomenon considered in the two cases is identically the same.[10]

This does not mean that the performance or utterance is in both cases similar. There is a similarity inasmuch as both sets of performance, the linguistic and the social, are regulated by codes or laws which underlie them without the performers being aware of them: and in the fact that they are regulated by a syntactic matrix. The main difference lies in the fact that, as we shall see in the discussion of Chomsky later on, the structures of kinship are a limited set of structures which generate a limited number of performances, i.e. a closed system; whereas the linguistic exchange allows an infinite and unpredictable number of utterances. The case is not simple, because the patterns of kinship attitudes are intermingled with a pattern of appellations, i.e. a linguistic pattern; and at both levels there is a return of the symbolic or semantic problem through the occurrence of overdetermination or polysemy.

But the basic novelty lies in a displacement of humanism, which could be formulated in this critique by Lévi-Strauss of Sartre's man-centred philosophy:

> In a century when man is bent on the destruction of innumerable forces of life, it is necessary to insist that a properly equipped humanism cannot begin of its own accord, but must place the world before life, life before man, and the respect of others before self-interest.[11]

In this statement there is an echo of Rousseau's thesis, in particular of this difference or shift which made Rousseau's quest so much at variance with the traditional humanistic claims of the Enlightenment: claims which were concerned with light, progress and reason. What one finds here is the difference stated by Rousseau between *amour propre* and *amour de soi, amour propre* – or love of self – being a corruption of *amour de soi*, and subsequent to it, whereas *amour de soi*, which is equated with pity, can be translated into English by 'love of the human species' as opposed to 'love of self'. In this contrast one finds an anticipation of that key contrast, between the general interest and self-interest, which will be the core of the political state in the doctrine of the General will.

In his second *Discourse* on the *Origin of Inequality*[12] Rousseau proposes *pity* as a basic passion from which all affective and intellectual movements of the mind will be deduced and derived, after a succession of stages which will be generated from one another not in a continuous pattern, but through a succession of discontinuities or splits or hiatuses. But this pity or natural goodness or *amour de soi* does not exist actually in what Rousseau calls the state of pure nature or pure state of nature. It is only a virtuality, a potentiality. What distinguishes his approach from all others is that he does not assume that there is a natural law which is of mutual love (as does Locke). Rousseau breaks the circular discourse in which jurists and philosophers used to enclose the formation of political laws, which were held to be mapped on a concept of natural law; whereas in fact the natural law was deduced from these social laws themselves. Rousseau goes back to a state of pure nature which is neither altruistic nor a state of war as in Hobbes, but a theoretical construct, a sort of degree zero of the state of nature, an absence of essence which cannot at its origin bear any predicate: man then is null and dull; he does not even assess his own existence in terms of time. As Alan Ryan has put it: in Rousseau's state of pure nature, men are mere isolated animals, isolated in space and time. For Rousseau, 'natural man is not the noble savage nor is he Hobbes's rational egoist. Both these conditions are social conditions and in an important sense non-natural. As an animal, man is neither moral nor immoral, but amoral.'

The consequence of this strategic move towards a degree zero will be to allow Rousseau to deduce another type of history than the one which has led to alienation, inequality, and injustice. By breaking this circle he avoids giving an undue legitimacy to existing laws in actual society. A superficial reader of both Rousseau and Lévi-Strauss would have been struck by the similarity that the legend of the Noble Savage in Rousseau bears to some allusions made by Lévi-Strauss to the tenderness, innocence and gentleness of the Nambikwara tribe, whose life is described in *Tristes tropiques*. This is one of the misleading analogies that have been drawn: to label Lévi-Strauss as a romantic and Rousseau as a pre-romantic. But there is no such thing as the Noble Savage in Rousseau, only this degree zero of nature. The gap between the two concepts is important because it allows Rousseau not only to invalidate the circular generation of unjust political laws, but also to fight the myth that there was a real evolution in time from primitive to civilized, from nature to culture. Genesis in the history of mankind as described in the second *Discourse* must be interpreted as an epistemology of discontinuity, an analogue of which appears in Lévi-Strauss. First of all Rousseau warns us against a possible misinterpretation of this genesis: it is not an anthropological chronicle but a theoretical problem embodied in the figure of a parable.

The fictional generation of the concept of culture through various rhythmic, discontinuous cycles ('*Commençons par écarter tous les faits*') is Rousseau's methodological recommendation. Lévi-Strauss follows this when he generates formally and theoretically some kinship structure or totemic relationships; and here he distinguishes himself from the culturalists or the empiricists as much as Rousseau did from the conventional Enlightenment philosophers.

But a convergence which is more striking is the one which can be traced between the battles that both Rousseau and Lévi-Strauss fight against a continuous evolutionary myth of history.

Rousseau, by destroying the anthropological circle and breaking his way towards the degree zero of culture and of nature, shows that faculties like imagination, or industry, and later the political state obtained through the contract, were born in *discontinuous hiatuses*. Culture emerges through discontinuity, and all at once. One cannot but quote here the famous passage in the *Introduction to M. Mauss's works*[13] where Lévi-Strauss writes:

Language was born all at once. Whatever the moment and the circumstances of its appearing in the range of animal life, language has necessarily appeared all at once. Things cannot have begun to signify gradually. After a transformation the study of which has no relevance in the field of social sciences, but only in biology or psychology, a change has taken place, from a stage where nothing had meaning to a stage where everything had.

But the strangest impact of this fight against evolution is to be found in the denunciation of the concept of history as an ethnocentric product of Western knowledge. The introduction of hiatuses and discontinuity patterns into the theoretical account of genesis had allowed Rousseau to destroy a certain ideology of natural law. Similarly, the use of discontinuity will allow Lévi-Strauss to destroy the linear evolutionist pattern according to which so-called primitive societies were conceived as earlier stages of a development of mankind whose Western culture would have represented the latest stage. Such a myth, which Lévi-Strauss denounces in *Race et histoire*,[14] is a consequence of this subtle Western ethnocentrism, a sort of intellectual colonialism in the process of which we try to annex the cultures of *other* peoples and consider their evolution as subordinated to the goal of reaching our own stage.

Against this ideology, Lévi-Strauss provides a pattern of discontinuity and differences: he shows in *La pensée sauvage* (*Savage Mind*) as well as in *Race et histoire* that cultures are various strategic moves in which mankind approaches and transforms nature according to the theory of games with different formal codes or deals, simultaneously. This helps to shatter the ideology of primitive as opposed to civilized cultures; it ruins the axiological hierarchies between savage, barbaric and civilized and it preserves at this stage ethnographic relativity. What Rousseau has achieved at the level of time, introducing discontinuity in genesis, Lévi-Strauss does in cultural space, introducing discontinuity between cultural codes and ruining the ethnocentric illusion of a common history of mankind. Lévi-Strauss denounces definitively what he calls the 'equivalence between the notion of history and that of humanity which is imposed upon us with the hidden aim of making historicity the last shelter of transcendental humanism.'[15] This allows us to see how opposed his views are to those of Sartre and of certain Marxists. His views have helped us to realize that history, and the difference between peoples within a history and those without an history, were ideologies rooted in a culture which would be wrong to take itself as an absolute. As a consequence, history will be seen only as a factor of degeneration of formal systems. For instance, those bodies of myth, which are built in cultures by networks of structural patterns are similar to musical scores which can be deciphered vertically as well as horizontally. Musical genres of the classical age and myths are mutually isomorphic, because they both provide a deciphering grid, a matrix of relationships which filter and process experience, substitute themselves for it and give the illusion that contradictions can be overcome and difficulties solved. This formal equilibrium is threatened by the erosion of history, that is lived by men, built by historians, and dreamt by philosophers.

In a beautiful passage of *La pensée sauvage* in the chapter called 'Histoire et dialectique',[16] Lévi-Strauss denounces the ethnocentric reductionism practised by Sartre when he continues to postulate history and dialectics as universal cultural predicates. Sartre is accused of letting escape the prodigious richness and diversity of fashions, beliefs and cultures; it is too often forgotten, Lévi-Strauss alleges, that

in their own eyes, each of the tens or hundreds of thousands of societies which have coexisted on earth, or which have succeeded one another since the appearance of man, has prided itself on a moral certitude – similar to that we invoke for our own sake – proclaiming that in itself – reduced though it might have been to the dimension of a little group or a village lost in the darkest forest – in that society were condensed all the meaning and dignity of which human life is capable. But whether it is in them or in us, much egocentrism and naïvety are necessary to make us believe that the whole of human nature is sheltered in only one of the historical or geographical modes of man's being, whereas the truth of man resides in the system of their differences and of their common properties.

So Lévi-Strauss not only destroys the ideology of a unified human nature in history in favour of a cultural polyphony, but he challenges the hierarchy between science and so-called primitive thinking when, at the beginning of *La pensée sauvage*, he writes: 'Two distinct modes of scientific thought exist, which are functions not of unequal stages of the development of human mind, but of the two strategic levels at which nature lets itself be attacked by scientific knowledge.'

Therefore the bodies of myth which are the result of these deep combinatory systems of logics are formal sets whose synchronic equilibrium is threatened by history. History is not, as in Hegelian, Marxist or Sartrian theories, a positive-oriented force which would gradually generate meaning; it is only a destructive power which brings disorder and entropy into the formal equilibrium of these networks of signs. And there is a striking similarity with Book VIII of Plato's *Republic*, where history and the succession of régimes are seen only as a degrading process damaging a synchronic purity. One could also notice that, once more, Lévi-Strauss is faithful to Rousseau's distrust of *history*, in Book 3, Chapter 11, of the *Social Contract*: 'Even the best Constitution will one day have an end, but it will live longer than one less good, provided no unforeseen accident bring it to an untimely death.' Both Rousseau and Lévi-Strauss see time and history as eroding factors, which the frail balance of structure and culture try desperately to arrest: we are far from the ideology of Progress in history shown by Marxists, Sartre and the philosophers of the Enlightenment.

The way in which Lévi-Strauss revisits classicism is a very anti-conformist way: it leads him back to a complicity with the most anticonformist of all the philosophers, Rousseau, the one who fights against a substantialist or empiricist determination of human nature and who demystifies the myth of history as orientated progress. We are now able to frame a new paradox which finds Rousseau and Lévi-Strauss akin in the same violation of the difference between nature and culture, although they have formerly proclaimed the methodological necessity of this split.

Prohibition of Incest as Human Nature
Once the relationship between nature and culture has been purified by Lévi-Strauss of all its substantialist and metaphysical

impact; once the illusion of a common substratum – which would supposedly lie bare after the shedding or stripping away of all particular or specific features – has been discarded; the only formal feature which remains universal is the prohibition of incest. The prohibition of incest, or exogamic imperative, is in Lévi-Strauss's view 'a fact or a whole set of facts' and he claims, siding with Geza Roheim against Malinowski, it is universally observable. But it is also a rule, and as such it is a methodological scandal. 'For,' Lévi-Strauss writes,

prohibition of incest presents, without the least equivocity, and indissolubly united together, the two characteristics where we have recognized the contradictory attributes of two mutually exclusive orders: it constitutes a rule, but a rule which, alone among all social rules, possesses at the same time a character of universality.[17]

The scandal is that in this rule/fact or fact/rule the two kingdoms of nature and culture meet, whereas they had been recognized as opposed to each other. Then, as in *Cratylus*, the legislator must have been self-contradictory. And not only do they meet, but their meeting is fecund. Prohibition of incest constitutes the archetype of all rules, the degree zero of syntax, the paradoxical place whence all rules can be considered as formal patterns, and above all, as a language, because by the transport towards an outside world, by the circulation between the *identical* and the *other*, the possibility of considering culture as a field of communication and transport occurs for the first time. Prohibition of incest may be the degree zero of the rules or law, it is a space where the field of the identical first escapes the monotony of a tautological repetition of itself and where the question of relationship with *another* begins. *'Je est un autre'*; but it remains an epistemological scandal, which defies the barrier erected between nature and culture by an Aristotelian logic of identity. Lévi-Strauss's concept of human nature, if assimilated to prohibition of incest – and it seems to be so – produces a logic which defies logical imperatives: *une logique qui se moque de la logique*.

Prohibition of incest is in the field of culture, and even constitutes the possibility of culture, because from it, an element (clan, ethnos, tribe, etc.) begins to communicate with another according to some rules and on a formal network. But it is also and at the same time *natural*, for it is universal. Lévi-Strauss, in fact, writes, in *Elementary Structures of Kinship*: 'Let us first suppose that all that is universal in man corresponds to the field of nature and is characterized by spontaneity, and all that is submitted to a norm belongs to culture and presents all the predicates of relativity and particularity.' Now prohibition of incest, or exogamy, in which one could find a manifestation of Lévi-Strauss's conceptions of human nature, remains a scandal because it presents these two aspects united together without the least doubt. Its universality remains in Lévi-Strauss's view a theoretical as well as a factual piece of evidence. By its privileged position as an archetype it does not prevent the following question being asked: 'Is this meeting-point that we name prohibition of incest a strange exception that one encounters as a challenge in the pure system of difference between nature and culture? or on the contrary, is not this system of difference between nature and culture to be conceived as a consequence of prohibition of incest? In that case this prohibition of incest would be outside the system, or prior to the system; and to think of it as a scandal would be an absurdity: it would mean already comprehending it into a system whose very condition it is.' This paradoxical situation is to be related to what Lévi-Strauss said in an interview published by *Le Monde* after the publication of *L'Homme Nu*: 'Structuralist thinking tries to reconcile the perceptible level and the level of the intelligible',[18] or to his view of myth as a shifter between concrete and intellectual levels: neither a concept nor an image.

At this point there is again a striking similarity with Rousseau's point of view; for, at the end of Rousseau's *Émile* the goal of the hero's education is assessed as the purpose of 'making' the pupil *'un sauvage fait pour habiter les villes'*, a savage able to live in cities. Such a formation of compromise, such a definition which overrides the logical imperative of non-contradiction, can be seen as an analogue of Lévi-Strauss's definition of the prohibition of incest as a source of rules and exchanges and a scandal at the same time.

And Rousseau is indeed acknowledged by Lévi-Strauss as the founder of ethnology: in *L'essai sur l'origine des langues* as well as in *Second discours: Sur l'origine de l'inégalité*, Rousseau provides 'the first treatise of general anthropology in French literature'. What Lévi-Strauss credits Rousseau with is having distinguished the object of the ethnologist from that of the psychologist or the historian: 'When one wants to study men, one has to look near oneself; but to study Man, one has to learn how to take a longer sight. One must first observe the differences in order to discover proprieties.'[19] For Lévi-Strauss, ethnological work achieves a fictional variation which is in quest of the essential invariant, beyond empirical diversity. And that justifies Rousseau's epistemological claim: '*Commençons par écarter tous les faits*' and refutes the objections made to Lévi-Strauss about his so-called contempt for field ethnography and empiricism.

No wonder we see in *le sauvage fait pour habiter les villes*, as well as in the scandal of prohibition of incest, the paradoxical result of this quest for the invariant. At this level the absolute split between nature and culture is challenged and contested. Lévi-Strauss writes: 'The opposition between nature and culture, on which we had insisted in the past, seems to us to offer now nothing more than a methodological value.'[20]

The dream of Lévi-Strauss as an ethnologist is now to reinsert culture into nature, but nature in a new key conceived in terms of a deep combinatory power. Yet this concept of nature is modified by the reductive detour accomplished:

> The idea of general mankind, to which ethnographic induction leads, has no relationship with the idea which was held about it before. And the day when one is able to understand life as a function of inert matter will mean the discovery that it possesses properties which are very different from those which were previously ascribed to it.[21]

This day has come, and modern biology has now started explaining life in terms of a combinatory process. For Lévi-Strauss it has become legitimate to confront the deep structures and logical systems of myths, of totemic operations, of kinship and commercial exchanges, which constitute culture, with life and nature. Life and nature are no longer opaque and dull; life is seen as the great combinatory power that modern studies in biology have now allowed us to recognize: Watson, Wilkins, Crick, Monod, Lwoff, Jacob and others have now made it intelligible in such a way.

Moreover, Lévi-Strauss is not naïve to the point of expecting to discover the formal invariants which underlie myths or totemism in the form of empirical evidence: a system of rules is not a fact. Similar to Rousseau's theory of a social contract which is not an historical event nor an empirical event but gives sense to historical or political realities which are conceived in its limits, Lévi-Strauss's invariant is not likely to be unveiled by the ethnologist in its complete and exhaustive clarity. In *La pensée sauvage*, in a chapter on the logic of totemic classifications, Lévi-Strauss writes that an underlying system can sometimes be postulated *de jure*, but might be impossible to reconstruct *de facto*.

Lévi-Strauss has been right to denounce the ideology of traditional humanism, such as triumphs in Sartre's fetishism of history and in a certain type of Marxism I have myself attacked elsewhere.[22] He has shown that ethnocentrism and a recourse to a transcendental Ego were hidden there. But in postulating a new type of formal congruency between culture and nature as decipherable with the help of a theory of codes and models, he has not completely avoided the risk of falling back into a regressive metaphysical attitude. Jacques Derrida has shown in *De la grammatologie* how Rousseau and Lévi-Strauss, by a privilege granted to the voice and spoken word as well as to phonological patterns, and by their shared dismissal of writing, were prisoners of Western metaphysics. One can also wonder whether in postulating a certain structural inherence of culture in nature Lévi-Strauss has not come back to the substantializing of a nature conceived in Spinozist terms as a *natura naturans* whose inherent tautology and whose generalizing power are somewhat alarming. In that case, all the shifts operated by Lévi-Strauss away from the usual self-deluding humanistic and anthropocentric concepts, would have only been an incestuous travel within metaphysical boundaries. This question deserves to be asked when we meet such affirmations by Lévi-Strauss as the following:

> It would not be sufficient to have absorbed particular mankinds into a general mankind; this first undertaking leaves the way open to others which Rousseau would not have admitted as easily and which fall to the exact and natural sciences: to reintegrate culture into nature, and eventually life into the whole set of its physico-chemical conditions.[23]

It seems that his criticism against history had led Lévi-Strauss to a curious rigid point of view where, formal though it is, this general network of patterns risks solidifying into an essence.

Chomsky and Transformational Grammar

It is against such a view that Chomsky has reacted; he has proclaimed the specific difference between human language and nature by affirming its main attribute: creativity. This concept is ambiguous and bears romantic connotations. We must resituate its scope in the very context of the revolution that Chomsky accomplished in the field of linguistics when he challenged conventional empirical and behaviourist approaches and licensed a new theoretical field for the investigation of language.

Behaviourists and empiricists held the view that the acquisition of language only comes from experience and that there is no linguistic mechanism, however complex, which has not been acquired through a process of learning from the outside world or environment.

A corollary of this view was that grammar was concerned only with the studying of data which were directly observable or physically measurable. The epistemological presupposition of this scientific school – 'scientific' in a restricted sense – came directly from Watson's behaviourism; that is, a school of psychology which acknowledged no need to postulate the existence of anything which was not observable and measurable: mind, etc.

Against this view, Chomsky's major contribution to linguistic theory consists of asserting the rights of grammar, i.e. of 'a device of some sort for producing the sentences of the language under analysis' (*Syntactic structures*).[24] A grammar thus is a machine, in the cybernetic sense of the term, whose models are to be conceived not only from the point of view of the speaker but from the listener's too. This model or device is not to be limited to the aspects which can be externally described: what accounts for the *creative* aspect of language is, on the contrary, that a grammar is to be conceived in terms of a system of transformations which is autonomous and generated from a certain number of patterns and structures which constitute the innate framework of the human mind.

Chomsky writes in *Cartesian Linguistics*:

A central topic of much current research is what we call the creative aspect of language use; that is its unboundedness and freedom from stimulus control. The speaker–hearer whose normal use of language is 'creative' in this sense must have internalized a system of rules that determines the semantic interpretations of an unbounded set of sentences; in other words, he must be in control of what is now called a *generative grammar* of his language.[25]

And in his first Russell lecture:

Furthermore, all known formal operations in the grammar of English, or of any other language, are structure dependent. This is a very simple example of an invariant principle of language, what might be called a formal linguistic universal or a principle of universal grammar.[26]

The main idea is that surface structures in language are derived through a set of transformations from deep structures. It is true that the surface structures of various utterances are different from one language to another. But Chomsky hypothesizes that at the level of deep structure all languages involve the same type of construction. This could lead to the idea of linguistic *universals*. Transformational grammar also refers to the idea of *innatism*: the linguistic ability would be innate to the child and would allow him the acquisition of his mother tongue. Given the fact that the child gets his information only from the utterances he hears around himself, and that these utterances appear to him in their surface structures, the question that behaviourism does not solve is: how does the child reconstruct their deep structure, i.e. how does he operate the transformations which are the reverse of those operated by the linguist? How for instance does he build *he will come* out of *I guarantee his coming*, if he does not have, *a priori*, built in his mind before any empirical datum, the innate patterns of deep structures? An *a priori* pattern of deep structure seems to be the condition of possibility for acquiring a language. Deep structures are thus not *discovered* by the child, but rediscovered, just as, in Plato's *Meno*, the argument of Reminiscence shows that to know is to recall to oneself.

We shall have to examine these claims later on. The novelty remains the postulate that the acquisition of language and knowledge, far from owing its result to the information gathered from the outside world or to a stimulus–response system, is facilitated by the presence in the subject's mind of a set of rules which is at variance with the vulgar empiricist position that remains the core of the behaviourists' thesis (in spite of their claims of scientific sophistication).

The second important feature consists of proclaiming the autonomy of grammar. Grammar had been too often mixed up with literature or anthropology. Even Boas's and Bloomfield's approaches were not completely devoid of interferences from anthropology. Chomsky, by contrast, proclaims the formal and epistemological purity of grammar: if, in the course of his studies, he resorts to psychology or biology, it is after having formally assessed the limits of their use and articulation as a result of a formal decision.

The scope of such a revolution in knowledge is comparable to that of Kant's achievement in the epistemology of physics in the eighteenth century. Fighting at the same time against rationalized and substantialist dogmatism and against empiricism, Kant in the famous 'Copernican revolution' claims the right of a rational subject who is conceived in terms of formal conditions of possibility of knowledge. This subject is constituted by a certain set of categories or *a priori* concepts which build human understanding and are not a result of information gathered in the empirical world, or a construct brought about by stimuli.

Knowledge, before this Copernican revolution, used to be subordinated to objects and turned around them, as in Ptolemaic astronomy the stars turn round the earth. Copernicus's model on the contrary shows the earth turning round the sun, and that provides an epistemological model to explain how the object of knowledge must turn round or be subordinated to the categories of a reason which builds *a priori* concepts. The question runs as follows: what must reason be to be able to know the world? Which implies that all this *a priori* and transcendental formal construction is a set of conditions of possibility for properly knowing the outside world: scientific experimentation is substituted for the random experience of the empiricists.

This implies in turn that external observation is not discarded but intervenes at the end of the rational process in a calculated way, and it answers properly the question asked by the *a priori* inferences supported by the set of *a priori* concepts which are independent from empirical data.

In a similar fashion, Chomsky allows a place to the behaviourist description of language, as a description of performances. But this place is limited and has to be accounted for in terms of formalist *a priori* models. The deep structures are inaccessible to behaviourist observation, and yet they make it possible. The similarity with Kant is striking, because both Kant and Chomsky fight against the dogmatism and ontology of the absolute, and against sheer empiricism: both of them show that these two systems of thought were accomplices of each other, and both denounce their hidden links. Both preserve formal purity: in the fields of physics and of linguistics respectively.

Chomsky is the author of a Copernican revolution as important as that achieved by Kant in epistemology of the exact sciences. Both have produced models of scientificity which do not dismiss perception but allocate it a predetermined scope in a theoretical system. Moreover, by recognizing that all rules of a grammar possessed by a subject are structure-dependent and cannot be otherwise, Chomsky poses a sort of requisitum to the acquisition of a language which is confirmed by factual evidence; otherwise it would be impossible for human children to learn in the normal way, though perhaps other systems might be learned as a kind of puzzle or intellectual exercise.

And Chomsky makes a definitely clear contribution to the debate between Cratylus and Hermogenes:

> The rules in question are not laws of nature nor, of course, are they legislated or laid down by any authority. They are, if our theorizing is correct, rules that are constructed by the mind in the course of acquisition of knowledge. They can be violated and in fact departure from them can often be an effective literary device.[27]

This kinship with a Kantian way of posing problems can also be recognized at the level of the formulation of Chomsky's questions. It is not only a quest which would concern the aspects of grammar as it is *de facto*, but the formal conditions of possibility of a grammar *de jure*. In the same fashion as Kant, he asks: 'What formal properties must a grammar have if we want it capable of automatically enumerating the grammatical sentences of a language and of assigning to these phrases in the same fashion structural description which could be represented in the form of a tree? More specifically, what form must the rules of such a generative grammar take?'

This concern for rules, and rules of the rules, which is common to Kant and Chomsky, leads to the recognition of a transcendental philosophy at the root of their approaches. Transcendental, not in the Husserlian sense of a substantialist Ego, but in the sense of a *formale quid sub lumine quo*, i.e. a formal set of rules or structures which permits the question *quid juris?* to be asked.

In the first of his Russell lectures, Chomsky has reverted to this very clearly: 'Knowledge of language results from the interplay of innate structures of mind, maturational processes, and interaction with the environment.' This statement is perfectly congruent with Kant's affirmation about the complementary articulation between *a priori* structures and *a posteriori* data in experimental physics. The following statement by Chomsky might even be mapped on a Kantian proposition: 'It is natural to postulate that the idea of structure-dependent operations is part of the innate schematism applied by the mind to the data of experience.'

And this Kantian feature is accentuated by the homage paid by Chomsky to Russell and Hume together for being, in spite of their myths, the introducers of a certain scope for innatism. Russell, quoted by Chomsky, writes: 'Part of empiricist theory appears to be true without any qualification'. Chomsky comments:

However, Russell writes: 'We need certain principles of inference that cannot be logically deduced from facts of experience. Either, therefore, we know something independently of experience or science is moonshine.' And Hume, in spite of his reputation as an empiricist had written too: 'Though animals learn many parts of their knowledge from observation, there are also many parts of it which they derive from the original hand of nature.'

It is not my intention here to discuss the validity of such a quotation by Chomsky: it may prove a difficult task to reconcile Hume's theory of knowledge with the Cartesian recourse to innatism. But after all, Kant himself has credited Hume for having opened the way to his own *Critiques*. Let us observe also that Chomsky's use of these quotations is polemical and rightly contests the claim made by some contemporary movements – behaviourism and empiricism – that Russell and Hume are their ancestors.

One must however ask a question which remains unsolved or not completely answered by Chomsky. What is, in Chomsky's view, the articulation between deep structures in language and deep structures at the level of the subject (the speaker–hearer)? One can accept the idea that to possess a grammar is to be able to perform a certain number of operations and transformations according to an innate set or bundle of structures. But how does this set of structures that a subject possesses (or *has*, or *is*) relate to the deep structures of a language? In other words, what is the area of impact of the subject on the deep structures of his code, given the fact that he has not internalized all of them?

Possible Objections to Chomsky

Chomsky uses the word competence or knowledge. But this word does not so far provide a satisfactory answer. Chomsky has not completely anticipated objections of this kind. When in his first Russell lecture he tries to preserve a certain relativity of the invariant, he does not show completely clearly the relationship, if any, between the invariant properties of human language as an *impersonal* code and the invariant that one discovers in the human subject in the form of those innate structures which underlie the knowledge and performance of a language for an *individual*. One cannot avoid thinking that Chomsky has generalized an idea from the field of Western culture to an ethnocentric concept of a universal human nature. And there he is liable to be criticized by anthropologists who could rightly invoke ethnological relativity and the diversity of cultures and codes.

There we could invoke Lévi-Strauss against Chomsky. However, that could not be done without our having first assessed the similarity and convergence between the two researches. The term *transformation* used by both can however be very misleading. When Lévi-Strauss in *La pensée sauvage* uses the word transformation ('*les systèmes de transformation*'), he alludes to the world of totemism and the combinatory processes which underlie it as a deep set of structures: but this logic is a logic of classification, a taxonomic network, whereas the system of transformations used by Chomsky concerns the *unpredictability* and *creativity* of speech. To assess the difference provisionally, one could say that Lévi-Strauss deals with performances or utterances which constitute a limited set generated from a finite set of deep structures (called the *totemic operator*, all of whose combinatory possibilities are systematically explored), where the individual subjects are only marks or signs combined in the general system. On the other hand, Chomsky deals with an infinite set of performances generated from a limited set of deep structures. Chomsky draws a careful limit between structure-dependent utterances and structure-independent utterances, which preserves the uniqueness or singularity of utterances and shows the limits of creativity and innovation in human language.

Moreover, whereas Lévi-Strauss is concerned with systematic combinatory powers (e.g. the totemic operator), Chomsky provides a linguistics of the sentence, i.e. of the *syntagm*. In this he is revolutionary because he challenges the dichotomy drawn by early linguists, who were only concerned by *la langue*, at the expense of *la parole* or speech. Deep structures control the production of syntagms, and the recognition of phrase-markers allows a description of all and any structural utterances. This does not reduce the structural inquiry to a combinatory account of the governing code, limited in its possibilities as in the Lévi-Straussian analysis of the totemic operator.

But the two major objections one feels entitled to address to Chomsky still hold:

(1) First, he provides a quest for the invariant which overrides cultural diversities of codes, and he there risks confining his search within the ethnocentric limit of human nature defined in a Western way and generalized by extrapolation to the dimension of universality. The great merit of Chomsky is, of course, to describe the sentence in syntactic terms: speech, *la parole*, is no longer the unwanted jungle of random and haphazard elements which Saussure had left to run wild when he decided to study *la langue* only. Chomsky conceives the generation of the terminal or concrete sentence on the model of a tree derivation from general grammatical categories; and in order to make it more accurate he hypothesizes a subtle system of transformations which will authorize or exclude a certain number of structural changes leading to the actual sentence. From this point, Chomsky concludes that under the surface structure of the sentence as it is pronounced or written there is a deep structure constituted by the whole of the derivation and of the transformations which have produced it. He has thus fulfilled his intention of providing a logic of the actual utterance, and he has been able to formalize *la parole*, which in itself is a revolution. The speech act, the relationship between *signifier* and *signified*, can no longer be satisfactorily described in empirical terms.

However, when, in the process of describing deep structures, Chomsky comes to the point of postulating a system of grammatical rules which would bind phonological and semantic utterances, and when he equates this system with a *universal* of language, it may be that this move leads him back to psychology, or to dogmatic metaphysics.

One of his disciples and major European exponents, Nicolas Ruwet,[28] goes even as far as wondering whether there are not *substantial universals*, given the fact that the deep structure of the sentences is less diversified from one language to another than the surface structure would induce one to imagine. (Hence the claim that syntactic categories are common to all languages.)

One can see easily where one is led through the question of the acquisition of language; and because linguistic competence is dependent on deep innate structures in the subject, there is a risk of reimporting here a substantialist concept of subjectivity. What would be the use of Chomsky's fight against descriptive psychology and behaviourism if it were to reimport a Cartesian psychology of the faculties of the mind? This would indeed be a regression from a Kantian formalist *cogito* to a substantialist one, which recurs in *Cartesian linguistics*.

(2) Thus the second question, that of innatism, is a key question. If one looks carefully into Chomsky's approach to innatism, one notices that the question of the insertion of a competence, or an individual grammar or knowledge of a language, into a code and into language in general, is still unsolved. Chomsky writes in his first Russell Lecture in a strictly Kantian manner:

It is natural to postulate that the idea of structure-dependent operations is part of the innate schematism applied by the mind in the sense in which Descartes argued that the 'idea of a true triangle is innate' because we already possess within us the idea of a true triangle and it can be more easily conceived by our mind than the more complex figure of the triangle drawn on paper; we therefore when we see that composite figure, apprehend not it itself but rather the authentic triangle.

This sentence starts indeed with a Kantian connotation, and ends up in a Cartesian style. The rediscovery of this classical Cartesian problem of the insertion of these seeds of truth, or clear and distinct ideas, into the mind of a subject seems to me to be a regression from the Kantian premisses and the Leibnizian relevance of Chomsky's epistemology.

Leibniz can rightly be invoked when one poses the question which Chomsky's work implies: is it true that among all languages, and among all the possible deep structures, only a few are actualized? Such a question would find elements of an answer in Leibniz's *Monadology*. And this is a legitimate question. But when Chomsky describes innatism in reference to the Cartesian idea of the triangle, one is disappointed, for a reference to Kant's categories would have been more welcome. Categories, or *a priori* concepts of the faculty of understanding, regulated by the transcendental activity of human reason, are not substantial but constitute a formal set of conditions of possibility of statements and knowledge. They remain forms, and they are in the field of law and rules. Chomsky seems to prefer innate schemas conceived in rigid terms which risk being mistaken for essences, and which reinstate the obsolete problem of interiority as opposed to exteriority. He is threatened there by the pitfalls of naturalism when he postulates human nature as an immutable concept in his paper *Changing the World* (second Russell lecture). He does not take sufficiently into account the changes that history has brought into the codes and the systems of culture. However, the polemical use of such a concept remains valid against empiricism and behaviourist reductionism.

Chomsky, by apparently dwelling in the field of normative psychology ('What must our thinking faculty be for its products to have such logical properties? What must our linguistic faculty be to allow such and such a transformation?'), reduces rationalist theory to the level of naturalism, or a hidden empirical trap, which is the ally of dogmatic metaphysics of a Cartesian kind. Similarly the notion of creativity – which has a technical sense as a result of the precise analysis of sentences treated as systems of operations and transformations – risks being somewhat arbitrarily projected into the field of metaphysical or ideological freedom conceived in Cartesian terms, linked with a concept of the subject as substance and substratum. Both creativity and competence, as well as the question 'Where to locate deep structures?', seem to send Chomsky back into an empirico-dogmatic situation that his linguistics and his criticism of behaviourism once avoided. (See *Cartesian Linguistics*.)

The notion of an unconscious conceived in Leibnizian as well as in Freudian terms, i.e. specified in terms of a structural network, is never touched by Chomsky. He provides a clear and effective criticism of Descartes's introspection (see *Cartesian Linguistics*, p. 58), but the notion of the unconscious status of deep structures is not elaborated. A relating of this unconscious to the Freudian formal unconscious determined as a language and a syntax by Lacan would be useful for Chomskian research; for it would have spared the determination of subjectivity as substance. Through the discovery that the Freudian unconscious remains structural while disobeying the Aristotelian principle of non-contradiction, Lacan and Freud provide a *split* in subjectivity which forbids any regression to idealist or substantialist concepts of the *Cogito*.

Human Nature and Biology

However, these innate principles of mind that on the one hand make the acquisition of knowledge and belief possible, and on the other determine and limit its scope, are related to biology and the new frontier opened by the neurophysiology of the brain. A temporary solution to the objections that one can put to Chomsky may be found in the relationship that Chomsky builds between his innate set of deep structures and Jacques Monod's approach to biology in terms of linguistic codes:

> These modern discoveries, Monod alleges, give support in a new sense to Descartes and Kant, contrary to the radical empiricism that has dominated science for two centuries, throwing suspicion on any hypothesis that postulates the 'innateness' of forms of knowledge.

Chomsky quoting Monod, and Monod quoting Chomsky, together assert a mutual fertilization of biology and linguistics:

> It is likely that the evolution of human cortical structure was influenced by the acquisition of a linguistic capacity so that articulated language not only has permitted the evolution of culture, but has contributed in a decisive fashion to the physical 'evolution of man'; and there is no paradox in supposing that the linguistic capacity which reveals itself in the course of the epigenetic development of the brain is now part of *human nature* itself intimately associated with other aspects of cognitive functions which may in fact have evolved in a specific way by virtue of the early use of articulated language.[29]

But one realizes here that as Chomsky's theory of innatism suffers from the risk of reinstating a substantialist view of nature through hazardous inductions, gradually building an invariant substratum and an innatism psychologically determined, Monod's work bears anthropocentric connotations which are not clearly elucidated and leave the way open to a positivist ideology which poses science as being able to provide an ethics of its own. These two moves entertain a certain similarity in their essentialist approaches.

A new classical age seems to offer itself as an opportunity of our century. Knowledge has been purified from metaphysical and substantialist imports or remainders; and, at the same time, it has not lost touch with the concrete data of experience, and has accepted the challenge of formal and structural theorization. A new Leibnizian harmony is at hand, exempt of any metaphysical pre-establishment. Departing from the dogmas of empiricism and narrow-minded behaviourism, science in our age allows an epistemological reflection which has many things in common with the Enlightenment, but freed from any illusion of a unilinear and always progressing history. Lévi-Strauss and Chomsky are among the artisans of this new approach to a demythified classicism. That is the reason why their approaches have to be all the more carefully scrutinized in order to prevent any regression to a metaphysical, substantialist view.

Against regressions of this kind towards a naïve view of human nature as invariant and of the subject as a substance, modern biology and Freudian formal and structural psychoanalysis are able to consolidate the results obtained by linguistics and anthropology. The new concepts of human nature must keep the formal purity of structural mobile networks able both to vary in their displays and to avoid the pitfalls of essentialism without neglecting the duty of dealing with diversity and otherness.

1 Plato, *Cratylus*.
2 F. de Saussure, *Cours de linguistique générale* (Payot, Paris 1967), p. 100, Première partie, Chapitre premier, § 2 ff, 'Premier principe: l'arbitraire du signe' (first publication: Lausanne 1916).
3 D. L. Bolinger, 'The sign is not arbitrary', 1949. For further investigations in this field, see *Problèmes du langage* (coll. Diogène, Gallimard, Paris

1966), and in particular, R. Jakobson, 'À la recherche de l'essence du langage'. Also E. Benveniste, *Problèmes de linguistique générale* (Bibliothèque des sciences humaines, Gallimard, Paris 1966).

4 C. Lévi-Strauss, *Anthropologie structurale* (Plon, Paris 1958), 'Langage et parenté', pp. 35–110, translated into English as *Structural Anthropology* (New York 1963, London 1968).

5 J.-P. Sartre, *Critique de la raison dialectique* (Bibliothèque des idées, Gallimard, Paris 1960).

6 Quoted by Lévi-Strauss, op. cit., p. 60 of French edition.

7 ibid., p. 61.

8 loc. cit.

9 Marcel Mauss, *Sociologie et anthropologie* (Bibliothèque de sociologie contemporaine, Presses Universitaires de France, Paris 1950), reprinted 1968.

10 C. Lévi-Strauss, op. cit.

11 C. Lévi-Strauss, *La pensée sauvage* (Plon, Paris 1962), 'Histoire et dialectique', pp. 324–57, translated into English as *The Savage Mind*, 1966.

12 J.-J. Rousseau, *Discours sur l'origine de l'inégalité* (Éditions Sociales, Paris), passim.

13 In Marcel Mauss, op. cit., 'Introduction à l'œuvre de M. Mauss' by C. Lévi-Strauss, pp. ix–lii.

14 C. Lévi-Strauss, *Race et histoire* (coll. Médiations, Gonthier publishers).

15 C. Lévi-Strauss, *La pensée sauvage*, loc. cit.

16 loc. cit.

17 C. Lévi-Strauss, quoted by Jacques Derrida, in *Cahiers pour l'analyse*, No. 4, published by Le cercle d'épistémologie de l'École Normale Supérieure, 'Lévi-Strauss dans le XVIIIe siècle'. 'La violence de la lettre de Lévi-Strauss à Rousseau', reprinted in *De la grammatologie* (Collection Critique, Éditions de Minuit, 1967), pp. 149–202.

18 Interview published by *Le Monde*, 5 November 1971, pp. 17 and 20.

19 J.-J. Rousseau, op. cit.

20 Quoted by J. Derrida, op. cit.

21 C. Lévi-Strauss, *La pensée sauvage*.

22 Jean-Marie Benoist, *Marx est mort* (Gallimard, Paris 1970).

23 C. Lévi-Strauss, *La pensée sauvage*.

24 Noam Chomsky, *Syntactie Structures* (Mouton & Co., The Hague 1957).

25 Noam Chomsky, *Cartesian Linguistics, A Chapter in the History of Rationalist Thought* (Harper & Row, New York and London 1966).

26 Russell Lectures, given in Cambridge in 1971 and first published in this country in *Cambridge Review*, Vol. 92, Nos. 2200 and 2201; also published as *Problems of Knowledge and Freedom* (Fontana, 1972).

27 ibid.

28 Nicolas Ruwet, *Introduction à la grammaire générative* (Plon, Paris 1967).

29 Jacques Monod, *Le hasard et la nécessité* (Seuil, Paris 1971).

Arthur Koestler

3 The Limits of Man and His Predicament

The first and most obvious limitation is the poverty of our sensory equipment. It is supposed to inform us of what is going on in the world, but it tells us very little about that exciting place. Our principal organ – the eye – responds to only a very small frequency-range of electromagnetic radiations. High-frequency cosmic rays may affect our body cells and low-frequency radio-waves activate our radio receivers, but only about a trillionth of a trillion of the total spectrum penetrates awareness as visible light. We walk around like knights in clumsy armour with narrow slits for the eyes. Until the thirteenth century man did not realize that he lived surrounded by magnetic forces; until fifteen years ago we did not know that showers of high-energy cosmic radiations – neutrinos – constantly traverse our bodies as if these consisted of gas, and we are as unaware of other unknown fields of forces, signals and messages that buzz around us as the citizens in H. G. Wells's 'Country of the Blind'. Our sense organs are biological filters which conceal more than they reveal.

These are facts known to every schoolboy, as the saying goes; but we do not always realize that the limitations of our perceptual faculties also limit and distort our reasoning faculties. The late Sir Cyril Burt has shown by a simple calculation that if our sense of touch were as delicate as our optical apparatus, then, 'when seeing light we should at the same time have *felt* the pressure of the impact of the photons; and mass and energy would from the outset have been regarded as merely two different ways of perceiving the same thing'. Yet we had to wait for Einstein to equate mass with energy. And although his equation worked – with unexpectedly sinister consequences – we are still unable to believe that a lump of matter consists of vibrations without a string. We are convinced that space can have only three dimensions, we believe in the substantiality of substance, in the sacramental ties which bind cause to effect, and other venerable superstitions based on, as we revealingly call it, 'the evidence of our senses' – although that evidence has been thrown out of court.

Eddington has given a vivid illustration of this conflict in his 'Parable of the Two Writing Desks'. One is the antique piece of furniture on which his elbow rests while writing; the other is the desk as the physicist conceives it, consisting almost entirely of empty space, sprinkled with tiny specks, the electrons whirling round their nuclei, but separated from them by distances a hundred thousand times their own size. And in between – nothing: apart from those few forlorn specks, the interior of the atom is empty. Eddington concluded: 'In the world of physics we watch a shadowgraph performance of familiar life. The shadow of my elbow rests on the shadow-table as the shadow-ink flows over the shadow paper . . .'

At this point we seem to perceive the shadow of little Alice walking through the looking-glass. 'But this is nonsense,' she exclaims indignantly. 'If I bang my elbow on the table it hurts very much.'

'And this is only the *beginning*,' says the Mad Hatter, ignoring her remark. 'Tomorrow I will prove to you that space is full of holes, that an object can have negative mass, and that time can flow backward when the fancy takes her . . .'

This conflict between naïve realism and its strong, seemingly self-evident beliefs on the one hand, and abstract reasoning on the other, is characteristic of our split mentality. Our native equipment being what it is, we can only get along by double-think. Eddington's two desks symbolize a relatively harmless conflict, and most people are barely aware of it. But at the same time it points to other conflicts at deeper levels which are of the very essence of the human predicament. I am referring to the split between reason and belief, the first ruled by the intellect, the second governed by emotion.

This conflict is reflected everywhere in the absurd and tortured history of our species. In one of the early chapters of Genesis we are told, with evident approval, how Abraham prepared for cutting his son's throat for the love of Jehovah. The rituals of human sacrifice, which arose independently in the most varied cultures from the South Seas to Scandinavia, are perhaps the earliest indication of the paranoid streak in man – of that perverted logic to which we are collectively prone. Anthropologists have paid surprisingly little attention to this phenomenon, perhaps because they are afraid to face its implications. Similarly historians, by long habit, seem to regard war as a more or less normal state of affairs, and not as an obvious proof that we are an aberrant species afflicted by some built-in biological disorder. I am not referring to the *moral* aspect of war, but to its *biological* aspect. As Konrad Lorenz keeps reminding us, other animals are also in the habit of killing, but they only kill prey belonging to a different species. *Within* a given species, conflicts are settled by ritualized forms of combat which, owing to some powerful inhibitory mechanism, nearly always stops short of inflicting lethal injuries. A hawk killing a field-mouse can hardly be accused of homicide. In man, however, the biological taboo against the killing of conspecifics is singularly ineffective.

But if we agree that something might have gone wrong in the evolution of our species, and search for an explanation, we always get the dusty answer that all evil stems from the selfish, aggressive tendencies in human nature. That is the explanation that has been offered by Hebrew prophets, Indian mystics, Christian moralists, by contemporary psychologists and in popular tracts like Lorenz's *On Aggression*. But speaking in all humility, I find this answer unconvincing and without support in the historical record. What the record indicates is that the part played by violence for selfish personal motives has always been negligibly small compared with the numbers massacred in unselfish devotion to one's tribe, nation, church or leader, in the name of metaphysical or abstract causes. Homicide committed for personal reasons is a statistical rarity in all cultures, including our own. Homicide for *un*selfish reasons, at the risk of one's own life, is the dominant phenomenon in history. Even the members of the Mafia feel compelled to rationalize their motives into an ideology, the *Cosa Nostra*, 'our cause'. Even the mercenaries of the French Foreign Legion displayed a proverbial *esprit de corps*, and their battle-cry was '*Vive la mort*'. Wars are not fought to satisfy individual impulses of aggression, except by a small minority of sadists. Soldiers do not hate. They are frightened, bored, sex-starved, homesick. They fight the mostly invisible, impersonal enemy either because they have no other choice, or out of loyalty to King and Country, to the true religion, the righteous cause. They are motivated not by aggression, but by *devotion*.

I am equally unconvinced by the fashionable theory that the phylogenetic origin of war is to be found in the so-called 'territorial imperative'. The wars of man, with rare exceptions, were not fought for individual ownership of bits of space. The man who goes to war actually *leaves* the home which he is supposed to defend, and engages in combat hundreds, or thousands, of miles away from it; and what makes him fight is not the biological urge to defend his personal acreage of farmland or meadows, but – to say it once more – his loyalty to symbols and slogans derived from tribal lore, divine commandments or political ideologies. Wars are not fought for territory, but for words.

Thus, in opposition to Lorenz, Ardrey and their followers, I would suggest that the trouble with our species is not an excess of aggression, but an excess of devotion. The fanatic is prepared to lay down his life for the object of his worship as the lover is prepared to die for his idol. He is equally prepared to kill anybody who represents a supposed threat to that idol. Here we come to a point of central importance. You watch a film version of The Moor of Venice. You fall in love with Desdemona and identify yourself with Othello (or the other way round); as a result the perfidious Iago makes your blood boil. Yet the psychological process which causes the boiling is quite different from facing a real opponent. You know that the people on the screen are merely actors, or rather electronic projections – and anyway the whole situation is no personal concern of yours. The adrenalin in your bloodstream is not produced by a primary biological drive or a hypothetical killer-instinct. Your hostility to Iago is a *vicarious* kind of aggressivity, devoid of self-interest and derived from a previous process of empathy and identification. This act of identification must come first; it is the *conditio sine qua non*, the trigger or catalyst of your dislike of Iago. In the same way, the savagery unleashed in primitive forms of warfare is also triggered by a previous act of identification with a social group, its rousing symbols and system of beliefs. It is a de-personalized, quite unselfish kind of savagery, generated by the group-mind, which is largely indifferent, or even opposed to, the interests of the individuals which constitute the group. Identification with the group always involves a sacrifice of the individual's critical faculties, and an enhancement of his emotional potential by a kind of group-resonance or positive feedback. Thus the mentality of the group is not the sum of individual minds; it has its own pattern and obeys its own rules which cannot be 'reduced' to the rules which govern individual behaviour. The individual is not a killer; the group is; and by identifying with it, the individual is transformed into a killer. This is the infernal dialectics reflected in our history. The egotism of the group feeds on the altruism of its members; the savagery of the group feeds on the devotion of its members.

Man has an apparently irresistible longing *to belong*, an urge to identify himself with a tribe, nation, church or party, to espouse its beliefs uncritically and enthusiastically. He is as susceptible to being imprinted with slogans as he is to infectious diseases. He has a peculiar capacity – and need – to become emotionally committed to beliefs which are impervious to reasoning, indifferent to self-interest and even to the claims of self-preservation. Waddington has called man a belief-accepting animal.

But how did this fateful peculiarity arise? Hypothetically speaking, it may have its origin in the new-born human infant's abnormally long period of helplessness and dependence. This earliest experience of total dependence may be partly responsible for man's ready submission to authority, whether it is exercised by individuals or communities, and his quasi-hypnotic suggestibility to doctrines, commandments, symbols and beliefs. Brain-washing starts in the cradle.

Another, related hypothesis invokes the critical period when our hominid ancestors emerged from the forests and took to hunting animals faster and more powerful than themselves. This must have led to a dramatic increase of mutual dependence, much stronger than in other primate groups. Here we may have the origin of tribal solidarity, *esprit de corps*, and their later, nefarious derivatives. Both factors – the protracted helplessness of the new-born, and the vital interdependence of the early hunters – may have contributed to the process of moulding man into the sociable, affectionate and devoted creature that he is; the trouble is that they did it only too well, and overshot the mark.

In so far as the vast majority of mankind are concerned, the belief-systems which they adopted, for which they were prepared to live and to die, were not of their own choice but determined by the hazard of birth and their social environment. Critical reasoning plays, if any, only a subordinate part in the process of accepting the imprint of a credo. And if its tenets are too offensive to the reasoning faculties, the art of double-think enables man to live with his split mind.

The next item in this inventory of possible causes of man's predicament is language. Let me repeat: wars are fought for words. They are man's most deadly weapon. The words of Adolf Hitler were more effective agents of destruction than thermo-nuclear bombs. Long before the printing press and the other mass media were invented, the fervent words of the prophet Mohammed released an emotive chain-reaction whose blast shook the world from Central Asia to the Atlantic coast.

Recent field-studies of Japanese monkeys have revealed that different tribes of a species may develop surprisingly different habits – one might almost say, different cultures. Some tribes have taken to washing bananas in the river before eating them, others have not. Sometimes migrating groups of banana-washers meet non-washers, and the two groups watch each other's strange behaviour with apparent bewilderment. But unlike the inhabitants of Lilliput, who fought holy crusades over the question whether eggs should be broken on the broad or pointed end, the banana-washing monkeys do not go to war with the non-washers, because the poor creatures have no language which would enable them to declare washing an ethical commandment, and eating unwashed bananas a deadly heresy.

Obviously, the safest remedy for our ills would be to abolish language. But as a matter of fact, mankind did renounce language long ago – if by language we mean a universal means of communication for the whole species. Other species do possess a single system of communication by sign, sound or odour, which is understood by all its members. Dolphins travel a lot, and when two strangers meet in the ocean, they need no interpreter. The Tower of Babel has remained a valid symbol. According to Margaret Mead, among the two million Aborigines in New Guinea seven hundred and fifty different languages are spoken in seven hundred and fifty villages which are at permanent war with one another. Our shrinking planet is split into several thousand language-groups. Each language acts as a powerful cohesive force within the group and as an equally powerful divisive force between groups. Fleming detests Walloon, Maharati hates Gujurati, French-Canadian despises Anglo-Saxon, dropped aitches mark the boundary between Them and Us.

Thus language appears to be one of the main reasons, perhaps *the* main reason, why the disruptive forces have always been stronger than the cohesive forces in our species. One might even ask whether the term 'species' is applicable to man. I have mentioned that Lorenz attributed great importance to the instinct-taboo among animals against the killing of members of their own species; yet it may be argued that Greeks killing Barbarians, Moors killing 'Christian dogs' did not perceive their victims as members of their own species. Aristotle expressly stated that 'the slave is totally devoid of any faculty of reasoning'; the term bar-bar-ous is imitative of the alien's gibberish or the barking of a dog; honest Nazis believed that Jews were *Untermenschen* – not human but hominid. Men show a much greater variety in physique and behaviour than any other animal species (except for the domesticated products of selective breeding); and language, instead of counteracting intra-specific tensions and fratricidal tendencies, enhances their virulence. It is a grotesque paradox that we have communication satellites which can make a message visible and audible over the whole planet, but no planet-wide language to make it also understandable. It seems even more odd that, except for a few stalwart Esperantists, neither Unesco nor any other international body has made a serious effort to promote a universal *lingua franca* – as the dolphins have.

So far we have been moving on fairly solid ground. My next point is frankly speculative. Earlier on, I referred to the paranoid streak in man. You may have taken that as a metaphor, but there is a serious possibility that it has to be taken literally.

Evolution is subject to trial and error; the fossil record is a litter-basket of misfired experiments. We cannot rule out the possibility that at some point in the evolution of *Homo sapiens*, too, something went wrong; that there is some engineering mistake built into the most delicate instrument of our native equipment, the circuitry of the nervous system, which would explain the mess we have made of our history.

Some turtles and insects are so top-heavy that if by misadventure they fall on their back, they cannot get up again – remember

Kafka's *Metamorphosis*. The *Arthropoda* were the most promising creatures long before the vertebrates appeared. But their evolution came to a halt because of a construction fault: their brains were built *around* their alimentary canal, whereas in vertebrates they are placed *above* them. So there was a narrow limit set for the growth of the arthropod brain, because if its mass expanded, the alimentary tube became more and more compressed until nothing but fluid pabulum could pass through into the stomach. End of invertebrate evolution; another start had to be made.

In our case evolution seems to have erred in the opposite direction. The human brain expanded, during the last half-million years, at an unprecedented speed – a phenomenon which, as far as we know, is unique in the history of evolution. The brain explosion in the second half of the Pleistocene seems to have followed the type of exponential curve which has recently become so familiar to us – population explosion, knowledge explosion, et cetera – and there may be more than a superficial analogy here, as both curves reflect the phenomenon of the acceleration of history on different levels. But explosions rarely produce harmonious results. In our case, the result seems to be that the recently-evolved structures in the human brain – the neocortex – did not become properly integrated with, or co-ordinated with, the ancient structures on which they were superimposed with such unseemly haste. I am following here the so-called Papez–MacLean theory of emotions, about which I have written in more detail elsewhere.[1] It is based on the structural and functional differences between the old and recent levels of the human brain which, when not in acute conflict, seem to lead a kind of agonized coexistence. MacLean has coined the term 'schizophysiology' for this precarious state of affairs in the nervous system. He defines it as

a dichotomy in the function of the phylogenetically old and new cortex that might account for differences between emotional and intellectual behaviour. While our intellectual functions are carried on in the newest and most highly developed part of the brain, our emotive behaviour continues to be dominated by a relatively crude and primitive system, by archaic structures in the brain whose fundamental pattern has undergone but little change in the whole course of evolution, from mouse to man.

To put it crudely: evolution seems to have left a few screws loose somewhere between the neocortex and the brain-stem. The hypothesis that this form of 'schizophysiology' is built into our species could go a long way to explain man's predicament. The delusional streak in our history, the prevalence of passionately-held irrational beliefs, would at last become comprehensible and could be expressed in physiological terms. And any condition which can be expressed in physiological terms should ultimately be accessible to remedies. Man may be a victim of his biological limitations, but he has also acquired the power to transcend his biological frontiers and to compensate for the shortcoming in his native equipment. Yet in order to neutralize the pathological side one has to start from a realistic base-line.

I have tried to enumerate a few of the pathogenic causes: the poverty of our perceptual apparatus which distorts our concept of reality; the explosive growth of the new brain and its insufficient ✓ control of the older, affect-laden structures; the protracted period of helplessness of the human infant, the strong mutual dependence and *esprit de corps* of the ancestral hunting tribes, reinforced by the enormous range of social and cultural differences within the species and by the fatal power of language to coin words into battle-cries. The overall result is indicated by the contrast between the tremendous powers of the intellect to master the environment, and its impotence when applied to the conduct of human affairs. It is decidedly odd that we can control the motions of satellites orbiting the distant planets but cannot control the situation in Northern Ireland.

My last point concerns the ultimate limitation of man: the awareness of his mortality, the discovery of death. But one should rather say: its discovery by the intellect, and its rejection by instinct and emotion. We may assume that the inevitability of death was discovered, through inductive inference, by that newly-acquired thinking-cap, the human neocortex; but the old brain ✓ won't have any of it; emotion rebels against the idea of personal non-existence. This simultaneous acceptance and refusal of death reflects perhaps the deepest split in man's split mind; it saturated the air with ghosts and demons, invisible presences which at best were inscrutable, but mostly malevolent, and had to be appeased first by human sacrifice and later by holy wars and the burning of heretics. The paranoid delusions of eternal hell-fire are still with us. Paradise was always an exclusive club, but the gates of hell were open to all.

In the middle of our century, however, events took a new turn. From the prehistoric dawn of consciousness until the year 1945, man had to live with the prospect of his death as an individual; since Hiroshima, mankind as a whole has to live with the prospect of its death as a species. This is a radically new outlook which has not yet sunk into the collective consciousness. There are periods of incubation before a new idea takes hold of the mind; the Copernican doctrine, which so radically down-graded man's status in the universe, took nearly a century to get a hold on European consciousness. The new down-grading of our species to the status of mortality is even more difficult to digest.

But there are signs that in a devious, roundabout way this process of mental assimilation has already started. It is as if the nuclear explosions have created a psychological fall-out, a sort of mental radiation-sickness, particularly among the young, which produces a distressing experience of meaninglessness, of an existential vacuum. They seem to feel that from now onward our species lives on borrowed time. All one can hope for is that out of this existential despair a new consciousness will arise, which will lead to a profounder insight into man's limitations and a more realistic and radical assessment of its causes. Biological evolution seems to have come to a standstill since the days of Cro-Magnon man; as we cannot expect in the foreseeable future a beneficial mutation to put things right, our only hope seems to be to supplant biological evolution by new, as yet undreamt-of, techniques. In my more optimistic moments my split brain suggests that this possibility may not be beyond our reach.

1 See A. Koestler, *The Ghost in the Machine*, Chapter XVI, 'The Three Brains' (1967).

Paul MacLean's relevant publications include the following:

'Man and his Animal Brains', in *Modern Medicine*, 95–106, 3 February 1964;

'New Findings Relevant to the Evolution of Psycho-Sexual Functions of the Brain', in the *Journal of Nervous and Mental Disease*, Vol. 135, No. 4, October 1962;

'Contrasting Functions of Limbic and Neocortical Systems of the Brain and their Relevance to Psycho-physiological Aspects of Medicine', in the *American Journal of Medicine*, Vol. XXV, No. 4, 611–26, October 1958.

Cornelius Ernst

4 The Vocation of Nature

There seem to me to be two sorts of contribution a Christian theologian might make to a series of lectures on 'The Limits of Human Nature'. In the first place, it is a matter of historical fact that the concept of nature has played a part in Christian theology, and, again as a matter of historical fact, Christian theology has helped in the past to shape many of our ways of thinking today. So a Christian theologian might make his modest but useful contribution by simply identifying some of the factors which have shaped some of our ideas about nature; it might turn out that merely by identifying these factors and indicating the way in which they interacted, connections might come to light which could help to explain the ways in which nature is problematic to us today.

In the second place, a Christian theologian might attempt to go further by trying to extend the Christian tradition of thought about nature so as to bring that tradition to bear on current discussions about nature. In this way a theologian might claim to contribute to the discussions not only as an historian of ideas but as a participant in an open discussion, the representative of a distinctive point of view. It is in this second sense that the present lecture is conceived, though the point of view it represents, by no means the only theological view possible, will have to be allowed to show itself by recourse to historical instances, with some fairly extensive quotation for the sake of particularity. The style will be historical, the aim constructive.

It should not be surprising that a discussion of nature and its limits should be offered in historical terms, even if one obvious sense of the word 'nature' contradistinguishes nature from history. Not so long ago Collingwood wrote an *Idea of Nature* in which he traced the history of the idea; and it is in any case obvious that 'nature' for Wordsworth was different from 'nature' for Pope, say. It isn't at all clear to me what defined use, if any, the concept of 'nature' might have for a modern natural scientist. As one turns the pages of J. Z. Young's impressive *Introduction to the Study of Man*, it is easy to pick out a familiar use of the word 'nature' in which it means no more than something like 'definite character', as in the phrase, 'an understanding of the origin and nature of this mechanism'. The phrase, colourless and unemphasized as it is, repays some attention.

Firstly, 'nature' is an object of understanding, not immediately evident, but prior to the activity of understanding. The world has its definite character or nature, which needs to be explored and can be ascertained progressively. Secondly, 'nature' is here coupled with 'origin', a peculiarly interesting conjunction, since it echoes etymological associations of both Greek *physis* and Latin *natura*, both of which are related (to put it cautiously) with birth and growth (*phuein, nasco*). It is clear that for Young the 'origin' is put somewhere in an evolutionary past, that the 'nature' to be understood is set in a history; and since the understanding looked for has its preordained schema such that this is the way and the only way in which the world of natures is to be understood, the particular nature is set in a universal history of 'Nature', or at least a general history of natures. Thirdly and most distinctively, the nature to be understood in Young's phrase is the nature of a 'mechanism', in this case the mechanism of homeostasis. It isn't only etymologically that 'mechanism' refers to a construction of human devising and ingenuity; it is central to the thesis of Young's book that 'mechanics', the immensely sophisticated mechanics of cybernetics and information theory, offers the most promising explanatory model for understanding the world and man as part of the world, in particular by the study of the brain (earlier books by Young, notably *A Model of the Brain*, have given special attention to this kind of explanation). All we need note here is that this 'model' – again an instructive notion – of understanding puts in question, to say the least of it, an older distinction between 'nature' and 'art', between what is prior to man and what he impresses upon it or elicits from it: a single style of particulate analysis is taken to be appropriate to both. If this view were to be pressed, it might seem that the limits of nature, including human nature, were those of combinatory analysis.

The point of this somewhat laborious examination of a casual remark in a recent book by a distinguished natural scientist was to suggest the historical dimensions implicit in any discussion of nature. The point could be made differently and perhaps more constructively. It is, I suppose, reasonable to assume that a discussion of the limits of nature is primarily concerned with human nature; and we might very well ask whether the concept of nature has any useful application in the consideration of man. Thomas Mann's phrase at the beginning of his great novel *Joseph and his Brethren*, where he speaks of mankind as a 'riddling essence', might I think help to pin down the inescapable ambiguity involved in speaking of man as 'nature', remembering that the 'essence' of the English translation stands for *Wesen*, a concrete nature. The whole passage deserves to be quoted:

Very deep is the well of the past. Should we not call it bottomless?

Bottomless indeed, if – and perhaps only if – the past we mean is the past merely of mankind, that riddling essence (*Rätselwesen*) of which our own normally unsatisfied and quite abnormally wretched existences form a part; whose mystery, of course, includes our own and is the alpha and omega of all our questions, lending burning immediacy to all we say, and significance to all our striving. For the deeper we sound, the further down into the lower world of the past we probe and press, the more do we find that the earliest foundations of humanity, its history and culture, reveal themselves unfathomable.

And so on through the immensely leisurely and yet dramatic meditations of the Prelude. This human *Wesen* is mysterious in its *historical* being, interrogates itself as riddler and riddle, makes and poses itself as question. Its immediacy to the past is to be assessed not by the procedures of scientific archaeology but by an archaeology of the spirit, where origin and *archê* can be recalled by poetic celebration, *memoria* and *anamnesis*; even if Mann had not himself publicly declared his kinship with Freud, we should have been able to discern his sense of a living continuity with origins, the presence and pressure of a more than individual past. And it does not seem to be fortuitous that Mann should have allowed the question of man's 'nature' to arise in the evocation of a biblical narrative, the re-telling of a biblical story.

It is a matter of linguistic fact that biblical Hebrew has no equivalent for 'nature' (modern Hebrew uses *ṭbᶜ*, which has the senses *coin, medal, impression on a coin, characteristic, substance, element, Nature, universe*). The registration of the fact ought, I think, to provoke an immense astonishment, to suggest vast perspectives in the history of ideas, and to raise in a new form the question of our self-identification. Once again, if Christian reflection has helped to shape reflection in the West, then the meeting of Jew and Gentile – Greek in particular –, which is the proper setting of early Christianity, is going to offer a privileged instance of the debate about the questionable 'nature' of man, where a search for understanding guided by a schema of *nature* has to try to come to terms with insights, revelation, about man and the world transmitted in quite other categories. It is certainly possible to examine the process of interdiffusion of cultures from the point of view of a sociology of knowledge, as a social anthropologist might try to present in a field study the categories of a preliterate society; only we should have to note that the sociology of knowledge itself is an instance of a historically-conditioned schema for the study of man. Again, the question about the nature of man is not one which necessarily admits a definite answer; it may turn out that the best we can expect to do is to provide a space in which we can go on asking the question.

The meeting of Jew and Greek had of course taken place centuries before the emergence of Christianity, after the conquests of Alexander the Great; the translation of the Hebrew Bible into Greek, the so-called Septuagint version, is a monument of this meeting. And in the greatest of the many Alexandrias founded by the conqueror, the Alexandria in Egypt, the process of Jewish self-understanding in Greek terms and the attempt to communicate this self-understanding as a contribution to Roman–Hellenistic culture reached its culmination in the writings of Philo, an older contemporary of Jesus Christ; there is no indication that Philo knew anything of his Palestinian contemporary. We can learn something of what is involved in the Greek interpretation of biblical revelation by looking briefly at Philo's commentary on the opening chapters of Genesis, *de Opificio Mundi*.

What we immediately notice is a lavish use of the word *physis*, in probably every one of the senses the word had acquired through centuries of Greek thought, and notably in the Stoic tradition. Philo himself could be described as a philosopher only in that very familiar sense in which men of letters who find systematic philosophy distasteful yet sustain large philosophical views, often in the language of systematic philosophy, but on the basis of literary experience. In the context of the creation of the world, then, Philo adopts that use of *physis* which it seems not to have had before the fifth century B.C., and speaks of Nature as immanent in the whole universe, the cosmos. Yet this world of Nature is administered not only by an immanent purpose but by the purpose of a transcendent Maker. To crown his creation, God made man 'and bestowed on him mind par excellence, life-principle of the life-principle itself, like the pupil of the eye: for of this too those who investigate more closely the nature of things say that it is the eye of the eye'. So the transcendent, god-like principle of intelligence animates this natural life of man, in a way compared by Philo to the natural scientist's or doctor's account of the pupil of the eye. Philo goes on to give reasons why man should have been created last, and one of these is worth quoting at some length.

God, being minded to unite in intimate and loving fellowship the beginning and the end of created things, made heaven the beginning and man the end, the one the most perfect of imperishable objects of sense, the other the noblest of things earthborn and perishable, being, in very truth, a miniature heaven. He bears about within himself, like holy images, endowments of nature that correspond to the constellations.

Even in this poetic account, the transcendence of man is still being exhibited in cosmic terms. Man is a 'little heaven', whose natural endowments are like the stars in heaven, the sacred images in a *Greek* temple.

The next reason given by Philo to account for man's place in the order of creation is worth noting, not so much for its style, which is still naturalistic and psychological, but for what can be discerned through the style. Man is represented as king, as ruler or master 'by nature' of all other animals, all sublunar creatures: a 'governor subordinate to the chief and great King'. In fact this probably represents more accurately the point of view of the first account of the creation of man in Genesis, the so-called P-version. The underlying image of this version, an image common to Egypt, Mesopotamia and even the early Greek cosmogonies (perhaps derived from Oriental sources) is the emergence of an island mountain of dry land from a flood. This island is successively populated by vegetation and animals, and finally by man, 'monarch of all he surveys', if I may be permitted the anachronistic quotation. The sense of the enigmatic phrase 'in our image, according to our likeness' describing God's plan in creating man may then be explained by the purpose of the plan, that man should 'have dominion' over the earth. What makes man the image of God is his royal dominion over the earth and its fullness.

Philo's picture of archetypal man is taken over and developed by the Greek Christian Fathers. At the end of this tradition St John of Damascus, living under Islamic rule in the eighth century, sums up the teaching of his predecessors. Man is the link between visible and invisible natures, he says, quoting the fourth-century Cappadocian St Gregory of Nazianzum, and goes on:

> God, then, made man without evil, upright, virtuous, free from pain and care, glorified with every virtue, adorned with all that is good, like a sort of second world or microcosm within the great world, another angel capable of worship, compound, surveying the visible creation and initiated into the mysteries of the realm of thought, king over the things of earth, but subject to a higher king, of the earth and of heaven, temporal and eternal, belonging to the realm of sight and to the realm of thought, midway between greatness and lowliness, spirit and flesh . . .

We might become so stupefied by this accumulation of contrasts as not to notice the sudden shift at the end of the passage, which concludes:

> Here, that is, in the present life, his life is ordered like that of any living thing, but elsewhere, that is, in the age to come, he is changed; and this is the utmost bound of the mystery, he is deified by merely inclining himself to God; becoming deified by participating in the divine radiance, not by being changed into the divine substance.

So man is presented as a paradoxical compound of two natures; and his destiny is to be transformed, deified by sharing in the divine radiance or glory; and this fulfilment of his destiny is open to him if he merely wills it. This last point is perhaps the most important: paradisal, archetypal man is in the image of God because he can freely choose to share in the deifying glory. Using a piece of Stoic vocabulary, Damascene calls man *autexousios*, in his own power; but the sense of the word has changed in

Christian use. It is God above all who is *autexousios*, free with unbounded power; man is *autexousios* only in a limited sense, free with limited power, free to choose a destiny offered him by God. Over and above the paradox of his divided natures, the riddling essence of man is a finite freedom called to be transformed into a divine glory which transcends him, called to a transcendence which he must receive as gift.

It is interesting to see how this connection between God's unbounded freedom and man's finite freedom might be at least hinted at in the Genesis story. The Hebrew word *br'*, to create, is used there once in the opening sentence, once at the close, once to speak of the creation of living things, and three times in the sentence, 'And God created man in his image, he created him in the image of God, male and female he created them.' *Br'*, used only with God as subject in the Old Testament, is a word which by the time the Genesis account was written (the P creation-narrative of chapter 1 is a good deal later than the J narrative of chapters 2 and 3) had acquired considerable force in the writings contained in the latter part of Isaiah, chapters 40–55, where Israel in exile is consoled and comforted by having recalled to her over and over again the transcendent power of God. For example:

> For thus says the Lord who created the heavens (he is God!), who formed the earth and made it (he established it; he did not create it a chaos, he formed it to be inhabited!):
> 'I am the Lord, and there is no other.
> I did not speak in secret, in a land of darkness;
> I did not say to the offspring of Jacob, "Seek me in chaos."
> I the Lord speak the truth, I declare what is right.'

This Lord, who is 'doing a new thing' in history, recalls the exercise of his power in liberating Israel from Egypt and in creating heaven and earth; his power is unbounded by any man or by any other god; and it is this Lord of unrestrained freedom who is three times said to 'create' man in his image.

The Damascene passage is recalled by St Thomas Aquinas in the thirteenth century, at a crucial point in his *Summa Theologiae* where he is about to begin his treatment of man's return to God by the exercise of his moral freedom. Characteristically, all the poetic imagery is omitted, and only the abstract terms of Damascene's account are recalled. Man is said to be in the image of God, because like his exemplar he is *per se potestativus* (the Latin translation of Damascene's *autexousios*). Using an argument from Aristotle's *Eudemean Ethics* to show that human rationality alone is insufficient to explain freedom, Thomas endeavours to show that this human freedom in the last resort depends on the divine initiative: that human freedom is most perfectly realized as the responsive choice by man of a transcendent God who in his own freedom has initiated the human choice.

The mention of Aristotle should remind us that Thomas was writing in the middle of one of those Renaissances which have marked the history of European culture; if the rediscovery of Plato was a feature of the fifteenth-century Renaissance, the rediscovery of Aristotle was a marked feature of the thirteenth-century Renaissance. Among the newly-available works of Aristotle, his *Physics* was one of the most influential and controversial; and Thomas's theology of human nature is intelligible only as a re-thinking of Aristotle's *physis*. Very briefly, and possibly misleadingly, it may be said that Thomas's understanding of Aristotle's *physis* is intermediate between the view of those modern commentators who hold (rightly, it seems to me, as far as the use of the word goes) that Aristotle never meant by *physis* Nature with a capital 'N', universal cosmic order; and the view of those modern commentators such as Heidegger, who see in Aristotle's *physis* a striking instance of his view that Being is a coming to light, disclosure, manifestation: there is some interest in the view of etymologists that *physis*, through the verbal form *ephun*, cognate with German *bin* and English *being*. It must at least be said for Heidegger's view that Aristotle's account of *physis* formed part of his view of cosmic order, and that Heidegger's intuitive interpretation may be eliciting presuppositions which Aristotle himself never stated. For Thomas, all natures find their place in a hierarchical cosmic order: describable in modern terms as a total environment. What on any account of Aristotle has to be allowed, that his *physis* is an intrinsic dynamic principle, a principle of change in each thing which gives it its proper intelligibility, is accepted by Thomas too.

Now while human nature belongs to this total order of Nature, it also transcends the universal order in a distinctive way; for while all other natures merely imitate their exemplar (in a Neo-Platonic rather than an Aristotelian way) by being finitely what they are and so partially exhibiting the fullness of being of their source, human nature has an immediacy of presence to the exemplar and source which allows it to reflect the source universally. Further, the whole system of nature depends on the free creative act which brings it into being at all. It is these two basic principles – man's transcendence of the cosmic order and God's freedom in creating it – that allow human nature on this view to have a *history*, and in particular a history of fall and redemption. Thus human nature can have 'states' corresponding to epochs of history; it can be 'intact' before the Fall and 'wounded' after it, 'restored' by insertion into the redemption offered by Christ and 'transfigured' in the eschatological fulfilment of the Redemption. Finite human freedom, exercised in positive acceptance of its unbounded source or by negative withdrawal from it, leaves its mark on the nature whose calling to a transcendent fulfilment it can either consent to as destiny, or by negation reverse upon itself as fate and judgement. On this view, 'nature' is intrinsically limited by being what it is; but for human 'nature', what it is to be is to be called to transcendence.

It may help to particularize this rather sweeping account if we look at some remarks of St Thomas on death, by any account a limitation of human nature. First of all, perhaps, we should remind ourselves that when we speak of the Fall we are, to use Thomas Mann's words, looking into the deep well of the past, with Aeschylus and Shakespeare as better guides, it may seem, than archaeology and palaeontology. Second, we should also remember that human death can never be simply a biological phenomenon; I write this among the echoes of the Londonderry shootings. I shall attempt what is very nearly impossible, an account of Thomas's position without the technical terms of his theology.

What is distinctive about human creatures, Thomas says, is that they are capable of reaching a transcendent fulfilment, but not by the powers of their own nature, only by divine gift. He looks back again to primordial, archetypal man, and sees in him that combination of diverse natures which could sustain stability and equilibrium, even in this world, only with divine assistance. For Thomas, then, the gift of divine assistance is needed both so that human nature might transcend itself, and also so that it might simply be itself, 'intact', before the Fall. So for Thomas, following the Christian doctrine that death is a consequence of the Fall, human death is both natural and non-natural. It is natural, if we look at human nature abstractly, disregarding its destiny in God's plan; it is non-natural if we take that destiny into account and see human nature as called to transcendence. Archetypal man, on God's plan destined for transcendence, is preserved in stable equilibrium in spite of the innate tendency to dissolution of his nature; the Fall deprives human nature both of its due access to transcendence and of its stability against dissolution, so that our dying is the symptom of our alienation from transcendence. The interest of this account seems to me that it does try to do justice to our experience of death, while subjecting the notion of nature to what is perhaps intolerable strain.

I like to see St Thomas's theology as the classical moment in the history of Christian thought; but we do not live in a classic balance, and in fact it was not long before his views were succeeded by more discordant ones. Both his idea of 'nature' and his idea of the 'supernatural' were given a kind of rigidity which deprived them of their Christian sense as *gifts* of a free Creator and Redeemer. There can be no question here, even if I were capable of it, of tracing the further history of the idea of human nature and its limits; instead I shall deliberately select, as a point of departure for a final survey of the problem of the limits of nature as seen by a Christian theologian, the writings of William Blake, for whom it can be not too implausibly maintained that he is in a special sense the prophet of modern consciousness, not least for his awareness of the constraints of Newton's 'single vision'. In view of the sophistication of the modern Blake industry, I had better emphasize that my simple home-made observations are meant only as a means of recovering in our consciousness today some sense of the perspectives of early Christianity.

Broadly speaking, Blake interpretation seems to fall into two streams, one interested in bringing out his place in the tradition of esoterism, the other in showing his place in the tradition of popular political revolt. E. P. Thompson, in *The Making of the English Working Class*, has well shown how, in certain circumstances, the life of the 'kingdom within' can seek liberation in the attempt to bring about a 'kingdom without', a kingdom of God as political liberation; and Thompson is surely right to seek Blake in the context of English Dissent. On the other hand, as perhaps his treatment of Methodism shows, Thompson is not very well qualified to judge the quality of life in the 'inner kingdom' and of the ways in which it might find public expression in its own terms: vulgar Freudianism is not a particularly precise instrument with which to gauge the quality of the life of the human spirit. What remains true is that the tradition to which Blake was indebted was precisely esoteric, insufficiently exposed to the common light of shared civilization; while again, this common light was available only within areas of permissibility defined by the conventions of that civilization. Blake, that is, belonged to a psychological and sociological 'underground', and had to be rediscovered much later in the nineteenth century when the conventions of English civilization had changed sufficiently to admit him to what Thompson calls the world of 'genteel culture'. It is perhaps appropriate and instructive to see a recent anthology of poetry of the 'Underground' in Britain, *Children of Albion*, edited by Michael Horovitz, placed directly under the patronage of Blake, and admitted to the genteel world of Penguin culture. Radicalism and respectability seem to need each other.

I am, then, proposing to see Blake's writings as a peculiarly significant expression of the 'riddling essence' of man, an expression which only rarely, above all in the *Songs of Innocence and Experience*, achieves an autonomy of poetic utterance and the pregnancy of contained ambiguity, but which elsewhere needs the kind of diagnosis offered by Blake-interpreters, the kind of diagnosis which sometimes illuminates man's riddling essence more tellingly than the symptom itself.

It may be useful to consider a couple of remarks made by Blake as marginalia to his reading of Lavater, himself described as a significant figure in the historical evolution of German Pietism on its way to *Aufklärung*, rational Enlightenment. The other direction in which Pietism evolved was of course Romanticism, well described as the 'apocalypse of the German soul', where the inner kingdom sought to interpret itself as the manifestation of immanent divinity, and so prepared the way for the secular eschatology of Marx, returning in this new guise to the light of common day and the public world.

On one of Lavater's peculiarly insipid aphorisms Blake remarks: 'Man is the ark of God; the mercy seat is above, upon the

ark; cherubims guard it on either side, & in the midst is the holy
law; man is either the ark of God or a phantom of the earth &
of the water.' On another aphorism, in which Lavater, surely in
terms of rational enlightenment, asks rhetorically, 'What nature
will he honour who honours not the human?' (underlined by
Blake), Blake declares: 'Human nature is the image of God.'
Later Blake remarks, again on a depressingly insipid aphorism:

It is the God in *all* that is our companion and friend ... God is in
the lowest effects as well as in the highest causes; for he is become a
worm that he may nourish the weak. For let it be remember'd that
creation is God descending according to the weakness of man, for our
Lord is the word of God & everything on earth is the word of God &
in its essence is God.

It is obvious that an intuition of the holiness of everything that
lives, but above all of man's inward being as ark of God, can have
political implications; but the intuition itself is surely the nerve of
significance. It is almost inevitable that on this view a God who is
discontinuous with his holiness in man, a Father-God, is seen as
limiting the freedom of man's inward holiness to expand and be
fruitful; it is precisely the human form that is divine ('the human
form divine' is Blake's expression).

There would seem to be no future, certainly not here and now,
in trying to say exactly what Blake meant by 'God' and 'divine';
the words are meant to be read not denominatively or referentially
but as the exploratory, prophetic reactivation of a tradition of
language, the opening up of a space in which the words 'man',
'God', can be released into new possibilities of semantic relationship. It is in this sense that I see Blake both as our contemporary
and as making freshly accessible the tradition in which he stands:
a tradition of Dissent, certainly, of vision suppressed or repressed,
a tradition which leads us back to an epoch in which visionary
experience was offered as the only key to the perplexities of
human history. The origins of Blake's tradition are in fact clear
enough; they lie in that period of history documented in the later
strata of the Old Testament, in the New Testament, and in a
quantity of literature now known as 'apocalyptic', the name being
derived from its purest New Testament exemplar, the Apocalypse
or Book of Revelation (*apokalypsis* is the Greek word for 'revelation'). The intermediate stages of Blake's tradition need not

concern us here; in some ways it is more profitable to look back at the beginnings from our own time, say from the point of view of a very remarkable novel (with an epigraph from *The Marriage of Heaven and Hell*) by Patrick White, *Riders in the Chariot.* (Perhaps it might be mentioned here that the title of the novel is meant to render the Hebrew *yordê merkabah*, an expression belonging to the first period of Jewish esoterism, prior to medieval Kabbalism, in which speculation and vision were playing with the chariot-throne of Ezekiel's vision; recent investigation has suggested that this throne and chariot speculation can be seen as a transposition into visionary terms of the liturgical cult centred on the ark – cf. Blake's note on Lavater quoted above – in the Jerusalem temple).

Let us for a moment suspend our everyday expectations and suppose that we too, like Patrick White's characters, are waiting for the manifestation of the glory, for a transfiguration latent in the world of our experience. How would a Christian of the first century have waited for the glory? The answer to this question is in essence extremely simple, and it brings us to the heart of Christian understanding of the limits of nature. The early Christian would have waited for the manifestation of the glory as the final expression of the Resurrection and Transfiguration of Jesus Christ.

Some hint of the implications of this identification may be found by looking at the uses, not very numerous, of *metamorpheo*, the Greek word for 'transfigure', in the New Testament. The most obvious set of uses is found in the three parallel accounts in the Synoptic Gospels of the Transfiguration of Jesus. In Mark's version we have:

> And after six days Jesus took with him Peter and James and John, and led them up a high mountain by themselves; and he was transfigured before them, and his garments became glistening, intensely white, as no fuller on earth could bleach them. And there appeared to them Elijah with Moses; and they were talking to Jesus ... And a cloud overshadowed them, and a voice came out of the cloud, 'This is my beloved Son; listen to him.'

Some modern scholars would argue that this account is a projection back into the life of Jesus before his Crucifixion of a post-Resurrection appearance; that it is at any rate offered as a disclosure of the divine glory of Jesus is clear. The overshadowing cloud is an unmistakable reference to the manifestation of God's glory as this is recounted in the Old Testament, what in later Jewish writing was known as the *Shekhinah*, the abiding presence of God. It can be shown fairly convincingly that the scene is conceived of as the advent (*parousia*) of the mysterious Son of Man from chapter 7 of the book of Daniel, a typically apocalyptic portion of the Old Testament, and at the same time the enthronement of the messianic King. But this King is not a king in the political sense. In the eschatology of contemporary Jewish apocalyptic, one can distinguish a political eschatology, where the Messiah is meant to overthrow the enemies of the Jewish people and introduce a victorious reign over all the world; and a transcendent eschatology, where God's new world transforms and transfigures the old. Early Christian eschatology, generally speaking, sees the first emergence of God's transcendent new world in the transfiguration of the risen Jesus.

But other uses of *metamorpheo* in the New Testament seem to evoke the kind of associations the word had in the pagan mystery religions. In the *Metamorphoses* of Apuleius, for instance, better known as the mildly salacious *Golden Ass*, Lucius is not only changed into an ass; at the end of the book he is also transfigured by initiation into the mysteries of Isis, and as such exhibited to the devout worshippers assembled in the temple. A great deal of rather dreary controversy has gone on about whether this so-called 'Hellenistic' sense of transfiguration can be accommodated to the allegedly pure Hebraism of the New Testament. We need to bear in mind the place of Christianity in the Hellenistic world of the Mediterranean, and the sense of Christianity as a transposition of revelation, apocalypse, from the Jewish to the Gentile world. In that rich and multivalent passage of the Second Letter to the Corinthians, where Paul has been commenting on the passage in Exodus in which Moses is described as wearing a veil over his face to conceal its blinding irradiation from the weak eyes of the children of Israel, Paul contrasts the condition of Christians: 'We all, with unveiled face, beholding [or reflecting] the glory of the Lord, are being *transfigured* into his image from glory to glory.' It is not necessary to go into the complex exegetical problems raised by this passage to see that the essential point here is the *communication* of the Christian believer in the transfiguration of Jesus into glory. The transcendent glory of God is made accessible to man in Christ, made accessible in the sacramental transformation of baptism, where the limitation of death is anticipated and overcome in the death and Resurrection of Jesus. For the Christian, metamorphosis is exhibited in symbolic action, anticipating the transfiguration of the world of experience already achieved in the nuclear entry of God's new world through the risen Christ.

The passage from 2 Corinthians just quoted is introduced by the general statement: 'Now the Lord is the Spirit, and where the Spirit of the Lord is, there is freedom.' In the immediate context, this freedom can consist only in freedom of access, openness to the transcendent glory of God; and it is the freedom of those who have been chosen with infinite freedom to be the sons of God, liberated into communion with transcendent freedom. There is no longer the danger of being consumed by the fire of the Lord; his consuming fire has been made a purifying fire in the death of Jesus, into which the believer enters. The disfigured are transfigured by death and resurrection.

The Christian hope is the conviction of the need for, and the possibility of, a transfiguration of a disfigured human nature. The riddling essence of man is to be interpreted as the enigma of this need and possibility. His 'nature', if the word is to be used at all, is the irreducible constant of an historical vocation to transcendence, a vocation which is identified primarily as anticipated transfiguration, secondly as the dark shadow left by the failure to accept it. We cannot precisely delineate the contours, boundaries, limits of this constant 'nature', any more than we can define the transcendence ('God') to which it is called, because the mystery of our being is one of finite freedom called, destined, to communion with an infinite freedom. Finite and limited, we cannot say just how we are limited. To quote the first letter of St John: 'Beloved, we are God's children now; it does not yet appear what we shall be, but we know that when he appears we shall be like him, for we shall see him as he is.'

John Casey

5 Human Virtue and Human Nature

Science and the Study of Human Nature

It has often been assumed – particularly in the last three hundred years – that science will one day be able to provide a complete and definitive picture of human nature. Ideas differ widely, no doubt, about what form such a picture might take; but they probably have in common the assumption that to form an ultimate picture of human nature, or to give an ultimate explanation of human action, is to bring human behaviour under general causal laws. Man can in principle be treated as part of the physical world, obeying the same laws as other physical objects. Even if man is regarded as part of the animal world, the same principle will apply. The teleological laws that traditionally were invoked to describe animal behaviour can also be replaced with causal explanations. The laws of physics are the paradigm of scientific explanation and provide, in principle, a method for describing all other phenomena.

This theory has indeed been challenged. In the later work of Wittgenstein, for instance, we find a sustained resistance to the intrusion of scientific ways of thinking into the description of human thought and action. In certain passages there seems to be the suggestion that there could never be such a thing as a 'science' of psychology. Such a science would presuppose the possibility of establishing general laws correlating mental states with their causes – a possibility which Wittgenstein seems to wish to deny. As for Freudian analytical psychology, Wittgenstein suggests that Freud's great mistake was to suppose that what he was doing had anything in common with science. Freud does not discover general laws for human nature: what he is doing is more like 'aesthetics'. And aesthetics itself is not a science of mental states and their causes, but more like a systematic account of the *reasons* for certain judgements and responses. In other words, while Freud thought of himself as investigating the causes of human behaviour in a scientific manner, he was in fact doing something else. He was trying to extend the language of reason, intention and desire in order to explain areas of human conduct that had previously seemed inexplicable. Freud extends, and perhaps enriches, our ordinary ways of talking about human thought and action. He does not depart from them.[1]

The question of a scientific account of man, then, is highly controversial, and I do not wish to go into it here. What I wish to do instead is to say something about an alternative approach, or at least about one aspect of it. This approach, unlike that of the natural sciences, is intrinsically anthropocentric. It is anthropocentric not just in the obvious sense that man is the object of study, but in the more important sense that the concepts it uses presuppose, irreducibly, the existence of human beings. That is to say, it uses the sorts of concept that man naturally uses in picturing to himself his own activities. It is impossible to imagine the writing of history, sociology, anthropology or aesthetics which does not make use, in however disguised a form, of such concepts as intention, desire, motive, reasons for action – indeed all that we can sum up under the general heading of 'mental concepts'. However general, abstract or technical any one of these disciplines might aim to be, or claim to be, it can never escape using, in its descriptions of human activities, essentially the same concepts as those we use in ordinary life.

This marks a profound difference from the methods and ambitions of the physical sciences, which aim to give an account of all natural phenomena in terms of causal laws. A systematic description of human nature in scientific terms might or might not be possible. Whether it is so is probably not a question of fact so much as a question of what one is prepared to accept *as* a description of human nature. A scientific account, subsuming human activities under general causal laws, would replace concepts like desire, intention and motive with some such notion as 'stimulus/response'. The specifically human concepts of thought and action would then have been resolved into something else. One might want to say that this is not to give an account of human nature, but to replace the idea of human nature with something different.

One of the reasons that might have encouraged the view that human nature must be described in scientific terms is this: physics aims at a complete description and explanation of events; every event will have a place in physics. Set against this standard of completeness, the system of mental concepts may seem incomplete and unsatisfying. Mental concepts apply only to a narrow range of events. Within this range, however, they allow of descriptions and explanations that are complete. There is no human action that cannot in principle be assigned a reason, a motive or an intention. The concepts of emotion, thought and desire seem to provide complete descriptions of human behaviour, and there is no area of human conduct to which they cannot, in principle, be applied. Indeed there is a clear sense in which the explanations they provide are ultimate: when an action has been made intelligible in terms of motive and reason then we understand it fully. There is nothing that could make it *more* intelligible.

A Philosophical Approach to Human Nature

But how can we present a systematic picture of mental concepts? Is there any way of talking about human nature, other than in scientific terms, that will be general, systematic and informative? The only other way would be to take our ordinary 'anthropomorphic' concepts of thought and action, and to try to see which of them are the most fundamental, in the sense that they are presupposed by all the others. One way of being systematic about human nature is to start from the most abstract of the concepts that apply to human beings, and see whether we can move from them, by a sort of natural transition, to the richer and more detailed concepts which we use to describe human behaviour in all its particularity. This would certainly not be a scientific procedure, since we would not be explaining human nature, in the sense of discovering what causes it to be what it is, but only describing it in very general terms. However, we would not be describing it in just *any* general terms, but in the most general version of the terms that we use in describing human thought and action. This is what we can call a philosophical procedure.

Now I shall devote most of my essay to an example of this

procedure. I shall take two ideas and see what relation there can be between them. These are the ideas of rationality or rational agency, and moral agency; man as a rational agent and man as a moral agent. I take these two ideas because there has been a very strong tendency in modern philosophy to separate them, whereas in ancient and medieval philosophy they were generally considered to have the closest connection one with another. I shall approach the idea of human nature from two of its opposite 'limits'. First, I shall take the general idea of rational agency – man as a creature with a mind and body – and see whether it somehow involves the idea of man as having desires and emotions, and therefore the possibility of virtue and vice. Secondly, I shall raise the question whether there is any sense in which animals can have such qualities as courage, cowardice and so on, and if not, what this means that they lack in terms of rationality.

The Embodied Mind

Let us start, then, with the most abstract picture we can form of a rational being. Descartes famously argued that we can imagine that everything is false about ourselves and our situation, except for the fact that we think. I cannot doubt that I am a thinking being. But I shall assume more than Descartes allows. I shall assume that, having acknowledged that I am a thinking being, then I must also admit that I have a body. The idea of a disembodied mind has, of course, a long and respectable history behind it. I shall merely say now that there are considerable difficulties in the way of imagining a disembodied mind. I shall mention only one. If we suppose, as Descartes allows, that such a mind can think (actually minds do not think, *persons*, whether disembodied or not, think) we have no way of identifying the thinking agent. We cannot say 'X is thinking', but only 'There are thoughts' or 'The following propositions are being entertained.' And we cannot really say that. If we cannot refer these thoughts to anyone then we might as well drop the idea of a disembodied mind altogether. Such a mind could not even refer the thoughts to itself. For what reason could it have for saying that *I* am thinking, when it follows from the fact that I am thinking that someone is thinking? The idea of 'someone' has no place in a disembodied existence.

We should reflect, next, on what follows from a body's being possessed by this particular mind rather than some other. What is it that makes it true to say that *this* body is connected with *this* mind? What is it that makes it true that this body is attached to this particular mind, rather than some other body, or some other physical object in the universe? Let us suppose that I am talking of my body and my mind: what are the grounds for saying that this body (an object which can be pointed to and given a location in space by others as well as by myself) is my body? Not in the sense that it belongs to me in the way that someone else's body might in some legal sense belong to me as a piece of property – if I were a Roman slave-owner talking of my slave – but in the sense that my body, my own body, belongs to me, such that I may truly be said, in pointing to my body, to be 'pointing to myself'. One point in raising this question is that someone might want to ask: could there be a mind related to a body, but in a way quite different from that in which human minds are related to human bodies? Could it, for instance, merely use a body as a means of observing, or experiencing, the world while not being related to it in any more intimate way? Such a question may seem absurd; it is, however, worth remembering that the picture of a mind which merely passively observes the world and happens to be located within a body is recurrent within the main British philosophical tradition. Many difficulties have arisen from this picture, not least about the place of morality.

In answering this question, I shall take as my starting-point some things that Stuart Hampshire says in *Thought and Action*.[2] In asserting that *this* body is *my* body, to what fact am I fundamentally appealing? I am appealing to the fact that I can, in principle, move this body at will. That is to say, that I can move it unless things happen of the following sort: I am prevented by external obstructions, am paralysed, or else (possibly) I am in some such state as a cataleptic trance. However these conditions which might prevent my moving my own body at will are radically different from what prevents me from moving someone else's body at will. If I could move someone else's body at will, then it would not be his body, but my body.

The possibility – or rather the relatively common actuality – of a body's being almost totally paralysed – and even the rare phenomenon of a body's being so completely paralysed that not even the eyes can be moved – is not really a difficulty for this thesis (although it is often assumed to be). The very fact that we regard such a man as 'paralysed' indicates how we must think of such cases. How, for example, could we think of a stone as 'paralysed'? In calling a human being 'paralysed' we have a very distinct sense of how he could move his body were he not paralysed. A man who is paralysed is *impeded* from moving: we regard paralysis as an obstacle. In other words, we have a sense of how his body could be moved at will. We cannot analogously imagine that a whole host of inanimate objects in the world are similarly paralysed: we could not imagine what it would be for them to move at will.

Now for me to be able to move my body 'at will' is not just the same thing as my being able to move it in any way I wish it to move. It is perfectly conceivable that some sort of contingent connection could be set up between my wishes and events in the external world, so that anything within, say, my visual field would move in any way in which I might wish it to move just whenever I wished it. But this ability – or, rather, dispensation – would not make any of these objects part of my own body. Similarly, if I moved my own body simply by wishing that the limbs would move (wishing that I might get out of the bath, for example) this would not constitute 'moving my body at will' and would not be a reason for calling this body *my* body. Indeed, if I tried to move my body by wishing it to move, I would never be able to move a single limb.[3]

So the idea of an embodied mind seems to involve the idea of Will. It does not seem possible to imagine an embodied mind which is a mere passive spectator of events in the world. To put the essence of the argument very briefly: one can observe events in space only if one has a point of view. One can have a point of view only if one is a body occupying space. A body which occupies space can be *my* body only if it is a body which I can, in principle, move at will.

Will, Intention, Desire

We can go further: not only must a thinking being have a will, but its will must be of a certain sort. If a being is to have thoughts, then it must also have a language. If I am able to think, then I am, in general, able to know what I think. And I only know what I think if I am able, on occasion, to say what I think, either to myself or to others. But once a being has language, it can make judgements not just about its present, immediate experience, but also about the past and the future. It is therefore integral to the concept of a rational being that it is capable not only of trying to do something – as a new-born baby that seizes a finger or a stick may be said to be 'trying to hang on' – but also of *forming the intention* of doing something. Its will does not arise simply as a response to its present situation, but also out of a conception of the future. In other words, a rational being has not only will, but also intention. A being that could move its body at will but which was incapable of forming and abandoning intentions would not be properly rational. A cat stalking a bird may be trying to catch the bird. Wittgenstein also thinks that this is the primitive expression of intention.[4] But the cat could not form and then abandon the intention of catching the bird, without ever moving a muscle. The full concept of intention would seem applicable only to the actions and behaviour of a rational being. That is to say, it has full application only to the actions and behaviour of a being capable of formulating judgements about the future, of choosing and abandoning courses of action.

Now if we imagine a being which forms intentions, we have, presumably, to imagine it as having wishes and desires. The notion of 'intention' quite independent of 'appetite' would be very odd. I can answer the question 'What are you doing?' by saying that I intend X in doing what I am doing. And I can answer the further question as to why I intend X by referring to some further intention Y. But could there be a whole series of questions and answers of this sort without at any point the intro-duction of a reference to a desire? We should notice how very unusual it in fact is to answer a 'Why?' question about an inten-tion by referring to a further intention. This is because, once it has been made plain what one's intention is in acting as one does – 'I am aiming at X' – then any further 'Why?' question is directed at one's motive. 'But why do you *want* X?' Further descriptions of one's own intentions may give an ever more complete picture of what one is doing – of what one is up to – but they do not show that one can dispense with considerations of motive altogether, or that the question why one has these intentions has no answer. For to fill out the picture by referring to a whole pattern of intentions is to give a picture of the motives from which the intentions spring. To have all these intentions is to have a motive. We know a lot not only about a man's beliefs, but also about his desires, when we are given some knowledge of his intentions. In other words, one cannot give an adequate account of what one is doing which excludes the possibility of reference to desires. Those cases where it seems that one can go on describing one's actions purely in terms of intention without any reference to desires are really cases where what is desired in what is done is understood. For instance, in describing my moves in a game of chess I might speak purely in terms of what I intend in what I do, with no reference whatever to any desires I might have. But it is all along understood that I *want* to checkmate or otherwise defeat my opponent. My intentions can only subsist against a background of desires (cf. Aristotle saying in *Ethics*, 1101*a*, that we desire the end, but *deliberate* about means).

Emotions of the Embodied Mind

Let us then suppose an embodied mind which has desires and intentions, and can move its body at will. Must it also have emotions? And if so, are there any *particular* emotions it must have?

Now if this creature desires certain ends, and is trying to encompass those ends, and can also intend to encompass those ends, with all that that includes in terms of envisaging future possibilities, then, if it is rational, it must be capable of envisaging the possibility that its attainment of some of its ends might be frustrated. We could, no doubt, place this creature in a world where Providence had so arranged things that its wishes and intentions were never frustrated. Even so, this would mean only that the notion of its ends being frustrated did not apply in this particular case. It would not mean that we could not imagine a change in the environment which would alter this fortunate state of affairs. Certain concepts would not be instantiated, but this does not give us a reason for saying that they could have no foothold. The description traditionally given, for instance, of prelapsarian Man is of a creature all of whose desires were in fact fulfilled, and in describing whose existence, therefore, we would have no need of concepts like 'frustration' of wishes. But the very fact that we can describe him as having wishes at all means that as soon as we envisage the situation radically changed (expulsion from the Garden) we have no difficulty in describing him as frustrated, disappointed in his wishes, balked in his intentions, and so on.

Now if we envisage this being as having certain ends which he desires and also having the expectation in a certain case that one desired end is going to be frustrated by some event which he foresees as possible or probable, do we not find that it is natural to use certain concepts in describing his 'state of mind'? For instance, if he desires an end, is not the event which will frustrate his attainment of the end, to be described from his point of view, as 'undesirable'? The point is that as soon as we introduce the idea of desire – which is necessary if we are to have the idea of Will, which is again necessary if we are to have the idea of an embodied mind – then we have already made room for the idea of things which are undesirable – for instance, the frustration of desires. But this means that as soon as one has desire, one has the possibility of *fear*. Aquinas makes this point, when he says: 'Because fear springs from love, the same virtue which governs the love of particular goods must as a consequence govern the fear of the contrary evils. For example liberality which regulates love of money, must logically control the fear of losing it' (*Summa* 2a2ae. 123.4).

In other words, fear is not an additional faculty which may or may not occur in a rational, embodied being with desires and ends. Although we can imagine a man having all the senses but one, the same does not seem to apply to the emotions. A man might have every sense but be unable to feel pain. But could a man have every faculty (every mental faculty, every faculty of desire, every other emotion) but simply be unable to feel fear?

What would a man also lack who lacked the emotion of fear? In his opera *Siegfried* (Acts I and II) Wagner attempts to represent a man who does not know what fear is. Mime tries to induce fear in Siegfried by giving him descriptions of frightening situations, but Siegfried is simply amused or pleased by what Mime tells him. Even the dragon, Fafner, mostly amuses him, and he does not experience fear until he is about to awaken Brünnhilde in Act III. But allowing that Wagner manages all this very ingeniously, can we really imagine a man who simply doesn't feel fear?

Surely a man who is incapable of fear must be incapable of conceiving that his desire might be frustrated. This presupposes either an overweening confidence – which is more or less Siegfried's case – or a combination of omniscience and omnipotence. (God, presumably, cannot feel fear.) A creature unable to fear must always be certain that it will get what it desires.

But the capacity for *fear* is not just a capacity for a certain sort of feeling – which is how Wagner represents it in *Siegfried* – in the sense of a capacity for being powerfully moved or terrified. Wagner construes fear simply as a *passion*. But a man who was incapable of fearing would also be incapable of certain forms of thought and expression. He would, for instance, be incapable of saying to himself: 'I fear lest his argument may be mistaken'; or 'If you do that I fear I shall have to punish you.' Now these are not cases of the 'passion' of fear – fear as Mime tries to make Siegfried understand it – but nor is their linguistic structure misleading. This is not a 'metaphorical' use of the term 'fear' (even in the second case). Bishop Blougram, in Browning's poem 'Bishop Blougram's Apology', always acted so as to give the impression that he believed implicitly in every last detail of Catholic doctrine. He feared that if he did not do this people might think that he believed none of it at all. This is a true case of *fearing*, although there are no feelings of trepidation, trembling, no shrinkings, pangs, tremors. Similarly, he *wants* people to think he believes, but he does not feel an appetite or longing that they should do so. We can elucidate the notion of fearing not only by referring to cases where people feel something akin to terror, but also where they fear lest so-and-so might happen, that so-and-so might have happened, etc. These are cases where we might say that people 'think with pain' (or with regret, or with disapproval) of what has happened, might happen, or might have happened.

What I hope is becoming clear is that fear is not a 'faculty' which some rational beings with desires and ends might have and others might simply lack. The possibility of fear is, as Aquinas implies, in the very nature of the *desire* for an end. Its possibility is involved in the very nature of intention. That is because if I intend to do something and am frustrated, the character of my reaction to the frustration will often illuminate the nature and seriousness of my intention.

Similarly a creature with desires is already in a position to feel hatred against whatever obstructs its desires, and anger against whoever unjustly obstructs its desires. And if it has a conception of the past – as rational creatures must have – then it can also feel regret, remorse, and perhaps guilt. Once we have introduced the concepts of thought, intention and desire we have introduced the possibility of all the emotions. And once we have introduced such emotions as fear, hope, regret, remorse and guilt, then we have introduced the possibility of a whole range of *moral* concepts.

Now let us suppose that the creature we are envisaging should on occasion strongly desire an end X. Event Y appears as a possibility, and if it occurred it would frustrate the attainment of X. This creature, on the mere thought of the possibility of Y, ceases to try for X. Let us further suppose that this event Y is not all that probable, and that even if it occurred it would not be a serious obstacle. What do we say of a creature who just abandons his attempt to get what he wants in these circumstances? Well obviously, without a good deal more filling-out of the case we cannot say with certainty. But we *might* be able to say things of the following sort: perhaps he was not serious in intending, or wanting or desiring, the end, so that any obstruction, however trivial, might turn him aside. Or perhaps he really did intend and want it, but exaggerated the difficulty of overcoming the obstacles. Or perhaps he really did desire the end, correctly estimated the difficulties, but because of the difficulties, which he did not exaggerate and which were small, he abandoned the intention of attaining his end.

Now these different reactions *could* be described in such a cumbrous, uneconomical way as I have just done. A more economical way of describing the three cases is to say that they are *prima facie* examples of Pusillanimity, Cowardice and Weakness of Will.

So we have now arrived at some moral concepts – the concepts not, indeed, of virtue but of vice. But it is easy to see that in doing that we have made room for an extremely important virtue – the virtue of Courage. Once it becomes possible to describe a creature's emotions, and if it is also possible to attribute aims to him – if, in other words, he has not only needs and desires but also definite intentions – then it is also possible to describe his behaviour in terms of the virtues or vices it exhibits, in this case Pusillanimity and Cowardice. The corresponding concepts of Virtue also become applicable to a rational creature that has desires and intentions. So where Cowardice, Pusillanimity and Weakness of Will are possible, then there is also the possibility of Courage, Confidence and Perseverance. (God, whom we suppose to have intentions, but neither emotions nor desires, can presumably not be called courageous or temperate in the pursuit of His aims. And here we have the perfect case of a Being to whom virtues and vices cannot be ascribed because He has no passions, and has unlimited knowledge and unlimited power. And I think it has been traditional for theologians not to ascribe any virtues to God except Justice and the theological virtue of Charity.) In elucidating the concept of rational action, we seem bound to mention virtues and vices. The possession of virtuous and vicious dispositions, along with desires, passions and intentions, seems to be a part of rationality, part of what it is to be a rational creature.

Rationality and the Virtues

But how are the virtues part of rationality? The answer we find in such medieval philosophers as Aquinas is this: nearly all the virtues, with the possible exception of justice, relate to various human passions. Given certain passions there is a rational or irrational way in which one may experience them. A rational creature does not, therefore, merely regard his own ends as objects of rational choice: he can also aim at cultivating certain dispositions. He may have a reason for being courageous rather than cowardly, for example. It will be part of his aim as a rational agent to bring his own emotions within the bounds of rational decision. Indeed, unless he to some extent aims at the cultivation of certain dispositions it is difficult to see how we can ascribe to him the kind of fullness of intention that is characteristic of a rational being.

We have therefore arrived at the conclusion that a rational creature is essentially a creature to whom certain determinate moral and psychological concepts are applicable. It is impossible to think of an idea of 'human nature' that lies outside the limits determined by these concepts. In particular, we may tentatively conclude that notions of virtue play a determining role in the description of rational (and hence of human) conduct, and this fact is of the greatest interest for any philosophical attempt to describe the limits of human nature.

Animals and the Virtues

Having arrived at the idea of a connection between Virtue and Rationality as it were from above, starting with the extremely abstract notion of a rational agent, I should now like, rather more briefly, to approach it from the opposite direction, from below. The particular virtue I have mentioned is Courage. So having asked whether a rational being – assuming that it has limited power and limited knowledge – must be capable of being virtuous and vicious, I should now like to ask the opposite question: could an animal have virtues? In particular, could an animal be brave?

Now we certainly have a temptation, in the case of some animals, to regard them as 'brave'. Some animals are colloquially called 'brave' as a species – lions and other predatory animals, for example. Or again, some people would wish to call a dog 'brave' if it tackled an intruder at the expense of its own safety. But in order to see whether or not these descriptions are merely anthropomorphic and colloquial, we must describe the case in greater detail. I propose to bring out the point by considering the case of an animal that is not normally called brave, but whose behaviour may be in some respects similar to that of the aggressive dog.

We are told that a male rat seeking to mate with a female is prepared (this being observed in laboratory experiments) to run over electrified plates, suffering considerable pain, in its eagerness to reach the female. Now I don't think we want to describe the rat as 'brave' on the grounds that it is prepared to undergo, or put up with, something in order to satisfy its desire.

And in fact there is something dubious about the locution 'being prepared to put up with something in order to satisfy its desire'. What, in the rat's behaviour, shows that it is 'prepared to put up with the pain in order to . . .'? Certainly what the rat is doing is pursuing the female – that is why it goes in the direction it does – and it does this despite the pain. It might show both its dislike and fear of the pain – through hesitancy, turning back, etc. – and yet still eventually get to the female over the electrified plates. But there is nothing so far which forces us to describe it as 'being prepared to put up with pain in order to gain pleasure' or 'gain the female'. There is a conflict of two passions – fear and the mating instinct; and the mating instinct proves to be the stronger passion (or 'drive') of the two. We could say that the urge to mate 'overcomes' the fear.

What it seems we cannot do is bring some reference to the pain into our description of the rat's intentional behaviour. Any reference we make to the pain would be, to use a piece of philosophical jargon, 'extensional'. What that means is this: if I say that the rat runs over the plates despite the pain, then my remark would have to be understood in such a way that someone could infer from it that the rat is putting its left foot before its right, despite the pain, or moving towards the far wall despite the pain, or moving away from the experimenter despite the pain. There is no unique description of what it is that, *despite the pain*, the rat is doing. We could say, noting an interesting fact about the creature: 'Look! It goes over the electrified plates despite the pain.' This, plus 'it is trying to get to the female', would be a sufficient description of its intentional action. The reason why the context 'it is doing . . . despite the pain' is extensional rather than intensional is that the rat is not 'putting up with the pain in order to reach the female'. Such a locution can have point only where it is possible to say 'its *reason* for putting up with the pain is that it wishes to reach the female'. That is to say, its course of action is a course of action which, out of possible courses of action, it chooses in order to reach an end which it desires. If we say of the rat 'it put up with the pain because it wanted to get to the female' the 'because' has the force of the giving of a reason. And of course once we have introduced the concept of 'reason' then we also allow for the concept of 'motive' and 'choice', and hence of the idea of virtue. As Jonathan Bennett says: '. . . if the concept of "reason" or "motive" could be brought to bear upon the behaviour of ants which march straight into the fire, they would have to be applied in such a way as to justify describing that behaviour as brave, self-sacrificing, etc.'[5] But for the rat to be capable of 'reasons' and 'motives' in this fashion, it would have to be capable of forming universal judgements; and, as Aristotle points out, animals are capable of forming judgements only in a limited sense: they can take account only of particulars, features of the immediate perceptual situation. For the rat's behaviour to be 'brave' or for the dog's behaviour to be 'self-sacrificing' we should have to be able to say of them, in describing their behaviour, not just such things as 'it went on, it didn't run away' (which are admittedly extensional constructions, allowing the substitution of any other correct description of the creature's behaviour, and thus reflecting merely a spectator interest in the proceedings), but also such things as 'it went on rather than run away' which would be a (rather ungrammatical) way of saying 'it *chose* [decided] to go on rather than to run away'. But only a linguistic creature could be described in that way. Although a non-linguistic creature – a creature which did not have a language – could do X rather than Y (at this moment my dog may be barking rather than standing on his hind legs) only a creature with a language could 'do X rather than Y' – i.e. only for a linguistic creature could 'doing X rather than Y' be a description of its intentional action. (That is to say, only a creature with a language could accept the description 'doing X rather than Y' – 'barking rather than wagging my tail' – as the description which he presents to himself of his own action and his own intentions. And a creature could say to itself 'I am barking rather than wagging my tail' only if it possessed a language.) But the possession of language is a defining feature of a rational being.

So once we talk of a creature 'putting up with pain in order to do such and such' or 'sacrificing itself' or 'overcoming its fear', we have introduced the language of reasons and choice. Only a rational creature acts from a motive, or for a reason: only a rational creature chooses to act, say, courageously. But of course, only if one has chosen to act as one does, and only if one acts from a good motive or for a good reason, can one be praised for what one does. And to attribute virtues and vices to people is to praise and blame them. (As Aristotle says, virtues are dispositions which we praise.)

Conclusions, Moral and Metaphysical

There are two sorts of conclusion which could be drawn from the approach that has been adopted in this essay, or perhaps we should rather say two further lines of thought. One can be called 'moral'; the other, which is more general, we can rather loosely refer to as 'metaphysical'. I shall end by sketching these two possible conclusions, without here arguing for either of them.

There has been a strong tendency in moral philosophy, particularly in the last seventy years, to believe that questions of value are fundamentally divorced from questions of fact. We cannot, so it has been thought, start off with a picture of human nature and then go on to derive certain moral values from it. But it is the tendency of what I have been saying to argue against this view. At any rate, the traditional picture of the virtues and the vices is of an extended, systematic way of describing man as a rational being. A rational being necessarily has a reason for cultivating certain sorts of disposition rather than others. If we take the notion of Courage – with which I have been largely preoccupied here – and if we connect it with the notions of rational action and rational choice, we may find that we can establish connections with some of the other virtues – with Temperance, Prudence (practical wisdom) and Justice. Courage might turn out not to stand alone as a virtue, but to be intimately connected with these other virtues. (Such was, of course, the general view in the medieval period and in antiquity.) Courage without Prudence and Temperance might be rashness rather than courage; without Justice it would be a form of bullying or egoism. The true character of Courage may come out in its expression as fully rational, chosen, properly motivated action. Temperance without Courage may be mere pusillanimity or priggishness.

Now if the full picture of the virtues is a picture of man as a rational creature, so that vicious actions are inherently flawed or vitiated, then it is very difficult to see how a man could knowingly and seriously choose to value vices more highly than virtues, or choose to regard such vices as Cowardice and Pusillanimity as virtues. It would, for instance, be difficult to imagine how a man could be *proud* of being a coward, since cowardice means such things as lacking perseverance and confidence; not persisting in a course of action although one desires the end; being overcome by the difficulties. I do not *achieve* something when I act in a cowardly manner, even if good results happen to follow from my cowardice. There is nothing, then, of which I can be proud in what I do.

It may then be that there are certain unchanging values that have their base in an unchanging human nature, and that these values are expressed in the traditional concepts of the virtues. It may also be that there are unchanging relations between these values. A good man is, perhaps, one who is courageous, temperate, wise, prudent, liberal and just; and whatever the moral or ideological fashion of the times, such a picture of the good man cannot change. We could never admire a man for cowardice, intemperance, sloth, envy and stupidity, however 'happy' such qualities might make him (if that were possible) or whatever pleasure the spectacle might afford to others. Even if I were able to find some grounds for admiring him on account of these qualities, I could not admire him as a *man*.

A second, and related, line of thought is this: reflection upon moral philosophy in terms of the virtues and vices in their connection with rationality may be a systematic study of human nature. If it is part of the notion of rational action that it should be virtuous or vicious, then the concepts of the virtues give one way of defining the field of rational conduct. It is therefore possible to impose certain *a priori* limits upon human nature. Human nature is the realm of thought, intention and desire. It further involves the whole range of emotions, and the dispositions to rational action that we describe as virtues and vices. It is impossible, therefore, to imagine human nature changing in these respects. People could no more cease to feel fear or desire, love or hatred, pleasure or anger, than they could cease to think; and they could no more cease to be brave or cowardly than they could cease to have intentions. At any rate, if they did cease to do these things or to have these feelings human nature would not have 'evolved' beyond its present 'limits', but would have ceased to exist. And it is the upshot of my argument that not only would it be difficult, perhaps impossible, to imagine such a change, but it would certainly be impossible to desire it. For human beings, to be what we already are is the only thing that is desirable. That is the true limit of human nature.

1 cf. Wittgenstein, *Lectures and Conversations on Aesthetics, Psychology and Religious Belief,* ed. Cyril Barrett (Oxford 1966).

2 Stuart Hampshire, *Thought and Action* (London 1959).

3 cf. G. E. M. Anscombe on 'willing' – *Intention,* section 29 (Oxford 1957).

4 Wittgenstein, *Philosophical Investigations,* section 647 (Oxford 1953).

5 Jonathan Bennett, *Rationality* (London 1964), p. 45.

David Bohm

6 Human Nature as the Product of our Mental Models

When we speak of human nature, we generally imply that we are talking about something that is more or less fixed in its qualities and properties, and that exists essentially independently of our thought about it. In this essay, however, I am going to propose that that aspect of behaviour which has been attributed to such a fixed and independently existent human nature is actually a continuously changing and developing artefact, created in the course of human work and social relationship, and very much dependent on how it has been considered in thought.

What is especially significant in this regard is that throughout all his activity man has developed a way of thinking about himself in terms of generalized models of what the human being is or ought to be. When accepted as true, these models have served to shape the character of the individual, who feels impelled to conform, either through fear of being stigmatized as abnormal or deviant, or through the sheer attractions of the models. Evidently such models not only act as positive stimuli to certain kinds of behaviour, but also function negatively as limits, tending to inhibit exploration of new modes of thinking and new forms of social relationship. That is to say, they are not merely structures of abstract thought taking place inside people's heads, but rather, they operate in the individual and in society as functioning realities which play a key part in helping to fix the bounds of that very human nature, of which they are supposed to be a model.

A cursory examination of human nature shows many such models, which serve in this way to shape and form human character. Thus there is the 'good boy' who obediently and virtuously does what his parents and teachers want him to do, and the 'bad boy' who naughtily and mischievously insists on doing whatever he himself may want to do. Then there is the industrious hard-working person who stands on his own two feet, and the lazy, shiftless person who depends on other people or on the state. Examples of this kind can evidently quite easily give rise to a vast totality of diverse models. All of these tend, however, to be assimilated into broader overall sorts of model, which can be seen to arise, develop, and die away in the course of the history of human society. One of the earliest of these is the strength, courage and other virtues of animals, the consideration of which was evidently especially significant to early man in helping to stimulate his hunting and fighting qualities. Then came the power, beauty and goodness of anthropomorphic gods, which served to give men a model more favourable to organized and civilized behaviour. And now, we have the precision, orderliness, efficiency and energy of machinery in the modern technological society, which each man is encouraged to imitate, in order to make it possible for such a society to function coherently and stably.

Such generalized models evidently tend to fit in with the prevailing world view, including the cosmology and the generally-accepted metaphysical notions. Thus the ancient Greeks tended, to a considerable extent, to look on the universe as a single organism, in which each part grows and develops in its relationship to the whole, and each part has its proper place and function. In this view, it clearly makes sense for man to try to play his part by acting according to the ideals embodied in his notions about the gods. On the other hand, in modern times, the prevailing world view has been one developed especially in physics: that the universe is like a vast machine, constituted of separately existent atoms moving mechanically, according to their inertia and their forces of mutual interaction. This view not only helped lay the foundation for modern technology, but also provided an intuitive theoretical basis for the assimilation of human nature to the mechanical qualities required of men in our industrialized society, in which neither the virtues of animals nor those of gods can be given first priority. Rather, as has already been indicated, the prime virtue in modern society is a kind of effectiveness, efficiency, or productivity similar to that of the machines which man has to operate. But this requirement goes far beyond the context of machinery and purely technological activities. Indeed, as there is

no room in the world view of modern physics for an organic order
of reality that cannot be revealed solely by measurements of
mechanical kinds of effect, so we are now discovering that in
modern society there is no room for regarding education or other
such activities as organic aspects of life as a whole, worth pursuing
in their own right. Rather, these activities have now to submit
ultimately to the test of whether they lead to useful results that
can be measured in terms of their contribution to the gross
national product.

Evidently, then, the notion of *effectiveness* or *efficiency* now
plays a key part in maintaining the present industrial society and
in shaping human nature into forms that are suitable for such a
society. But every *effect* must issue from a cause, so that, more
deeply, what is implied in the current notion of efficiency is an
acceptance of that aspect of the prevailing cosmology and general
world view having to do with cause.

Such notions of cause have in fact changed in fundamental
ways throughout human history. These changes can be brought
out in a manner relevant to our discussion by considering certain
key differences between modern notions of causality and some of
those held in ancient Greece. To do this, we may begin by review-
ing briefly Aristotle's distinction of causes into four different
kinds:

> *material*
> *efficient*
> *formal*
> *final*

A good example in terms of which this distinction can be understood is obtained by considering something living, such as a tree
or an animal. The *material cause* is then just the matter in which
all the other causes operate and out of which that thing is constituted. Thus, in the case of a plant, the material cause is the
soil, air, water and sunlight constituting the substances of the
plant. The *efficient cause* is some action, external to the thing
under discussion, which allows the whole process to get under
way. In the case of a tree, for example, the planting of the seed
could be taken as the efficient cause.

It is of crucial significance in this context to understand what
was meant by the *formal cause*. Unfortunately, in its modern con-

notation, the word 'formal' tends to refer to an outward form that is not very significant (e.g. as in 'formal dress' or 'a mere formality'). However, in the ancient Greek philosophy, the word *form* meant, in the first instance, an inner *forming activity*, which is the cause of the growth of things, and of the development and differentiation of their various essential forms. For example, in the case of an oak tree, what is indicated by the term 'formal cause' is the whole inner movement of sap, cell growth, articulation of branches, leaves, etc., which is characteristic of that kind of tree, and different from that taking place in other kinds of trees. In more modern language, it would be better to describe this as the *formative cause*, to emphasize that what is involved is not a mere form imposed from without, but rather *an ordered and structured inner movement that is essential to what things are.*

Any such formative cause must evidently have an end or product, which is at least implicit. Thus it is not possible to refer to the inner movement from an acorn giving rise to an oak tree, without simultaneously referring to the oak tree that is going to result from this movement. So formative cause always implies ✓ *final cause.*

We also know final cause as *design*, consciously held in mind through thought (this notion being extended to God, who was regarded as having created the universe according to some grand design). It must be emphasized, however, that design is only a special case of final cause. For example, men often aim toward certain ends in their thoughts, but what actually emerges from their actions is generally something different from what was in their design, something that was, however, *implicit* in what they were doing, though not consciously perceived by those who took part.

In the ancient view, the notion of formative cause was considered to be of essentially the same nature for the mind as it was for life and for the cosmos as a whole. One can understand this notion in more modern terms by considering the flowing movement of awareness. Thought can then be perceived within this flow as a series of momentary product forms, continuously being created and dissolved in the whole movement, as ripples, waves and vortices are created and dissolved in a flowing stream of water. In this process, one can in the first instance discern associative thoughts, in which one step follows another relatively mechanically, through association determined by habit and conditioning.

Each such associative change is external to the inner structure of the thought in question, so that associative changes act rather like a series of efficient causes. But to see the *reason* for something is not a mechanical activity of this nature. Rather, one is aware of each aspect as assimilated within a single whole, all of whose parts are inwardly related. Here one has to emphasize that reason is essentially a kind of perception through the intellect, similar in certain ways to artistic perception, and not merely the associative repetition of reasons that are already known. Thus one may be extremely puzzled by a wide range of factors, things that do not fit together, until suddenly there is a flash of understanding, and thereafter one sees how these factors are all related as aspects of one totality. Fundamental scientific discoveries generally involve perception of a similar nature. For example, there is Newton's well-known insight into the law of gravitation, in which he saw that as the apple falls, so the moon falls, and so everything falls, under the influence of the universal force of gravity. Such acts of perception cannot properly be given a detailed analysis or description. Rather, they are to be considered as aspects of the *forming* activity of the mind. A particular structure of concepts is then the *product* of this activity, and these products are what are linked by the series of efficient causes that operate in ordinary associative thinking. Likewise, in this view, one regards the forming activity as primary, in nature as it is in the mind, so that the product-forms in nature are also what are linked by efficient causes.

In modern physics, formative and final causes are not regarded as having a primary significance. Rather, law is generally conceived as a self-determined system of efficient causes, operating in an ultimate set of material constituents of the universe (e.g. elementary particles subject to forces of interaction between them). These constituents are not to be regarded as formed in an overall process, and thus they cannot be considered to be like organs adapted to their place and function in the whole (i.e. to the ends which they would serve, in this whole). Rather, they tend to be conceived as separately existent elements of a fixed nature. Similarly, in society, each human being tends to be regarded as separately existent and likewise of more or less fixed nature. He acts on other people and on society as a whole, in much the same way that he acts on nature, to produce effects that he wants, and these in turn act on him in a corresponding way.

In earlier phases of the development of this point of view, the human mind was regarded as something completely separate from the outwardly visible substance of matter, so that, in principle, room was left for a non-mechanical sort of formative and final cause in man's 'innermost soul and spirit'. But what is implicit (and often even explicit) in the dominant trend of development in modern science is that ultimately even life and mind will be seen as reducible to nothing more than an aspect of the movements of elementary particles, according to the mechanical laws that govern these movements. This whole trend is evidently in complete contrast with the ancient view, in which people regarded the entire universe, including external nature and man, as continuously growing and sustaining itself in each part through its inner formative activity (e.g. the very word 'nature' comes from a Latin root, meaning 'that which is being born', while the corresponding Greek word '*physis*' is based on a verb meaning 'to grow').

In recent times there has been an increasing realization that the modern technological society has certain inherent defects of a very serious nature, which may even prove to be insuperable in the long run, if there is no fundamental change. Some signs of these defects are the widespread occurrence of pollution and destruction of the balance of nature, in a context of growing overpopulation and the creation of a general environment that is neither physically nor psychologically healthy for the people who have to live in it. More and more people have thus been led to question the modern technological model of human nature, some implicitly and others explicitly. Such questioning naturally leads to the consideration of alternative models. Thus, could we revive some form of the organic model favoured in ancient times? Such a model might, for example, help us to see the proper limits of the notion of effectiveness or efficiency, by making it clear that this notion is a sensible one only in the context of a rational and coherent common *end*, which really acts as a kind of general formative cause that pervades all of our activity. The difficulty with the modern technological view of human nature is indeed that *efficiency itself* has tacitly been taken as the ultimate end of all human activity, so that it has not been noticed that what is called efficient in one context may actually be fragmentary and destructive in a broader context. Evidently some sort of organic view of reality could at least in principle help not only in this regard, but also more generally, to orient men toward a sense of unity and common purpose, in which material and mental aspects were not divorced.

Nevertheless, a closer inspection shows that such an organic view may also have certain very serious inherent defects. For example, in ancient times, slavery was often justified by comparing different kinds of men to different organs of the body (e.g. the master to the head and the slave to the limbs). The more modern mechanical view evidently tends to favour the notion of the essential equality of all men. What is perhaps even more important is that the mechanical view made possible a technological development that enabled the vast body of mankind to look forward to a life free of back-breaking and soul-destroying toil. Moreover, the ultimate decline of ancient societies, basically through various forms of fragmentation, conflict, and inner decay, would tend further to show that their overall world-view was in some deep sense highly inadequate.

Perhaps, then, one could seek yet another model that would combine the virtues of the organic model and the mechanical model, allowing man to 'have the best of both worlds'? At this point it is necessary, however, to give pause and to ask whether it is wise to go on with this process of exchanging one model for another. Is the human mind actually capable of conforming to any model at all? In view of what has been said about the formative movement of the mind revealed in reason and in the act of understanding, does it make sense to try to construct a model of this movement?

Even if one does decide to adopt such a model, one first needs an intelligent and rational perception, which indicates whether any specified model is suitable or not. In any case, after adopting a particular model, one needs further perception of this kind to see its limits. For example, people who carry the model of a courageous man too far are described as foolhardy; those who try always to put other people's welfare first, without considering their own, are criticized as improvident; and those who carry efficiency too far are said to be cold and inhuman. Only intelligent and rational perception from moment to moment can deal adequately with seeing how far any model should be carried in a given case. So it is clear that such intelligent and rational perception is the prime necessity, even when it comes to dealing with models. For models are fixed, and reality is eternally changing, going beyond the limits comprehended in particular models. Moreover, the ability of the mind to see contradictions between model and reality evidently also has to go beyond any particular model.

As indicated in the discussion of formative cause, reality may be likened to the flowing movement of a stream, producing eternally-changing forms, such as vortices, ripples, waves. Our thoughts can model these forms, but cannot model the flowing movement in its totality. This is so not only with regard to the physical universe, but, even more, with regard to the flowing movement of awareness, in which our thoughts are themselves merely evanescent forms. When these forms recur systematically, then we have organized ideas; otherwise, only ephemeral images. What can it possibly mean for such superficial forms to model the whole movement that creates, sustains, and eventually dissolves them?

Scientific, technical, and practical experience over the ages has indeed shown that the attempt to impose a firmly-fixed model upon the flowing movement of nature eventually leads to contradiction. Clearly this is even more apt to occur when the mind attempts to impose such a fixed model on its own flowing movement. The resulting contradiction brings about conflict, which is the attempt of one aspect of the mind to impose its pattern on another, with a resulting split of the mind into opposing fragments. This process, in which the mind divides against itself by attempting to conform to a model, is in essence the root of what has in other contexts been called neurosis. Such neurosis, which is present in all of us to a greater or lesser degree, evidently impedes a generally relevant and appropriate response to life as a whole, by breaking up thinking, feeling, and outward action into parts that work against one another.

We are thus led to give serious attention to the fact that the mind is not a 'thing' of which one can sensibly form a model. Rather, we may explore the notion that the mind is to be considered primarily in its formative activity as a flowing movement, and only secondarily through the relatively fixed forms of ideas and concepts, which are the product of this activity, and which are the essential basis of all models. Note here that we are not proposing the notion of formative cause as a model of the activity of the mind. Rather, this notion is to serve as a sort of metaphor, that 'points to', or indicates, a movement of which we can all be immediately aware. This movement cannot be specified in detail; but nevertheless, from it emerge all the specifiable forms, ideas, models, etc. that can be entertained in thought.

It is clear, then, that what is under consideration here is a thoroughgoing change in the nature of thought itself; i.e. a change in which the mind ceases to try to shape and control its own activity by thinking about a model of human nature and trying to impose this model on its own thoughts, feelings, and outward actions. This change has to be explored and experimented with; for the deeper nature of the mind is essentially unknown. To try to specify this change in detail at the outset would be like trying to anticipate the content of a flash of understanding before the latter has actually occurred. Indeed, it would in effect be an attempt to make a model of what it means to think without being dominated by a model, a procedure that would evidently be meaningless in terms of what is being suggested here.

To consider such a change properly, one has rather to understand thought more deeply. As has been seen, one may distinguish two poles, between which all thought moves: thought following mechanically through associations which constitute a series of efficient causes, and thought forming creatively in new totalities, through that aspect of intelligent perception that is called reason.

We shall begin with a discussion of the more mechanical aspect of thought; i.e. with thought that proceeds through a series of efficient causes. Clearly any sort of efficient cause involves the *order of time* in a fundamental way. Now, quite generally, the order of time is abstracted from movement and change. But this abstraction is itself present only in the content of thought, and does not correspond to some directly and immediately perceived reality. Thus, if one reflects a bit, one sees that the past is gone. It is in fact known only in memory. Memory itself is active in the present moment, but the content of its imagery refers to a past that no longer exists. Similarly, the expected future is always known only in thought, operating in the present, but referring to what is to come and does not yet exist (and, indeed, to what may never exist). If we take the ordinary view of time as a sort of linear order, however, the present is to be regarded as a dividing-point between past and future. Since neither of these exist, it would follow also that the present does not exist either. In other words, there is no past, no present, and no future.

This paradoxical conclusion has its root basically in the fact that time is not a reality that exists independently of thought about it, but that, as indicated earlier, it is an abstraction, knowable only in thought, and thus not capable of being perceived directly and immediately. Indeed, as is quite evident, one never observes time as such. One observes the position of a clock indicator, or a star, or some other such thing, or one observes changes in the structure or state of being of some object or system. All of these are forms produced in the universal flux or flowing movement of reality as a whole, and abstracted in thought. As pointed out earlier, in so far as the features abstracted are recurrent and stable, an overall order of cause and effect may reveal itself in the way in which the various forms succeed each other, with effect following cause in a regular way, always at a later time. But to understand the whole process deeply, one cannot begin with the sequence of abstracted product-forms; rather, one has to begin with the whole flowing movement, which carries the formative activity that creates these product-forms, and explains the order in which they succeed one another.

Such an understanding has to comprehend not only the formative activity underlying natural process, but also the formative activity underlying thought itself. For if we treat thought as some sort of ultimate truth beyond the limits of the mutability of natural things, we will fall into contradiction, because we ignore the evident fact that thought is inseparably involved in that process of change from which time has been abstracted.

The illusion that the content of thought may have a validity beyond time is given some apparent support by the fact that one's thought at a given moment contains an image in principle capable of covering all time. As one thinks, one can, as it were, sweep over the whole of time without limits, in a single glance. But in doing this, one is liable to ignore the fact that thought is not only *about* the order of time in the way just described, it is *of* the order of time as well. One thought succeeds another through association or through response to new perceptions, and in this way what seemed to be an eternal truth is seen later to be limited, or even false, so that it falls under the dominion of time. In other words, our thought is itself a functioning reality, a process that is taking place in the order of time.

The process of thought may be regarded in the first instance as containing a model of a time-order. But what is more important is that the time-order that is modelled in the *content* of thought is in essence the same as the time-order that is actually created in the *functioning* of thought. We have learned through much re-enforced habit and conditioning to project this order into those fairly regular and recurrent aspects of natural process (e.g. day and night, the seasons, etc.) which can be seen to be, in a certain sense, similar to the order of thought.

It is important, however, to consider the fact that in primitive stages of development the organization of human society tended on the whole to be much less based on the order of time than is our own, so that men did not then give the time-order nearly so great a significance as we do now. But later, as man developed his civilization and arranged his technology according to the order of time, he created an apparently universal and pervasive environment that is built into a time-structure. Thus, his overall experience seemed to confirm him in the belief that the time-order is not merely a useful and perhaps necessary way of co-ordinating practical, technical and other social activities, but, much more, the universal ground of all existence. So man was led to project this time-order into the totality of his being, physical and mental, and to suppose that this projection covered all that could possibly be significant about the whole of life. That is to say, man made a mental model of himself, in which he saw himself entirely within the framework of a time-order.

To do this leads however to very important consequences. For as has now been seen, any thought in the framework of time is not just a potentially informative abstraction. Rather, it is a functioning and operating reality, that continues and maintains itself in a process, in which one association leads automatically to another. So, to develop a model of the self, conceived in the order of time, is to create a mechanical order of real activity which is a product of the model. This means however that such a model of the self does not remain a mere model, but that it actually *becomes* the self.

This sort of effect is indeed already well known in common experience. Thus, if a child is systematically frightened, he develops a model of a timid, fearful, inadequate self. This model contains fear-sensations similar to those that may arise in the presence of real danger, which include even physiological effects, such as the release of adrenalin, and increase of the rate of beat of the heart. In other words, a mental model of fear *is* fear. Similarly, a mental model of a time-order *is* a time-order. And a mental model of a self *is* a self.

This sort of complication need not arise in connection with models of things that are essentially independent of the process of thought (which are to be understood as recurrent and stable forms in the totality of the flowing movement). Thus, one can have in one's thoughts all kinds of models of objects (e.g. tables, chairs, houses), and their possible relationships, extending onward to engineering models of machinery and to scientific models of the atomic structure of matter, planetary orbits, galaxies, quasars, etc. One may have mechanical models, organic models, or models of any other kind that one may be able to think of. In this domain (the limits of which have to be seen in each case through intelligent perception) models are evidently both useful and necessary, so that it would be absurd to try to do without them.

However, to make a model of the self is, as has been seen, to allow one's thought to create the very reality of which it is supposed to be only a model, in such a way that in this reality one part of the mind is trying to split off from the rest, and to impose its pattern on the whole flowing movement. To do this is evidently a form of fragmentation and confusion, resulting from an attempt to carry out a contradiction. Put explicitly, the contradiction is this: thought, which is fixed and limited in the form of particular models, is attempting the impossible task of controlling the unknown and unlimited flowing movement of the mind, which continually produces and changes all the content of the mind in unforeseeable ways, including even the very thought that is trying to maintain control.

Is it not then possible for models of the self to cease to operate, and thus to bring to an end this contradiction, with its attendant general fragmentation and confusion?

When a leaf dies, one can still see its form, which serves to reveal its whole structure and the order of development from which it has arisen as a product. But its inner formative activity has ceased, so that it will gradually wither away and dissolve.

Our question is thus equivalent to asking whether the general formative activity underlying all models of the self can die in a similar way so that this activity too will wither away and dissolve.

The ending of the formative activity that creates a model of the self (or of human nature more generally) implies a very deep change in the order of operation of the mind, which could perhaps be called a mutation; i.e. a beginning of a new evolution, in which intelligent and rational perception, rather than the automatic and repetitive function of models of the self, would be the main formative cause of man's activity. As indicated earlier, it makes no sense to try to give a detailed description of this evolution before it takes place. But one can perhaps give some sort of over-all feeling for what is to be meant here by saying that, in general, it implies that what one does is less important than why one does it. That is to say, the question 'Why?' points to the inner formative activity, while the question 'What?' points in a much more restricted way to a particular product of this activity. Even if this product is right on a given occasion, the long-run implications will be wrong if the universal formative activity is wrong. To be aware of this requires an intelligent perception which can reveal directly and immediately (i.e. not in terms of a time-sequence of associative changes) how the formative activity arising in models of the self is actually an attempt to carry out the general contradiction that is implicit in all such models. When this contradiction is perceived not merely with regard to content, but also in the actual formative movement of one's own thinking and feeling, then (as happens with any contradiction perceived in this way) the activity in question withers and dies.

Of course, to suggest such a notion of man's nature as contingent and capable of fundamental change when the deep contradictions in thought are perceived and understood raises enormous issues, which could be discussed adequately only in a sustained and serious work of common inquiry. Here we can touch on only a few salient points.

Among these, we may consider the question of how we may regard morals and ethics. It is well known that, for the most part, men have in this domain attempted to conform to various models of right behaviour, right thinking, and right feeling. But it is also well known that these models have not worked very well. For example, man has for thousands of years accepted the elementary injunction not to kill, and along with this has gone the model of the good man, to whom killing is abhorrent. Nevertheless, killing in every conceivable form has continued over these thousands of years, often reaching a vast scale. What is especially significant here is that man has never lacked for models that make killing seem necessary and right (e.g. honour, glory, duty to family, country, God, etc.).

Given any model, man can always conceive of a different model, which may be anything between a small modification of the original one and something that is opposite to the original in essential respects. Thus, for example, the injunction against killing may be modified to the form 'Do not kill, except in certain cases'. Within these exceptions, men may first place defence of what is sacred, defence of the security and interests of the nation, of the family, of the self, etc., until finally they may in effect be able to go as far as to think: 'I must not kill, except when someone is preventing me from getting something I want very much.'

One can see by looking at what is known of history over the past five thousand years or so that this sort of process of steady sliding away from the meaning of moral and ethical injunctions has been extremely common. Indeed, a major part of this history would be a chronicle of how men who were fairly moral and ethical in ordinary times somehow found themselves engaged in countless wars, large and small, with their attendant massacre, pillage, robbery, enslavement, mass starvation and death through plague, senseless destruction of material resources, and so on.

The key difficulty is that clear and intelligent perception is needed, particularly in times of stress or when strong passions are at work, for under these conditions men can easily be swayed to adopt any model that assuages their sense of fear, rage, hurt pride, etc., or that otherwise justifies them in doing whatever it is that they may happen very strongly to want to do. It is evidently very hard to keep the mind clear under such critical conditions. This is made even more difficult by the fact that, at bottom, models are arbitrary, so that in times of stress and conflict no unshakeable reason can actually be found for adhering to any particular set of moral or ethical models. Why, for example, should a man hold to the model of civilized kindly co-operative human behaviour, when inwardly he may be burning with indignation and hatred for those who have treated his nation badly, trampled on all that he feels to be sacred and dear, etc.?

As indicated earlier, the real question to raise in this context is not 'Which model is right?' but rather 'Why is one behaving as one is?' Here we are not merely asking for some superficial reason that is ready to hand, but rather for the deep forming movement that has to be seen in an act of perception as revolutionary as that which Newton or Einstein needed to set physics on a new course of development.

I would like to emphasize that at this depth the source of irrational, violent, and ultimately self-destroying reactions is a wrong mode of functioning of the general model-making activity, which has been caught up in models of the self. As has been seen, to adhere to a model of the self is to create and give sustenance to an actual time-process of a rather mechanical kind in which there is a confused attempt to split the mind into one part that tries to maintain control and another part that is apparently being controlled.

What is, in the first instance, such an inward division in each man then goes on, in further development, to give rise to a division between one man and another, one group and another, one religion and another, one nation and another, etc. For different people with different backgrounds of experience and conditioning will in general come to different models of the self. But since these models imply an overall definition of what is good, what is right, what is true, and, in general, what is the necessary form of all human life, then ultimately men cannot do other than fight to the death over them. That is to say, man's attempt to model his own nature has, built into it, an inner logic leading to a split of the mind for the individual and to general destruction for society as a whole.

In this regard perhaps one of the most important models is that of different human beings, and groups of human beings, as separately existent, and divided, as it were, by a deep chasm that has somehow to be bridged, or that is perhaps even unbridgeable. Evidently, as long as such models are generally accepted, there is little or no real scope for a common co-operative endeavour of people all over the earth which is now needed if the natural resources of this planet are not soon to be destroyed in a mindless scramble of each group to get what it can for itself while something still remains to be got in this way.

With regard to the question of how this separative mode of looking at oneself and the world originates, one may perhaps speculate that at a certain stage a young child realizes that as he calls himself 'I' and other people 'you', so each person calls himself 'I' and other people 'you'. This implies that 'I' and 'you' are the names of every man. Such an insight could in principle point to a general formative activity, which might be called the universal essence of humanity as a whole of which each person is a particular case. Actually most children probably do sense something like this, which could be expressed by saying, for example: 'If I had been exposed to all the conditions and experiences of another person, I could have thought, felt, and acted as he did.' In other words, at the deepest level we all participate in one inner formative movement, which we may be said to observe and experience from different points of view. But just as one person can understand why things look physically different to another person who is differently placed, so mentally we are all potentially capable of understanding the deep formative cause underlying human behaviour in general which is seen and experienced differently by each person.

But when a child grows up in a world in which the notion of separateness is accepted as truth, he is gradually conditioned to operate according to the corresponding models of divisions among men. In this way his potential insight into the oneness of humanity is blocked. Thereafter his experience will be such as apparently to prove and confirm the reality of the divisions among men, as portrayed in the model. What is missed in this is a perception of the fact that the behaviour which seems to prove and confirm the model is mainly a result of the operation of the model itself. Thus before young children have learned about the model of races as fundamentally different sorts of human being, they generally have no difficulty in relationships with people of different skin colour. But afterwards they may, in such relationships, experience a sense of fear and revulsion, which serves to create the very barriers that the model claims merely to represent and describe.

Evidently this sort of reaction is only a special case of the general activity of models of the self. Such models lead to an impasse, in which the problems of humanity cannot be solved because attempts to solve them are confused by mistaking the activity produced mainly by the model of the self for an independent and substantial reality that appears to have to be given first priority in any acceptable solution.

The only way out of this impasse is for men to see the meaninglessness of all these models, so that the confusion can die away. Men may then be able to understand one another deeply, and so, to act from a sense of the oneness of humanity. What is needed here is not an action from a 'model of oneness', but rather an action from the direct and immediate perception that the deep cause of all human action is a universal formative movement. Such perception allows each man to have a sense of what it is that moves other men and makes them act as they do, which arises from an immediate feeling for their conditioning as potentially or even actually his own. When people who have such a perception get together, they will be able to come to a common understanding that is not blocked by the meaningless models to which each person has been conditioned.

More generally, in all human relationships, we have to be free of the constraining and distorting notion that human nature is some well-defined sort of 'thing' that can in principle be known and specified in terms of models of the self. Human nature in its totality – and all the essential abstractions from it, such as beauty, truth, rationality – are not 'things', but aspects of a whole movement. 'Things' can properly be conceived in terms of models. But the whole movement of human nature cannot be contained in any models. Rather it is capable of continually revealing itself anew in fresh and unexpected ways that are in essence inexhaustible.

When we are aware of both the contradictory content of our models of human nature and their limiting and distorting influence in the deep formative activity of the mind, these models will drop away, and there will be no specifiable limits to human nature.

The real question – which has to be explored deeply rather than given a ready answer – is then: can we live without depending on models of human nature?

ADDENDUM: RÉSUMÉ OF DISCUSSION

An extensive discussion followed the lecture on which this essay is based. This discussion will be summarized here not in detail but rather with regard to presenting what seemed to the speaker to be the essential questions that it brought out.

A great deal of the earlier parts of the discussion centred on the question of how far models could properly be used. In the beginning it was necessary to emphasize that in the practical, functional, technical and scientific domains there is a vast scope for models of all kinds. But then more subtle questions were raised. Thus: can we not make models of the thought process itself?

If we have in mind the process of associative thought with its relatively mechanical sequence of efficient causes, a model of it may well give us important insights into how it works. But we have to be careful here, or else we may slip into trying in a similar way to develop a model of reason as a whole, i.e. of the creative movement of perception through the intellect which gives rise to new totalities of concepts and ideas. To try to make a model of reason would be meaningless, because reason is the formative movement that creates all models and ultimately shows their limits.

What is perhaps even more important in this context, however, is that if we attempt to make a model of mental processes or states of feeling with which we identify our whole being (as is implicit in models of the self) this will lead to all the contradiction and confusion already discussed earlier. Consider, for example, a person who is given to dishonesty and self-deception. Suppose that on suddenly realizing that he has such tendencies this person were to try to construct or find a model of honesty and truth to which he would attempt to conform. This would evidently make no sense. For since this person is in the habit of self-deception he will inevitably deceive himself further about his attempts to 'become an honest man'. Rather, the right question in this context is: 'Why am I caught in self-deception?' This question, if asked seriously, may point to what is going on at the deep formative levels of the mind. Generally speaking, one can, through such a question, see that self-deception originates in the automatic, habitual and largely unconscious operation of models that was picked up in early childhood. A typical model of this kind is that the self is highly inadequate, but that to be aware of this is almost unbearably painful, because the self ought to be essentially perfect. So the mind covers up the sense of inadequacy, and seeks any form of self-deception (e.g. accepting flattery from others) that momentarily eases the sense of pain produced by the operation of the model of an inadequate self.

A great deal of confusion originates in men's efforts to identify themselves with models of truth, honesty, courage, power and effective-ness, kindliness, love, etc. Thus, it is well known that in battle most men are afraid but feel impelled to conform to a model of courageous behaviour. The fear then comes out in confused behaviour in other contexts, of which the person is largely unaware. Similarly, parents commonly imply to their children that love consists of modelling themselves on what the parents think is right, good, true, etc. Such conformity is not real love, but rather a form of fear. Moreover, it must evidently destroy originality and intelligence: once a child learns to accept a notion of the self because not to do so would displease his parents, then he has started an overall movement of undiscriminating conformity in the deep activity of the mind as a whole. A child should never be asked to accept a model of love, truth, honesty, etc., because these are not specifiable 'things', which can sensibly be modelled, but rather, have to be discovered in the unlimited flowing movement of life as a whole. Indeed, he should not really be asked even to accept a technical or practical model before he understands the reason for doing so. Otherwise (as has been brought out in some modern in-quiries into the education of children) he is being taught the habit of unquestioning conformity in the deeper levels of the mind, and this is incompatible with true intelligence.

The question was then raised about the validity of psychological analyses, such as those of Freud, Jung and others. Evidently these contain models of the mind, such as, for example, Freud's division between conscious and unconscious layers in terms of the concepts of Id, Ego and Superego. Such models have to be considered with the utmost care and attention. Thus to assert that in some general sense a large part of the operation of the mind is not consciously known is one thing; but to give the content of a particular model to the uncon-scious is another. Here there is the distinct danger (proved very often in practice) that the operation of the model will (as generally happens with models of the self) tend to create the very thing of which it is supposed to be only a model. To do this, however, is to add to the confusion rather than to help to clear it up.

Further questions were raised about the possibility of making models of a person's knowledge. For example, one can say of a certain person that he is a physicist, a plumber, or something else. To do this is to make a mental model of him as possessing a certain knowledge (or skill).

Such a model may be appropriate, provided its use is limited to a suitable context (which has to be seen in each case anew, in an act of intelligent perception). For knowledge is part of the associative side of thought, and is thus only some limited aspect of the mind as a whole. However, if a person identifies himself with such knowledge and skill, then this becomes part of a model of the self with all its attendant fragmentation and confusion. For example, a man who identified himself with his knowledge of physics would feel very uncomfortable on learning that key aspects of his knowledge were wrong or mistaken. As a result he would tend to deceive himself by overlooking or distorting evidence of error in his knowledge, so that his ability to work properly in physics would be greatly impeded.

Similar difficulties with models arise when a person tries to be completely certain, or sure that he is on the right track. For example, it was asked in the discussion what are the criteria for knowing whether or not one has transcended models of the self. This is equivalent to asking for a model of a self that has transcended models of the self. One has to consider first why such a question is asked. The reason is easily seen to be that the prevailing model of the self is one with great uncertainty and insecurity, one that evidently calls for a new model in which this uncertainty and insecurity are removed.

Actually the attempt to be sure that one is free of models of the self is irrelevant and a source of distortion. Thus, for example, if Einstein had begun by asking himself how he could be sure that he had transcended Newtonian mechanics, this would have so blocked his mind that he could never have inquired freely without fear of failure, as is needed for any original discovery. In fact, creative work can generally take place only when attention is totally devoted to whatever is being done, and this is not possible when one is thinking about the self, which always brings in an irrelevant fear of the unknown, that tends to keep the mind a prisoner of its old way of thinking. A similar creative freedom, but at a yet higher level, is needed to discover how our models of the self produce this fear of the unknown.

In this connection, it may be added that we have a wide range of models of death, which are aimed largely at easing the sense of fear of the unknown that is implicit in models of the self. Our understanding of the functioning of such models can play a key role in determining whether we live in creative freedom or in fear. Thus it is quite easy to see, when someone dies, that the inner formative activity of the body has ceased, so that the latter must start to dissolve and disintegrate. But generally speaking this is not the aspect of death that must interest us. Rather the main question is usually 'What will happen to *me*?', meaning by 'me' some 'inner spiritual essence' or 'soul' concerning the fate of which there is usually a great deal of fear.

In earlier times men came to propose that in one sense or other the 'me' survives death and goes on living in some other realm or domain. This model evidently helped to assuage the deep fear that is often raised by the notion that the 'me' does not survive (though it led to further uncertainties as to how the 'me' would be treated in the life to come after death). On the other hand, in more modern times, death has become a topic that people would prefer to avoid, though evidently the fear connected with it is as deep as ever. For death is both universal and necessary, so that if fear prevents us from considering it in a clear and rational way there will be a pervasive effect on how the whole mind works and thus on how we live.

If one looks at this question carefully, one sees that there is as little reason to make a model of death as there is to make a model of life as a whole. The ultimate meaning of death is unknown. The model that we will go on after the death of the body evidently has no basis in fact. What is perhaps less evident, though no less true, is that the model of death of the body as the absolute end has also no basis in fact. Actually we have no way of knowing what, if anything, happens to the individual after death. To suppose that he comes to an end may give rise to an easing of tension that results from seeming to know, which removes the unpleasant sense of uncertainty about the future. But to accept this notion as true is a form of self-deception, not deeply different from accepting the notion that one is certain of survival after death. The two notions are basically equivalent, in that they create a confused movement in the deeper formative activity of the mind, which tends to destroy both real intelligence and true feeling.

Why is it generally difficult to remain with the simple fact that one does not know what, if anything, follows death? Is it, as was suggested in the discussion, simply that one is curious to know? Or is it not that the mind is seeking a sense of security, and is ready to take what is false as true if to do so will make things seem certain and secure so that one feels more at ease in oneself?

Without this meaningless search for the illusion of security about death, the mind may then perhaps be able, naturally and spontaneously, to cease to make models, in the whole of that domain in which models have no proper function.

At this point, the question was raised: if freedom from models is equivalent, in a certain sense, to spontaneity, does this mean that our social institutions, being based on models, have to be dropped, if we are to be what we really are, rather than what our social institutions require us to be?

Here, it is first of all necessary to point out that a great deal of what is *called* spontaneity is illusory. Thus a person conditioned to identify with a model of power and dominance will feel urges that appear spontaneous to him, to assert himself and to insist on his own way. What is at issue here is *true spontaneity*. This cannot be defined, specified, or sought, as to do so is, in effect, to make a *model of spontaneity* – which is absurd. It may, however, be said that true spontaneity is what arises naturally and of its own accord when models of the self have ceased to impede it. In other words, the problem is the *negative one* of discovering the (largely though not entirely) unconscious models that prevent spontaneity.

With regard to the establishment of social institutions, the key question is (as always): '*Why* do these prevent spontaneity?' rather than '*What* is wrong with them?' If one is at all observant, one will see that one has a strong tendency to identify with such institutions and thus to incorporate them into one's model of the self. All of us can, if perhaps only fleetingly, sense the hollowness of the model of the self, which from time to time 'frays at the edges' and thus lets through a glimpse of the fact that there is no solid and substantial reality beneath it. Therefore men have sought to identify the self with something broader, deeper, and more stable, such as social institutions. Thus when one feels that one belongs to such institutions, and that in them one has a place in which one's existence and value are outwardly and publicly recognized, the unpleasant sense of 'being a nonentity' is assuaged.

The difficulty with this sort of reaction is that one can no longer rationally consider serious changes in social institutions. When such changes are proposed, it seems that one's whole being is threatened. And when the institutions start to develop insoluble contradictions and inner conflicts, the mind engages in self-deception, to cover up this fact and to make it appear that the problems are not serious. This not only prevents institutions from adapting to a changing situation, but more important, it tends to create in the formative activity of the members of the whole society a destructive movement of self-deception and general confusion that ultimately invades every aspect of life.

The real trouble is then not mainly with social institutions as such but rather with our models of the self, which tend to incorporate these institutions and thus to make them unworkable. We *need* some kinds of social institutions and organizations, to enable us to co-operate in a generally orderly way. Thus it is clear that unless everyone drives on the same side of the road, chaos will ensue, and that nobody really wants this to happen. For everyone to agree to keep to the same side of the road is then not really a significant barrier to spontaneity. On the contrary, to have cars driven at random on both sides of the road would be a truly serious interference with one's spontaneous wishes to travel from one place to another. Similarly, all can see the need for establishing a certain common social order in which each person has to co-operate in maintaining essential services such as food, water, sanitation, electric power, communications. Without these services, our possibilities for true spontaneity would evidently be greatly decreased. In principle, the forms of the institutions and organizations which are needed to make such activities possible have to be subject to unceasing free discussion; for otherwise they will soon fail to adapt to the ever-changing situation in which they operate. What prevents this free discussion now is the identification of the self with these institutions.

Evidently no change of society which leaves people identified with their social institutions will really end the basic contradiction in such institutions. So to understand the role of models of the self is crucial if we are ever to understand the chaotic structure that society has rather generally shown throughout recorded history, and thus to begin to bring this chaos to an end.

Finally, a question was raised concerning possible means of favouring and furthering the awareness of the workings of models of the self. It was suggested that the consideration of history and studies of other cultures would show up the relativity of particular models, their dependence on special conditions and contexts of development, so that our thinking could, in some degree, cease to be based on such models. Studies of this sort could evidently be helpful, as could also attempts to communicate with the higher animals, such as dolphins and chimpanzees, whose way of thinking may be different from our own and yet ultimately comprehensible to us in essence. But more than this, what is primarily required is a growing realization that models of the self are actually operating, so generally and so pervasively, to confuse almost everything that we try to do. Such a realization would give the inquiry into the overall operation of these models that sense of urgency and energy which is needed to meet the true magnitude of the difficulties with which such models are confronting us.

Raymond Williams

7 Social Darwinism

Social Darwinism is the conventional term for a variant of social theory which emerged in the 1870s mainly in Britain and the United States, and which I'm sorry to say has not entirely died out. I shall describe the ideas in question in the context of an analysis of various applications of evolutionary theory to social theory, and of its use in creative literature. And so I shall be describing, first, the Social Darwinism which is conventionally known by that name, and which has been so well studied by Richard Hofstadter in *Social Darwinism in American Thought*; and then looking at some of the other variations.

In a sense, you can provide a very adequate analysis of Social Darwinism in terms of the errors of emphasis it makes in extending the theory of natural selection to social and political theory. You can say: this is a false extension or a false application of biology. But while that is true, I think it simplifies the matter a little too much, in that the biology itself has from the beginning a strong social component, as Robert Young's contribution to this series expounds in detail. Indeed, my own position is that theories of evolution and natural selection in biology had a social component before there was any question of reapplying them to social and political theory. We have to think of this dialectical movement between the two areas of study as a fact from the beginning. For example, in the case of Darwin himself, we have the impressive note on his reading of Malthus, whom he picked up to read for amusement: it's not the most likely motive for reading Malthus but there we are. He writes:

Being well-prepared to appreciate the struggle for existence which everywhere goes on from long-continued observation of plants and animals, it at once struck me that under these circumstances favourable variations would tend to be preserved and unfavourable ones to be destroyed; the result of this would be the formation of new species.

And Darwin's co-discoverer of natural selection, Wallace, says that Malthus gave him the long-sought clue to the effective agent in the evolution of organic species. This has been disputed: many historians of science have argued that the Malthus clue was a very minor element. But to me it is significant that a theory about the relation between population and resources – an explicit social theory which had great influence on nineteenth-century social thought – was at any rate one of the organizing elements in the emergence of the great generalization about natural selection.

But then one must make clear that Social Darwinism, the popular application of the biological idea to social thought, comes not so much from Darwin as from the whole tradition of evolutionary theory, which is much older than Charles Darwin, which indeed goes back at least to his grandfather, Erasmus, at the end of the eighteenth century, and which, in the first half of the nineteenth century, is already a well-founded system of thought. The explanation of the means of evolution might have to wait on further discoveries, but the idea of evolution was there. It was in many cases built into systems, and – above all for the purpose of understanding Social Darwinism in the narrow sense – it was built into a system by Herbert Spencer. Indeed, it was Spencer, as a social philosopher, who first, in 1864, coined the phrase which was to have such a history in this debate, 'the survival of the fittest'.

Spencer's view of progress – which, he said, was not an accident but a necessity, a visible evolution in human history – carried some consequences which are the real origins of the narrow kind of Social Darwinism. He believed, for example, that there was a principle of social selection operative in human history, and that because this was so it was extremely important that men didn't interfere with it, and in particular that governments didn't interfere with it. He opposed state aid to the poor on the grounds that this would preserve the weaker and less successful members of the race.

Whatever we may now think of the social ethics of this position, it was seen as a logically deducible consequence of the theory of progressive evolution by social selection. The weaker or less able members of society should not be artificially preserved, because the process of social selection which was creating the most vigorous and self-reliant types was something that ought not to be interfered with: its ultimate achievement would be human happiness of a general kind. So he was specifically against what he called artificial preservation of those least able to take care of themselves: a Spencerian theory which has, I suppose, survived to our own decade in the concept of the lame duck who must stand on his one and a half feet or presumably fall. If you really believe this, if you really believe that there is a system of progressive social selection going on, it can seem wild infamy to interfere with it. And it is the confidence that evolution is leading to this development that forms the ethical or quasi-ethical component of what becomes Social Darwinism. Otherwise it seems the merest random cruelty and rationalization.

The idea of competition as a fundamental social principle is, of course, not new. It was most powerfully prefigured in English thought by Hobbes, who believed that our life is the war of all against all, until some sovereign power intervenes and takes control of what would otherwise be a self-destroying horde. Until the intervention of the power to control men and to prevent them destroying one another, that is the natural condition of man. A critical constituent of the full Social Darwinist theory was the growing nineteenth-century belief that character was in a simple sense determined by environment: the doctrine of Robert Owen, for example, that you could wholly reform the moral character of the entire population in a short period of time by altering their environment. If you put the two things together you still don't have Social Darwinism in its full sense, but you have competition, inherent competition, as a natural state; and the idea of character being influenced by circumstances can very easily modulate into its being selected by favourable circumstances and unfavourably selected by unfavourable circumstances. Add to that the theory of historical progressive development and you have Social Darwinism in its developed form.

Darwin himself did not take a consistent position on any of these applications. In a letter he observes ironically that he has just received 'a squib', printed in a newspaper, showing that 'I have proved might is right and therefore that Napoleon is right and every cheating tradesman is also right' – obviously a reaction to one of the first and one of the crudest kinds of Social Darwinism. He was against anything which smacked to him of selfish and contentious policies. However, he did from his long early experience of the breeding of domestic creatures, the famous pigeons, take the view that a society was in some peril which didn't in a conscious way select and discard. He did say: 'We civilized men do our utmost to check the process of elimination. This must be highly injurious to the race of man.' In other words, if the weak or the unfavourable variations are, as Spencer would have put it, artificially preserved, the general condition of the race is likely to deteriorate. On the other hand, Darwin was much too humane a man to think in terms which were later to become possible – of the elimination of unfavourable variations, or of social policy in this conscious sense, to which he never fully applied himself.

Almost at once, however, the extensions began to be made: traced back to the social ideas of Spencer, and gaining a lot of support from the general climate of harsh competitive individualism as a social ideology at that stage of industrial capitalism and general industrial development. And we can trace the process, in part in the work of particular thinkers, but as much in the groundswell of a certain kind of public opinion. Look, for example, at Bagehot's *Physics and Politics*, published in 1876. Bagehot was a country banker, editor of the *Economist*, literary essayist, author of *The English Constitution*. In *Physics and Politics* he wrote a work which he subtitled 'Thoughts on the Application of the Principles of Natural Selection and Inheritance to Political Society'. It is one of the first conscious attempts to do just this. And in a sense it comes surprisingly from Bagehot, who was always a moderating man. His famous analysis of the English Constitution was in its way a superb piece of demystification, but of a rather special kind: demystification in order to remystify. He analysed the English Constitution in terms of its theatrical show, which is designed to produce deference in its subjects – he wrote quite sharply about the Widow of Windsor – and the whole panoply of the British State as a means of creating deference in its subjects. He then argued with a quite new tone in Victorian social argument that this was nevertheless necessary to any well-ordered state. In a way, the conclusions of *Physics and Politics*, after what seem some rather bolder speculations, are essentially similar. He takes from Spencer the idea of the progress of human society by certain well-ordered stages. Primitive or preliminary: the military stage in which human relations are basically those of armed conflict. And then a stage of civilization which he thought he was living in, a stage of order in which conflict is resolved by discussion. He did believe that in human societies there was intrinsic competition: not so much of all against all, individual against individual, but rather an intrinsic competition for the best shape of the society. This or that notion of how the society might be had to engage in competition with all other notions, and in a sense what emerged as the constituting notion of any particular state was the superior notion. This was so, however, precisely in a period of ordered discussion, rather than in a period of military conflict in which a better idea might be destroyed by a physically stronger enemy. Europe, having been the central area of conflict between states founded on different notions, different ideas of the social polity, different ideas of religion, was also the centre of progress. The conflict and the progress were directly correlated.

This is soon overtaken by something which has a more sinister ring, although many of the ideas of the next stage can already be found in Spencer. Sumner in the 1880s offers what becomes, if you read in the period, a very familiar definition: that civilization is the survival of the fittest, that the survival of the unfittest is anti-civilization. Socialism is an absurd notion because it proposes both the development of civilization and the survival of the unfittest, which are manifestly contradictory, he argues. Competition is a law of nature and to interfere with the results of competition is radically to undermine civilization. So let no one pretend to believe in civilization if on some other grounds he argues for intervention. Millionaires, Sumner said, are a product of natural selection. You can see that within twenty years of the formulation of the biological idea of natural selection you have got a quite new phrase – not that earlier phrases had been lacking to rationalize rich men – to describe the internal logic and necessity of the social process.

Not surprisingly, Sumner was almost at once echoed by John D. Rockefeller, who said that the growth of a large business is merely the survival of the fittest and made a rather pretty analogy with a prize rose bloom which has to be debudded of its subsidiary minor blooms before it can come to its perfection. The processes of industrial monopoly which were occurring at this time could be rationalized as the production either of the most beautiful blooms or of the next stage in the social species.

Of course, this was an ideology: it was consciously in opposition to liberal egalitarian tendencies, to measures of social welfare and reform, and classically to ideas of socialism. Because it was an ideology, not all the implications of this rather stark and powerful theory were always welcome even to some of its exponents. It is very significant that along this line – the line through Spencer to Bagehot, Sumner and others – the main inheritance function which is assumed biologically is still that of Lamarck rather than Darwin: in other words, the physical inheritance of acquired characteristics rather than the kind of variation in adaptation to environment which Darwin relied on. Spencer continued to believe in Lamarck long after Darwin, and the concept of physical inheritance in this sense gave the ideologists of Social Darwinism a particularly fortunate opening for modifying competition of an absolutely open kind when it came to the preservation of family property. After all, if you take their argument quite seriously, the war of all against all should never stop, because to interfere with it would prevent the emergence of the strongest types: so that family property, which means that somebody who may not have strong individual talents which are going to evolve the higher kind of man starts with an advantage, is a kind of interference with competition. But if you have a Lamarckian notion of physical inheritance, then you can rationalize the family and family property as precisely the continuation of what you can now see to be the strongest and best species.

So, too, with the inheritance of capital: nobody could look at the nineteenth century and suppose that it was a society in which one day somebody fired a pistol and said: 'Go on, compete economically, and the strongest will come out at the top of the heap.' Quite evidently, huge fortunes were there at the start of play, and the great majority of the players came to the table bearing nothing but their hands. If there is to be competition in the full ruthless sense, then you must all come to the table with empty hands. So financial inheritance is defended within the ideology because the possession of capital provides a measure of continuity. It is really rather painful to follow the convolutions of men who'd committed themselves to a rhetorically powerful theory which rationalized competition as a principle of society, dismissing as sentimental all apparently ethical and moral objections to it, and then find them having to turn to defend things which were quite evidently qualifications of the competitive principle as such.

Nevertheless, the survival of the fittest, the struggle for existence – nobody had to invent these as descriptions of nineteenth-century society, it was most people's everyday experience. Millions of men in Britain alone went out each day knowing they had to be stronger or more cunning than their fellows if they were to survive or take anything home to their family. The idea is in a way as popular among the victims of that kind of competitive process as it is among its promoters, because it corresponds very directly to their daily experience of life: whether or not anybody can conceive a better social order, the idea does seem to fit the experience of life as it is ordinarily lived. The popularity of phrases like 'the rat race' to describe our own society is a direct continuation of these earlier descriptions among the victims. And, of course, anyone who has succeeded, whether or not he's had advantages, has been very willing to invoke the principle of 'the survival of the fittest'.

There are two particular applications of this principle which ought to be noted before one goes on to some of the other variants. First is the development of eugenics as a movement. It's a natural consequence of this theory that you should breed only from the most perfectly endowed types. The whole future of man was thought to depend upon this kind of selective physical inheritance. Although there are signs of it throughout the second half of the nineteenth century, it is in the nineties, and especially up to the period of the First World War, which did a little selection of its own, that eugenics gets put forward by a whole range of people otherwise sharing different views. Eugenics as a positive policy is one thing: it amounts to very little more than the argument that every encouragement to breed should be given to the most physically and intellectually favoured. The negative side of eugenics is a more serious matter. There's a direct link back to Malthus and to the thought that the unfit should be prevented from breeding.

Everything depends on the concept of fitness. It is one thing to hear the eugenic argument about the breeding of children from the physically malformed or those carrying some hereditary disease: it is quite another to hear the eugenic argument against breeding from the disfavoured, the unsuccessful, the socially and economically weak. And yet it gets entangled with this, because very quickly it combines with theories of race, which again don't have a specific origin in the biological argument. Gobineau's argument about the inequality of races had appeared in 1853, well before this phase, but it is readily applicable to race because Darwin had at times used race as a biological term for species, and so the idea of a particular human race – the Anglo-Saxon was a particular favourite – as the vigorous stock, the survivor in the competitive battle, inheriting a certain natural right to mastery, became a very powerful component of the ideology of imperialism. In imperialism, it was perfectly possible to argue, and many did, that the strongest, the best survivors, the Anglo-Saxon race, had a duty to humanity to continue to assert itself, not to limit its competition with weaker peoples out of some false ethical consideration for them or out of some legalistic notion of their rights. If the competitive struggle produces the strongest human types, then clearly the strongest race must in no way be limited.

You get an interesting variant of this in the North American theory that an even more vigorous hybrid of the Anglo-Saxon race happens to have established itself in the United States, and its turn will come. The general idea of the Aryans as a race with these attributes becomes intensely popular, and in a natural fit of self-defence somebody reinvents the Celts. If you follow the logic of the crude argument of strength through competition, then you do arrive at imperialism, you do arrive at racist theories, although there may be different choices as to the most favoured race, according to where you happen to live. You also arrive at the rationalization of war. Von Moltke argued that war is the supreme example in human history of the Darwinian struggle for existence, because here, under the most intense conditions, men are set against one another, and the strongest survive, and it is right that it should be so, because only if the strongest survive can the future of humanity be assured.

Social Darwinism in this sense was not the only product of the application of these theories. It is very interesting to see that Marx in 1860, looking into *The Origin of Species*, wrote to Engels saying: 'Darwin's book is very important and serves me as a basis in natural science for the class struggle in history.' And immediately you turn it that way round you see that you can provide a total basis for a theory of class struggle on the same analogy. Once again, human history is a struggle – but now between classes rather than races or individuals.

Bagehot was to introduce the idea of a competition between groups rather than individuals: clearly this could be defined as involving classes as well as nations, and the class struggle could be seen as something inherent in the natural history of man, with the survival of the strongest and the highest type as the future of humanity. Marx himself could see in Darwin what he called 'the basis in natural science' for a view he had developed from social and economic evidence: once again, the law of struggle as biologically inevitable was taken as underpinning for a social theory.

One of the results of Spencerian ideas of political development had been the belief that although progress is going to happen by a natural evolutionary mechanism, it can't be hurried. There's nothing you can do about it. In the natural processes of social selection higher types eventually emerge: this is the whole process, but you can't hurry it along. Therefore evolution becomes a way of describing an attitude to social change. If somebody says to you, 'Here is a wicked condition, a case of poverty or corruption or exploitation,' you say: 'Yes, it is very bad, but there is nothing we can do about it. The evolutionary process will eventually take us beyond it and if we interfere now we shall merely prevent that happening.' Then this led to a popular contrast between evolution and revolution, and the half-rhyme helped. You could not bring about change in society by intervention, let alone by violent intervention. 'We believe,' so many thousands of people must then have started to say, 'in evolution, not revolution.' And given the bizarre nature of the application to biology, it is not surprising that when De Vries established the evolution of species from mutations, socialist writers who engaged in the argument against the theorists of social evolution quickly seized on the mutation as the justification precisely for the sharp revolutionary break. 'There you are, you see,' they said: 'nature does not work by the inevitability of gradualism,' which had been the ordinary assumption and which was built into the ideology of the Fabians. 'It works by the sharp mutation which establishes a new . . .' And then you say 'species' or 'order of society' according to which argument you're involved in. The argument between evolution and revolution, which ought to have been a social and political argument because it is really an argument about particular societies and about means of changing them, thus attracted very early a strong biological or pseudo-biological component.

Now let us look at some of the reactions from within the same tradition to some of these applications. Veblen, for example, in 1899, in *The Theory of the Leisure Class*, said, 'It is quite true that our social system selects certain men,' granting the point that Sumner had made, that millionaires are the product of natural selection: the point is, Veblen argued, does it select the right human traits? May not our social system be selecting altogether the wrong human qualities – for example, shrewd practice, chicanery or low cunning? Granted all your arguments about the mechanism of selection as inevitable, may not the social system be producing precisely the wrong emphases, and giving success and power to the wrong human types? This argument was very much developed around the turn of the century.

Benjamin Kidd in his *Social Evolution* said in 1894: 'We must above all take social action to preserve real competition.' At the moment the mass of men are shut out from effectively competing. They don't have the means to compete in society, they're not educated, they don't have money. He therefore uses a social democratic or liberal kind of argument about extending education, giving opportunity, but its purpose is to promote competition, to make the competitive struggle more active and more general. W. H. Mallock, on the other hand, taking a conservative view in his *Aristocracy and Evolution*, argued against democracy and the extension of education on the grounds – more in line with conventional Social Darwinism – that the one desirable product of the competitive process was the great man, the leader, and the one condition of a leader was that he should have enough power, that he should be instantly obeyed, that he should have the means of control to put his great visions into operation, because if the great man cannot put his visions into operation, dragged back by the mediocrity of the mass, human society will never solve its problems. This theory, with its biological component, became, in the twentieth century, first a theory of élites and then a theory of Fascism.

Meanwhile, however, there had been a response of a rather surprising kind. For Kropotkin, in *Mutual Aid* in 1902, said in effect: 'Yes, let us indeed learn from the order of nature. If we look at nature we find it full of examples of mutual aid. Look at the herds of deer, or of cattle. Look at the ants, look at the bees, look at all the social insects. We will find that everywhere there are examples of mutual aid.' Of course, this was co-operation within species. Most of the competitive theories had been based on struggle *between* species, and then covertly applied to competition within one species – man. Kropotkin reversed this: the order of nature, he argued, teaches us mutual aid, collectivism, a quite different sort of social order.

Thomas Huxley made a point of some importance in his *Evolution and Ethics* in 1893. He said: 'The whole confusion has arisen from identifying fittest with best.' 'Fittest', after all, in the Darwinian sense, although not in the Spencerian sense, had meant those adapted to their environment. If 'fittest' had meant strongest, most powerful, then presumably the dinosaurs would still be here and masters of the earth. 'Fittest' meaning 'adapted to the environment' didn't mean any of the things which it meant in the social analogy – the strongest, the fiercest, the most cunning, the most enduring. It meant that which in its situation was best adapted to survive. If this is so, Huxley argued, we realize that we can derive no ethical principle from a process of largely random survivals. If we look at the real process of the origins and survivals of species, we learn that fitness to environment cannot be based on any central principle and, therefore, that ethics cannot be founded on biological evidence.

Advanced societies, Huxley argued, develop ethical systems whose precise purpose is to modify natural law. Huxley assumes, which I would take leave to doubt, that natural law, the order of nature, is a process of unrestrained struggle, and ethics is then a qualifying mechanism to what, unrestrained, would be a cosmic law. Huxley is as firm as many of the others that there is such a cosmic law, but he proposes social ethics, cultural development, as a way of modifying it. This position has been repeated by his grandson Julian, for example, who would argue that cultural evolution is now the main process, cultural evolution within man.

Meanwhile, this climate of ideas had been pervading imaginative literature in ways that went very deep, but in many different directions. You can pick it up, for example, in Strindberg, especially in the preface to *Miss Julie*, that remarkably powerful play about a single destructive relationship which he wrote in 1888. Strindberg in the preface describes the servant, Jean, as the rising type, the man who is sexually on the upgrade. Risen from a poor family, he is vigorous, adaptable and will survive in his struggle with Lady Julie, the weak aristocrat belonging to a fixed and therefore rather decadent strain. A powerfully-observed sexual relationship of a direct kind is interpreted in terms derived from the context of the Darwinist or pseudo-Darwinist argument.

I cannot think how many successors there have been to that proposition: the idea of a vigorous, rising working-class male, or a male from a submerged racial group, who enters into a relationship of love and conflict with the representative of a comparatively weak, comparatively declining or fixed social stratum. A resolution which might be seen as destructive, as in the kind of imposed suicide of Julie which is Jean's culmination, can be ethically rationalized as the emergence of the most vigorous stock. The metaphors for such a process are everywhere apparent in subsequent imaginative literature.

There were more direct applications of the idea in, for example, Jack London, a socialist, a man deeply influenced by Spencer and Darwin, with experience of struggle under very primitive conditions and with experience of the jungle that was the late nineteenth-century city. London develops a characteristic imaginative structure in which struggle is a virtue. The survival of the most vigorous type is seen at once in terms of a kind of individual primitivism and also in terms of the rising class, the class which had hitherto been submerged. In some of his work – for example, *White Fang* – it is the emergence of the powerful individual who has competed under wilderness conditions: in *The Iron Heel* it is the emergence of the class that has been long suppressed but is historically due to rise.

H. G. Wells's ideas on the subject derive most directly from Thomas Huxley's, but imaginatively he reaches well beyond them. Think, for example, of *The Time Machine*, which is the imaginative projection of a particular phase of evolution operating at several different levels. It is in one sense a projection of the division between the rich and the labouring poor in the nineteenth-century industrial society. When the time traveller goes far into the future, he discovers two races of creatures sharing the earth. The race that he first finds is pretty, doll-like, plays games with flowers, has charming manners, has a playful but weak kind of life in the sunshine, like children. Unnoticed at first, but eventually emerging from below the ground, there appears the other race, the Morlocks, who are dark and bestial.

You can see in all this the evolutionary projection of an idle, playful rich and a working population submerged in the darkness and reduced to animal conditions. But the whole situation is imaginatively reversed because the Morlocks keep the Eloi as food: the pretty playmates on the surface of the earth are not the dominant race, the Morlocks are waiting their time, in evolutionary terms, to come back to the surface again, and meanwhile they feed on the playful ones as cattle.

The idea of the struggle for existence, projected from deep social stratifications, resulting in a branching of the race of man into these two extremes, is one of Wells's most powerful ideas, unforgettably expressed, with the kind of horror with which so many of these ideas of the inevitable struggle for existence were imaginatively received. Wells uses everywhere in his imaginative fiction (and a whole tradition of Science Fiction and scientific romance has followed him) the idea of evolution into new physical types of man, the idea of differently evolving intelligent species on other planets and the idea of competition between them.

When alternative races meet they make war: this idea is deeply established in Science Fiction. *The War of the Worlds* and the whole vast tradition of intergalactic war that we've had ever since in books and magazines represent to some degree a reaction to twentieth-century experience of war. But the tradition begins before the epoch of major wars, and represents also a reaction to the idea of the fundamental struggle for existence: if one species meets another, it will inevitably compete with it and try to destroy it. The extraordinary physical beings that we have been regaled with in Science Fiction are the product of this idea of evolution playing on situations of great tension, great fear.

Utopias have been quite differently projected. Instead of the static Utopias of pre-nineteenth-century writing, when men would find an ideal condition, an island or some point in the future, where their social problems would have been solved, Utopias now, as Wells observed, must be dynamic: they will not stand still.

That is what we learn from Darwin, he said: there has to be progression through higher stages. Moreover, they are fraught with great threat: there is inherent danger and conflict in them. Wells's Utopias characteristically are arrived at only after a period of destructive conflict.

A few other writers may be mentioned. Shaw, I'm afraid, takes a version of creative evolution which is, one might say, more naïve even than Spencer's. The evolution of the final ideal type in *Back to Methuselah* one would be happy to read as a caricature of Spencer. But one is afraid, from the preface, that one is asked to take seriously the emergence of those He-Ancients and She-Ancients (and I think it isn't only the pronouns which remind one of goats) who have pressed on to human perfection, which is, guess what, the goal of redemption from the flesh: pure intelligence has emancipated itself from the body. This is the sort of thing that Wells imagined in his extraordinary race of Selenites on the Moon, with the enormous brain case and the tiny legs: but with Shaw it really was a kind of evolutionary idea that man should get rid of this flesh stuff.

In Ibsen and Hardy there is a very interesting preoccupation with heredity, directly influenced by Darwin and the evolutionary debate, but in each case the critical imaginative difference is this: survival is not seen as a criterion of value. Ibsen and Hardy were perfectly prepared to accept that there is intense struggle and competition, that people do get defeated, often the most aspiring being the most deeply defeated. Nearly all Ibsen's heroes aspire, climb (spiritually in most cases) and are defeated in the very act of climbing, overwhelmed because they aspire.

In Hardy it is very often the aspiring or the exceptionally pure character, the Jude the Obscure or Tess, who is the most absolutely destroyed. You cannot read Ibsen or read Hardy without realizing that survival is not the criterion of value: struggle is the criterion of value – but struggle in a rather different sense from the rationalized struggle of the simple Social Darwinists. It is man's constant self-urging towards the light, towards a different, higher kind of human life, which is repeatedly imagined in Hardy and in Ibsen: the attempt is defeated, but the manner of the defeat is such that what is confirmed is the impulse to the light, with a very sober, very sombre look at the possibility or probability that the darkness will win. It is not a teaching of darkness, nor is it any kind of rationalization of the results of crude struggle.

The final example I can give – and it is a surprising one in this context because he used to say he didn't believe in evolution and didn't believe in science much at all – is D. H. Lawrence. Like Strindberg, he uses the idea of the vital rising type and a rather decadent or fixed or imprisoned alternative social type: generally the vigorous rising man and the sexually imprisoned, socially imprisoned or socially declining woman.

He makes of the encounter a cosmic process: it is precisely the cosmic character of the Lawrence sexual relationships of this kind that gives them their place in this tradition, for these are not simple personal relationships: they have something to do with the future of the race, and the physically rising vigorous type is strongly emphasized. But beyond that, at the end of *Women in Love*, having reached a kind of deadlock in human relationships, having seen the failure of one cold, willed relationship between Gerald and Gudrun, having recognized that the relative warmth and friendliness of the relationship between Birkin and Ursula had its limits, that it was more decent but not necessarily complete, Lawrence suddenly in a very surprising version repeats the imaginative conclusion of so much of this tradition, that perhaps we shall have to evolve beyond being human: the merely human is the merely disappointing. He puts it in direct evolutionary terms: just as the horse, he writes, has taken the place of the mastodon, so the eternal creative mystery would dispose of man:

> Races came and went, species passed away, but ever new species arose, more lovely, or equally lovely, always surpassing wonder. The fountain-head was incorruptible and unsearchable. It had no limits. It could bring forth miracles, create utterly new races and new species in its own hour, new forms of consciousness, new forms of body, new units of being.

It is a positive transforming idea that the creative mystery could evolve beyond man, if man in his present condition failed to attain an adequate consciousness. It is in that sense at the very opposite pole from the pessimistic rationalizations of struggle. But all these matters, issues of societies, of social, economic and political relationships, issues of human relationships between individuals, have been affected, both fundamentally and at the level of their persuasive content, by ideas of what is held to be a scientific process – which, as we have seen, can be applied in many different directions according to the main bearing of the argument or the work.

One does come back (or I at least come back, particularly remembering the social component in the biological theories themselves) to saying that man cannot derive lessons and laws from the processes of what he sees as a separated nature, lessons and laws supposed to be conditions of himself, conditions to which he must in some way conform. This whole perspective of a man learning from a separately observed nature is deeply false. The correlative is that in the end it is best if we discuss the problems of social and human relationships in directly social and personal terms.

Part Two

Evidence

John Maynard Smith

8 Can we Change Human Nature?
The Evidence of Genetics

For a geneticist, the word 'nature' has a technical meaning,
although fortunately this is not too far from the colloquial one.
Geneticists are interested in the causes of the differences between
the members of a species, or of closely related species. They
classify these causes into two categories: a difference between
two individuals is said to be one of 'nature' if it is caused by a
difference between the fertilized eggs from which those individuals
developed, and of 'nurture' if it is caused by factors acting after
fertilization. In the vast majority of cases, differences of nature
are caused by differences between 'genes', which are now known
to be molecules of DNA. It is one of the most startling conclusions
of genetics that a difference between a normal and a mentally or
physically handicapped individual may be caused by an alteration
in a single molecule in the fertilized egg.

Notice that it is meaningless to ask whether a characteristic
owes most to nature or to nurture; to have a nose, an individual
must have both genes and an environment. But it is sensible to
ask whether a difference owes most to nature or to nurture; two
noses may be of different shapes because their possessors have
different genes, or because one nose has been broken.

In this essay, I shall discuss how far human nature can be
changed. It is impossible – by definition – to alter the nature of an
individual once conceived, but it may be possible to alter the
frequency in the human population of individuals of different
genetic constitutions. It is this possibility I shall discuss. But first
I must say something of my competence to do so. The trouble
with experts is that having become experts in one subject they
assume they are expert in all. My own work has been primarily

in the field of animal genetics, and in particular in the genetics of populations and in the theory of evolution. My knowledge of human genetics is largely second-hand, and of medicine is almost non-existent. I am therefore more likely, although by no means certain, to be right about the effects on populations of particular eugenic measures than about the details of particular human diseases.

Unhappily, before I turn to the main topic of this essay, there is an aspect of human genetics which, because of its topicality, I cannot altogether ignore. This is the relation between race and intelligence, which has recently been raised by Jensen in the U.S. and by Eysenck in this country. I say 'unhappily' because the whole controversy is based on a misunderstanding of a problem which has been fairly well understood by geneticists, but apparently not by psychologists, since the writings of Hogben and Haldane thirty years ago.

I will confine myself to the causes of the differences in average test scores in intelligence tests by blacks and whites in the U.S. I will not discuss the more difficult problem of the relation between such test scores and behaviour which in other contexts would be regarded as intelligent, because I have no competence to do so. It is agreed that there is a substantial difference between the average scores of blacks and whites; what is at issue is the relative importance of nature and nurture in causing this difference. Jensen and Eysenck have argued that nature plays the more important role. I think that their arguments are mistaken, and that the evidence they adduce is irrelevant to the issue.

If we test the members of a single population – for example the white population of England – we find individual differences in test score (as we do for any other character). We also find that the members of a family resemble one another more closely than do individuals chosen at random. Unfortunately this does not tell us anything about the relative importance of nature and nurture, because members of families not only resemble one another genetically, but also share an environment. There are two main kinds of evidence which enable us to get round this difficulty. The first is a comparison of pairs of identical (i.e., developed from a single egg) and non-identical twins. The second is a comparison of adopted children with their adoptive and their biological parents. Using these lines of evidence, Jensen and Eysenck (and others before them) have concluded that within a population both nature and nurture are relevant, but that nature is responsible for more than half the total variance in test score. The word 'variance' is here being used in a technical sense, but it amounts to saying that nature is somewhat more important than nurture in causing the differences in test score between members of a population. The conclusion is not absolutely watertight, but few conclusions are. Personally I find the arguments which lead to it persuasive.

Jensen and Eysenck argue that because the major part of the variance of test scores within a population is genetic, so too is the major part of the difference between populations, and in particular between blacks and whites. This argument is clearly fallacious. An analogy will make the fallacy clear. Suppose that a batch of seed containing a mixture of different strains of some plant species were sown on a single uniform plot of ground. Most of the differences in height between the resulting plants would be genetic in origin. Suppose then that a similar batch of seed, containing the same strains in the same proportions, were sown on a second plot, differing from the first in having a higher content of fertilizer. The average height of plants on the second plot would probably be higher than on the first. If so, the difference would be entirely one of nurture. Yet by the Jensen–Eysenck line of argument, we would be justified in concluding that it was largely one of nature.

This argument does not prove that there is *not* a genetic contribution to the difference in test score. We simply have no evidence to enable us to decide. If it were a matter of analysing the causes of the differences of height in an agricultural plant, we could settle the question by raising a sample of each population in the environment normally occupied by the other. It should not need a geneticist to tell two psychologists that there is at present no way to bring up a black child in the environment normally experienced by white children.

If geneticists are unable to say anything one way or the other about the causes of racial differences in intelligence test scores, are they equally helpless when faced with other problems of human genetics? In particular, do we have the knowledge which would enable us to change 'human nature'? Previous discussions of this question have concentrated on two very different objectives, which I will call 'negative' and 'positive' eugenics. The aim of negative eugenics is to prevent the conception or birth of individuals with severe mental or physical defects of genetic origin. The aim of positive eugenics is to increase the frequency with which individuals with particularly desirable characteristics are born. Of these two aims, that of negative eugenics seems to me important and increasingly practicable; that of positive eugenics of no immediate importance, and either impracticable or practicable only by unjustifiable interference with personal liberty.

I will discuss positive eugenics first, and will do so briefly. There are two methods which might in principle be adopted. The first and most obvious is some form of selection whereby individuals with characteristics regarded as particularly desirable are enabled to have more children, and those with undesirable characteristics to have fewer children. Such a programme is faced by two difficulties: who decides what is desirable, and how do we influence differentially the number of children people have? I know of only two suggested solutions to these difficulties which are not ruled out on social and political grounds. The first is that we should use social inducements; the simplest form of this suggestion is that we should impose a tax on children. The logic behind this proposal is that, by and large, society rewards those it approves of by giving them more money, and therefore a tax on children would be a relative encouragement to the socially desirable to breed. I regard such proposals as irrelevant and untimely; their genetic effects would be small or non-existent and their social effects undesirable.

An alternative method of selection was suggested by H. J. Muller and also by Julian Huxley. It is that we should encourage women to have children by artificial insemination by donors of their own choice. Here the logic is that if women were free to choose the genetic father of their children, the effect would be eugenic. This proposal ignores the psychological difficulties which would arise for the woman, her husband if any, the donor and the child. Also, as I have argued in detail elsewhere, the proposal would probably have negligible effects genetically.

The second method of positive eugenics is that of 'cloning'. This is a procedure which is not at present possible in man or in any mammal, although it has been achieved in frogs. It is by no means certain that the procedure will ever be practicable in man, but I think it likely that it will be. If so, it would enable a woman to bear a child genetically identical to a living 'donor', male or female. Briefly, the nucleus of an unfertilized egg would be removed and replaced by the nucleus of a body cell of the donor. The egg would be placed in the uterus of the woman, who would bear the child in the normal way. The child would then be genetically identical to the donor of the nucleus, just as two identical twins are genetically identical.

Again there are obvious psychological difficulties associated with such a procedure. Its effectiveness in producing outstandingly gifted individuals depends on the relative importance of nature and nurture in determining genius. But I see no reason to be alarmed if what is at present a theoretical possibility becomes practicable.

I want now to turn to negative eugenics, which is the real and important field of application of human genetics. The effectiveness of negative eugenics depends on the detailed type of genetic causation. But before I consider the main classes of genetic defect, there are two general points I would like to make. First, before we can hope to cure a disease we must be able to diagnose it; genetic analysis has already played a large part in the classification and diagnosis of disease. Second, the fact that a disease is genetic in origin does not mean that it is incurable. We cannot change the genes responsible for the defect, but we can sometimes change the environment of the individual so that the defect does not develop.

Clear-cut defects of genetic origin fall into four main categories as far as their causation is concerned: recessives, dominants, chromosomal abnormalities, and a residuum of cases of more complex causation. Recessive conditions are most easily understood by considering an example. A classic case is phenylketonuria. Individuals who at fertilization receive from both parents the same particular kind of a defective gene – so-called 'homozygotes' – cannot make a particular enzyme. A trivial consequence of this which enables the condition to be diagnosed is the presence of an abnormal substance in high concentration in the urine. The important consequence is that the homozygotes are mentally defective. 'Heterozygotes', who receive a defective gene from one parent and a normal gene from the other, develop normally, but can be recognized because of a somewhat lower level of the enzyme. Although homozygotes usually develop as mental defectives, if they are recognized at birth and brought up on a diet with a very low level of a particular amino acid, phenylalanine, then their mental development is normal, or almost so. The disease is therefore in a sense curable, but only with great difficulty, because it is not easy for a child never to eat what other children are eating.

Phenylketonuria is typical of a numerous class of defects, but is better known than most. Thus we cannot always identify the abnormal enzyme associated with a particular defect; often we cannot recognize the heterozygotes or 'carriers' of the abnormal gene; usually, although we can recognize the condition, we cannot cure it.

What if anything can we do about defects caused by recessive genes? Clearly we have to try to cure individuals who are born with such defects, and it is important to find methods of treatment less difficult to maintain than the dietary restriction required in the case of phenylketonuria. But it would be far better if we could prevent the conception or birth of affected individuals. The possibility of preventing the birth of such individuals once conceived arises because it is sometimes possible to recognize affected foetuses three to four months after conception. The technique, known as amniocentesis, is to withdraw fluid from the amniotic cavity. This fluid contains cells of foetal origin which can be cultured outside the body. If they lack an enzyme, this fact can be recognized in time for an abortion to be performed. At present only a minority of recessive defects can be recognized in this way, but the number is certain to rise.

What use can we make of this technique? It is not at present sensible to suggest the routine testing of all pregnant women for all recognizable defects. Apart from the high cost of such testing, we have to weigh the risk to mother and foetus against the gain in preventing the birth of defective children. The risk is low, but is not negligible. It therefore seems justifiable to perform amniocentesis if there is a high risk that the foetus will be defective. In the case of recessive conditions, this means that there is a justification for performing amniocentesis if both parents are known to be carriers of the same defective gene, since it is only in such cases that a homozygotic foetus can arise. This emphasizes the importance of learning to recognize carriers of recessive genes.

The use of amniocentesis rests on the assumption that it is justifiable to abort a foetus which suffers from a sufficiently serious genetic defect. I accept this assumption, but with great reluctance. It amounts to saying that life is not sacred until after birth, and that we do not owe to a foetus the duty of charity and compassion which we owe to other human beings. I accept the assumption because not to do so would add enormously to the amount of suffering in the world. But methods which prevent the conception of unwanted children – unwanted because genetically defective or for other reasons – seem to me greatly preferable to methods which require us to kill them after they have been conceived.

At first sight it might seem that the simplest way of preventing the conception of individuals homozygotic for harmful recessive genes would be to discourage the carriers of such genes from having children. Indeed, from time to time the more rabid and less numerate eugenists have proposed the compulsory sterilization of all those known to be carrying such genes. There is a simple numerical reason why such a proposal is impracticable. Suppose that for some condition such as phenylketonuria we were able to 'count' the genes in the population of Britain, counting one defective gene per heterozygote and two per homozygote. Suppose further that we found of the one hundred million genes counted in the population of fifty million individuals that exactly 1 per cent were defective and 99 per cent were normal. Then (if for simplicity we ignore the marriage of close relatives) the chance that an individual would receive a defective gene from both parents is $1/100 \times 1/100 = 1/10,000$. This frequency of one per 10,000 is fairly typical for the frequency in the population of individuals born with particular recessive defects. The frequency in the population of heterozygotes will be approximately $1/50$, since each individual has a $1/100$ chance of getting the defective gene from either parent. Thus to eliminate one particular recessive gene from the population we would have to sterilize one person in fifty. Since there are many different kinds of defective gene in the population, it is likely that each of us is carrying at least one. There is therefore no point in preventing or discouraging carriers of harmful recessives from having children.

Fortunately a much less drastic measure would almost eliminate individual homozygotes for such genes. If we could prevent the marriage of pairs carrying the same harmful recessive, few such homozygotes would be conceived. This raises an intriguing problem. If two people who already plan to marry discover they are carriers of the same harmful recessive, the chances are that they would not be deterred by the discovery. But if two people when they first met were aware that they carried the same recessive, it is likely that they would avoid a degree of intimacy which would lead to marriage. It is, on the other hand, difficult to imagine a custom whereby a boy making his first date with a girl was expected to add 'and by the way, I'm carrying galactosemia and Tay-Sachs disease'. A solution I first heard from J. B. S. Haldane, but which I cannot find in his published works, is that everyone should wear a jewel which indicated symbolically the harmful genes for which they were heterozygous. This suggestion may at first sight seem odd, but is greatly to be preferred either to widespread amniocentesis and abortion, or to the birth of large numbers of mentally and physically defective children.

One last point must be made. If we prevent the conception or birth of children homozygous for harmful recessives without reducing the fecundity of their parents (and both the methods discussed could have this effect) we remove the natural selection which keeps the harmful gene rare. The consequence would be a gradual rise in the frequency of the harmful gene in the population. This is not a consequence which need seriously concern us, because the rate of increase is very slow; no detectable change of frequency would occur in a century. Although I am in general opposed to the practice of unloading our problems on to our descendants, a change of this kind seems tolerable, if only because with the advance of knowledge we may find more direct solutions before the change is significant.

In some cases a defect develops if an individual inherits the corresponding defective gene from only one parent. The defective gene is then said to be dominant. Normally an affected child will have one affected parent, unless the defective gene has arisen by mutation in a parent. Examples are achondroplasia (a form of dwarfism) and Huntingdon's chorea (a fatal degeneration of the nervous system accompanied by involuntary jerking of the limbs, appearing in middle age). There is at present little we can do to reduce the frequency of such genes, other than to discourage people affected by the more serious conditions from having children. Unfortunately, none of these conditions can at present be recognized by amniocentesis.

A third and numerically important cause of defect is chromosomal abnormality; that is, the production of gametes and hence of fertilized eggs containing abnormal numbers or arrangements of chromosomes. The processes leading to chromosomal abnormality need not concern us here. What is relevant about them is that, with some important exceptions, they cannot be predicted from a knowledge of the parents. In many cases foetuses with chromosomal abnormalities are aborted naturally. The commonest types of which this is not true are Down's syndrome (or 'mongoloid idiocy'), and various abnormalities associated with the sex chromosomes.

It is usually possible to recognize chromosomal abnormalities in cells obtained by amniocentesis, but there is in most cases no way of predicting which pregnancies may be abnormal, so that the routine testing of all pregnancies is open to the objection discussed earlier that the risk is not justified by the gain. There is, however, one case in which routine testing would be justified. The frequency of Down's syndrome rises sharply among the children of older mothers. If all pregnancies in mothers over 35 were investigated and selective abortion practised, the frequency of Down's syndrome among all births could be halved. In economic terms alone, it has been calculated that the cost of such a programme would be less than the cost of caring in institutions for the children who would otherwise be born; there are obviously other criteria which need to be taken into account.

There is one last category of abnormality which must be mentioned. When I first started work on fruit flies in a genetics laboratory, I learnt that in addition to well-behaved abnormalities caused by recessive or dominant genes, there was a class of abnormality (known in our lab as 'goofies', but I fear this term has no general currency) which occur more often in some stocks than others, but which never appeared in all the members of a stock, and whose frequency could be altered by environmental means, but which could never be pinned down as caused by a particular environmental factor. Such abnormalities are best understood as requiring for their appearance both a particular and sometimes quite complex genetic constitution and a correspondingly complex environment. Such abnormalities occur also in man; examples are hare lip and spina bifida. At present we know of no way in which the frequency of such conditions could be reduced.

I must now make some effort to sum up. Schemes of 'positive eugenics' designed to improve the nature of man are, at the very least, premature. Either they are likely to be ineffective, or they call for interference in our personal lives which we would rightly refuse to tolerate. On the other hand, schemes of 'negative eugenics' designed to reduce the frequency of children with crippling mental or physical defects are already practicable in some cases, and the range of possible applications is likely to increase rapidly. Such schemes are desirable because of the unhappiness at present suffered both by the affected children themselves and by their families. These schemes are becoming increasingly important because advances in medical science are enabling us to keep alive – and often to keep suffering – more and more such children. Two main methods are open to us; foetal diagnosis and abortion, and the avoidance of marriage between carriers of the same harmful recessive genes. Both methods will be needed, because there are important categories of defect, particularly those caused by chromosome abnormalities, which cannot be predicted and which can therefore be dealt with only by abortion. But when we can, we should surely rely on knowledge and choice of marriage partners rather than on retrospective abortion.

For further reading

I. M. Lerner, *Heredity, Evolution and Society* (Freeman, San Francisco 1968).
V. A. McKusick, *Human Genetics* (Prentice-Hall, 1964).

Vernon Reynolds

9 Man Also Behaves

Introduction

If by the term 'human nature' we put the emphasis on the word 'human', and mean the capacities of man which are unique to him, such as ideas, inventiveness, imagination, concept formation, symbolic thought and language, then I think it can well be argued that there are no limits to human nature. The philosophies produced by our own and other cultures, the world's religions, arts, scientific discoveries and technological inventions, cannot be explained by any kind of determinism; nor can the actions and changes in the historical past of our society, and we are aware of the unpredictable nature of our own experiences and the actions of others. For man, unlike other species, does not interact with his environment directly, as an individual or as a group. Man alone organizes the data of experience and the environment into *hypotheses* of how things work, he constructs within his mind *conceptualized working models* of the relationship between himself and his environment, between man and man, between group and group. With new information or new experience he can modify these conceptual models, and with symbolic tools he can think and communicate and discuss and plan and decide. Response to the environment, physical or social, is *mediated* by the hypothesis, the conceptual working model of reality; with purpose man can, because he conceives of it, seek to change, and succeed in changing, the reality in which he lives.

For some people human nature means *human* nature, man's unique capacity to respond to the world in terms of his own ideas, concepts and hypotheses. I agree with Koestler and other contributors to these essays that such qualities are exclusively human, the hallmark of our species. I should like, however, for present purposes, to look at the other side of the coin, and to interpret the term in the opposite manner; that is, to mean that part of *nature* which is human. As man is undoubtedly a product of evolution, we can expect to find a continuity and affinity between humans and the rest of nature. Within this framework man's unique capacities can then be seen as emergents in the course of evolution, rather as Teilhard de Chardin saw the 'noösphere' as emergent from the 'zoösphere'. Since their emergence they have assumed immense significance for the development of the human species, but the question remains: does it inevitably follow that the other human characteristics and capacities, which we *share* with other species of primates, are not equally important in any consideration of human nature? I refer here mainly to our postures, gestures and facial expressions, the sounds we make, and also the kinds of friendly and hostile relationships in which we get involved.

For man the thinker is only a part of man; however meaningful our actions they contain a strand of behaviour. We are flesh and blood and nervous system organized in very much the same way as the apes with whom we share a common evolutionary origin. We share the same kind of limb structure, skull shape, blood groups, hormones as they. The emotional needs and ontogenetic development of the young ape and human infant follow similar patterns. These characteristics have not evolved in a vacuum but as the instruments and motivational sources of behaviour: running, climbing, gesturing and vocalizing, caring for the young, mating, fighting, foraging. Behaviour too has not evolved in a vacuum, but is there because it has been functional in the survival of our evolutionary ancestors in their ecological context. And the survival we are talking about in the case of social species such as man and the other primates is the survival of the *group*. The group and the relationships which structure it, in man as in other primates, are, or have been, functionally related to subsisting and surviving in a particular habitat.

Let us begin then by looking at the circumstances of our own prehistory.

Man's Past

Man has a past, but there isn't a skeleton in the cupboard, a naked brutish killer whose existence embarrasses us. We are related to our pre-human ancestors not by a series of terrible battles in which only the strong survived, but by a vast number of acts of copulation and subsequent births. These stretch back in an unbroken chain from each of us now through the Ice Ages to pre-human times some four or five million years ago when *Australopithecus* was just beginning, despite his ape-sized brain, to use tools as he scavenged a living on the African savannas. *Australopithecus* was the last of the pre-humans. Living from South Africa to Ethiopia, he was a successful primate who had colonized the grasslands millions of years before and was by now well adapted to them, walking and running upright on strong, specialized back legs very like our own, feeding on vegetable matter and as much meat as he was able to get hold of. We have no evidence of his behaviour or the form of his society but we know his brain was chimpanzee-sized and we do know something of the behaviour and society of living apes such as chimpanzees. The studies of Jane Goodall and others such as Adriaan Kortandt and myself have shed a lot of light on the subtle complexities of social life among our nearest living relatives.

A few years ago I observed some chimps interacting with one another on the sensitive matter of food distribution. These were captive chimps living, if you like, in a sort of apes' prisoner-of-war camp, with two feeding-times a day. This is quite an abnormal situation for apes, and it tends to heighten the level of stress and arousal produced by food. Plates 1 to 5 are in sequence as they were taken, and show some of the ways apes today, and perhaps our ancestors millions of years ago, may have behaved towards one another. These illustrations give us some idea of the nature of anthropoid behaviour. It is probably on the basis of some such system of postures, gestures and facial expressions that our own interaction processes have developed. Chimpanzee behaviour is extremely complex. There are great differences between individuals, and sometimes one has, as an observing human, a real feeling of non-verbal understanding with the animals themselves.

This understanding extends beyond what one can see, to the impact of chimpanzees' calls. While in Africa my wife and I made tape-recordings of chimpanzees in the Budongo Forest, Uganda.

We found that their calls had some features in common with the noises produced by human beings. In particular this was true of the noise produced by a group of wild chimps unaware of our presence but excited by the prospect of feeding on a tree full of ripe figs – their favourite food. Such chimps hooted together in a noisy chorus. This was a sound produced by excitement, but not frightened excitement. It was more a case of happy excitement or enjoyment. If we compare it with the noise produced by humans enjoying a good joke there are enormous similarities – so much so that it is easy to compare the two. I am not suggesting that chimps have a sense of humour. This I doubt. What I am saying is that we express our enjoyment in a similar way and with a similar vocal apparatus to that possessed by modern chimpanzees, suggesting common inheritance.

For some five million years or so, our Australopithecine ancestors occupied the African grasslands, foraging and developing their hunting skills. Quite how their social groups were organized is a matter for speculation and those who have read Desmond Morris's *The Naked Ape* will have come across some well-informed speculation already. Mother–offspring relationships must have been very basic and central to any social organization. These mothers with their young probably clustered together in a home base, while males developed co-operative hunting skills, leaving their mates and offspring for periods of hours or days as they went off in search of carrion or game. Kinship relations, as in living monkeys and apes, were recognized beyond the mother–infant level to include three generations and brother–sister relationships; incest was avoided, especially between mothers and sons, and outmating preferred. The question of whether or not there was an emergent 'pair bond', and the extent to which groups were friendly to one another, exchanging members, as opposed to being 'closed' and hostile, is more contentious and is very much subject to debate.

Within the group, mothers would have cared for their children up to the age of 5 or more, establishing bonds which would last throughout life. As for sex, there was perhaps not much courtship but a good deal of directly sexual behaviour, as females became receptive for more and more of the time. Greeting behaviour when individuals met, especially in the case of subordinates towards their seniors, consisted most likely of baring the teeth and touching the partner's hand, while hunger could be expressed by begging for food, with the upturned palm outstretched.

In due course of time, within the last one million years, man (that is the genus *Homo*) evolved, a genus already adapted during millions of years of evolution, by its behaviour and social organization, to living off the land by hunting and gathering. And by now the ape-like capacities for recognizing relationships over space and time, and understanding the functional possibilities of simple tools to work the environment, had been developed to a new organizational level; man had become able to select and assess the data from the environment and from his experience, to perceive regular patterns and relationships, and to organize these data into conceptual models of how things worked. He applied his new abilities to conceiving of his own relationship with the environment, his relationship to others in the group, the relationship of living members to dead ones still remembered, and the relationships between one group and another. In this way, man became able to act on his physical and social environment by means of his working hypotheses, instead of behaving in direct response to it; and as his use of symbolic language developed, he was able to organize the things of his environment, of his group and beyond, into conceptual categories, and eventually to create new categories out of his own imagination. This, as Lévi-Strauss has said, was the time of the great geniuses, long, long before the dawn of history. Culture, religions, morals and customs are the ways they classified and organized the data of life and past experience into hypotheses of the basic functional relationships of man to habitat, man to man, man to the past, and group to group. Man's unique capacities thus evolved out of potentials in the inheritance he shared with apes and earlier forms of hominids; they were selected in the long period of struggle for survival by hunting game.

There are today in a number of places people who still subsist on the basis of a hunting-and-gathering economy – some groups of Eskimos, Kalahari Bushmen, Congo Pygmies, Australian Aborigines (until recently), and some of the Indians of the rain-forests of South America. These people are still living in ecological balance with their habitat, by the same means as did our ancestors for more than 99 per cent of our entire existence as humans; for it is only in the last ten thousand years that we have devised alternatives to hunting and gathering as means of subsistence: we are the blatant *nouveaux-riches* of the natural world.

What is most interesting about these surviving hunter–gatherer societies, and what makes them relevant to our theme, is the number of basic features of their social organization they have in common with one another. Despite the great variety of areas they inhabit, their totally diverse languages, their utterly different conceptions of the universe and man's place in it, their varying moralities, their intriguing technologies, all of which serve to distinguish them clearly from one another – when it comes to social organization they have much in common, and we can talk without distortion of the basic pattern of hunter–gatherer society. The largest unit in this pattern is the regional *community*, all the people an individual gets to know in his lifetime and whom he identifies with and beyond which people are 'strangers'. This community totals some 500 persons as a rule. These people do not live together, though. Living arrangements are based on a number of nomadic *bands*, which camp, hunt and forage together. Such a band is usually made up of around twenty-five persons, and consists of a few nuclear *families* related to one another by kinship ties.

Thus we have, as our basic hunter–gatherer pattern, families within bands, and bands within communities. This whole arrangement seems to be important in giving the necessary degree of flexibility for exploiting the shifting food supply on which hunter–gatherers depend, and as a social security system in time of need. It is the nearest we can get to envisaging the kind of society of our human precursors. Knowing as we do how long man has lived this way of life we can propose it as man's 'natural' kind of social organization. That is, man is adapted to life in a family, living with other families in a small band or co-residential task group which co-operates to solve the basic problems of living. Beyond his immediate social environment of twenty-five people or so, he has a much wider acquaintance of up to 500 people living in the surrounding areas, all of whom he identifies with as members of his own community.

This is not to say that we are stuck with any particular kind of social organization *today*: clearly we are not; we can, and have, modified our societies in all sorts of ways, especially since the advent of agriculture. There has been the conquest of one group by another, the establishment of class systems, colonial exploitation, the advent of minor and then major wars, the flow and flux of peoples migrating hither and thither as pioneers or refugees. All these developments, which have taken place in the last few thousand years, have been the outcome of economic and political forces, in turn resulting from conscious planning, hypothesis formation and subsequent action, negotiations and the failure of negotiations. Nevertheless, there is still a person-to-person level of human existence: what Kropotkin called 'mutual aid'; there are still bonds of affection linking people who live and interact together into co-operative groups. There are antagonisms, jealousies, and hates, and to balance these there is sexual attraction, maternal love, paternal care, infantile dependence. The question is: despite the reorganization of society by man and the re-casting of everything in a cultural mould, how much of our own personal time and energy does not in fact go into the age-old channels, which vastly pre-date modern society and even to some extent man himself, of loving and hating, of caring and avoiding, of seeking dominant status and appeasing those who dominate us, of looking for sex and other kinds of excitement, of fearing and fighting against the unknown that threatens to upset or destroy ourselves or those who are dependent on us?

How do we Interact?

From this general survey of social relationships, let us now turn to some recent studies of the details of human actions, and look at some of the methods that have been used and some of the results that have been obtained.

Anthropologists such as E. T. Hall have taken the trouble to observe people in social situations and to measure how close they come to one another and how often they actually touch one another and where and how they do it when they do. Hall calls this study 'proxemics'. In his book *The Hidden Dimension* he distinguishes various distances people keep apart from one another for different culturally-defined purposes. He starts with what he calls the 'intimate distance', when, as he puts it, 'sight (often distorted), olfaction, heat from the other person's body, sound, smell and feel of the breath all combine to signal unmistakable involvement with another body'. From this, the intimate distance, which extends from 0 to 18 inches, we go through 'personal distance' ($1\frac{1}{2}$ to 4 feet) and 'social distance' (4 to 12 feet) to 'public distance' (over 12 feet) Each distance is regarded as appropriate to certain circumstances and these differ from culture to culture.

I remember being surprised in East Africa to see people talking to one another quite quietly across the main road. We would normally walk to the same side of the road to talk, and regard it as a sign of lack of enthusiasm not to do so, but this is not at all the case in Bunyoro. On the other hand, when we do meet close to, we may not touch one another at all or we may shake hands, in which case it is usually a fairly quick process. But in East Africa if you do shake hands it can be quite a long and involved process. First you shake hands with a man palm to palm, then he grasps your thumb and presses it backwards, then you shake palm to palm again and finally you press his thumb back. While this is going on you exchange smiles, look into each other's eyes, and exchange a long series of ritual greeting phrases in a very leisurely fashion. It all seems very odd at first but after a number of disastrous failures I got the hang of it and came to enjoy it; it certainly broke the ice and made for peaceful and friendly relationships.

These examples, of spacing and of greeting actions by humans, show two things. First they show the differences between cultures and give clues to the different ideas and feelings underlying the overt patterns. Second they show that in different places human beings are faced by similar problems (how to space out, how to greet one another) which they solve in ways that, though different in many respects, do nevertheless have certain features in common. Greeting, for instance, did involve hand-to-hand touching and teeth-baring in each of the two cases we looked at. Some observers have been more inclined to stress the common features at the expense of the differences. Such for example is the case with Eibl-Eibesfeldt, who, working with the cameraman Hans Hass, has done one of the major cross-cultural studies of human action in recent years. His approach is ethological, and he is in search of the basic repertoire of human species-specific behaviour, just as would be the case if he were studying any other animal species.

Hass used a ciné camera that had a lens pointing sideways to obtain records of the responses of people who did not know they were under observation. Among the clearest findings of this two-man team was the fact that in all cultures studied, in India, the South Seas, France, East Africa, New Guinea and the U.S.A., greeting behaviour, that is, behaviour when two individuals met, included a quick but definite raising and lowering of the eyebrows, or as it has been called eyebrow 'flash'; see Plate 6. This certainly also goes for ourselves, and once one becomes aware of it it is surprising how often one sees it among one's acquaintances when one had never really noticed it before. One isn't conscious of giving this signal until one has become aware of it. Nor is one actually instructed by cultural agencies such as the family and the school to do it, so on the face of it (to coin a phrase) it looks as if this might be a good contender for an item of pan-human, non-cultural, species-specific behaviour, perhaps having ultimately some appeasing function or other function to do with the business of coming face-to-face with a known conspecific, whether on the Palaeolithic plains of Africa or in the crowded confines of a London bus.

This eyebrow flash was also a part of an elaborate series of facial expressions that Eibl-Eibesfeldt and Hass found to be associated with flirtatious, or, to be more biological, courtship, behaviour directed towards them by girls. While Hass was apparently filming something else, Eibl smiled at girls of nubile age whenever a suitable opportunity for study arose; subsequent film analysis showed that his smile drew a series of glances at him, alternating with lowered eyes and eyelids, a series of eyebrow flashes, smiles of increasing intensity, and the occasional blush. This language of love was apparently quite universal.

As everyone knows, eyebrow flashes also occur during the course of ordinary conversation. Clearly in this situation they cannot be classed as 'greeting' nor, necessarily, as flirtation. Take for example those familiar faces reading the television news. Why do they flash their eyebrows? It has been suggested that what the eyebrow flash basically does is to draw attention to a face, to indicate or create or sustain interest. In conversation it acts to keep the attention of the partner (or should I say opponent?) from wandering, to stress the significance of what is being said. Perhaps the newscaster, unable to see his victims, fears that they may be about to switch off or turn over to a livelier channel, and does what he can to prevent this.

Quite clearly the study by Eibl-Eibesfeldt and Hass was no more than a pilot survey, but it certainly indicates that there may be a common 'language' of non-verbal facial expressions and gestures by which human beings anywhere can communicate with one another. This would not be to deny that such a 'language' or signalling-system is everywhere to a greater or lesser extent modified by cultural inputs about exactly how and when to smile or to touch or how close to stand or how loud to talk. Nor would one want to deny that culture can introduce new items, such as the one-eyed wink well known in Britain but possibly incomprehensible to a Pygmy or an Eskimo, or the habit which I understand is prevalent in continental Europe of tickling a lady's palm when shaking hands if you want to make love to her.

But as before, where we have cultural modifications we are dealing with modifications of a common core. One could perhaps claim that all our ideas and ways of interacting non-verbally have certain common features because they are all modifications of a system dreamt up by earlier generations and diffused over the world like the knowledge of windmills or the plough or Coca-Cola. But this is unlikely to have produced the degree of uniformity that does now appear to exist. If we look at the growth and diversification of verbal languages we can see the products of wholly cultural diffusion. In Europe or Africa one has only to travel a few hundred miles (a short distance, these days) in almost any direction and one enters a zone in which the native language is almost wholly different from one's own. This simply is not the case with non-verbal communication. On the other hand, those who have travelled to distant parts will know that even where language is an almost insuperable barrier a level of communication can be achieved by the use of non-verbal signs, such as pointing, smiling, making physical contact in friendly or unfriendly ways. In fact it would not be wrong to say that all peoples everywhere *can* in fact communicate with one another. We are all members of one species, we are all interfertile, we all have much in common in terms of our physical and emotional needs, and we all have common ways of getting together to satisfy them.

This claim – that we can all communicate – may on the surface

Penny (*left*), an adult female, approaches Gracie, another adult female, who has food. Penny is hungry

2 Penny sits close to Gracie who gives her a neck-kiss

Gracie pushes her head underneath Penny, who gently bites her back

4 Tommy, a young male, approaches. Gracie greets him by holding out a finger, which he takes in his mouth. Penny has succeeded in obtaining an apple

5 Tommy sits beside Gracie, taking her protruded lips into his mouth. Penny has now left. Tommy has been very successful in obtaining food from Gracie

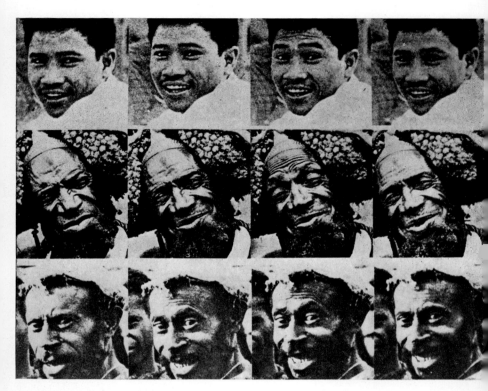

6 Eyebrow-flash during greeting:
Upper row Balinese—Island Nusa Penida (19 frames)
Middle row Paupa—Huri tribe, New Guinea (45 frames)
Lower row Paupa—Woitapmin tribe, New Guinea (85 frames)

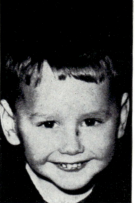

7 Simple smile (*left*) and upper smile (*right*)

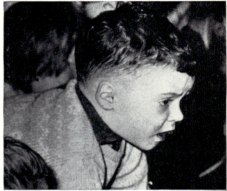

8 Aggressive frown—note central furrowing of forehead (*right*) and protusion of lips (*left*)

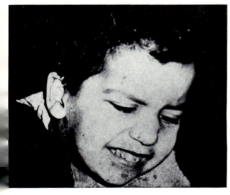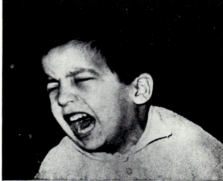

9 Fear grimace—note eyes downcast, lip corners turned down and drawn back, and head evasion

10 At the funfair

11 Mussolini

12 Bangla Desh

of it sound rather obvious, but I think this is far from being the case. It will require a long and difficult uphill struggle to make it scientifically respectable, or alternatively, to disprove it. The *Zeitgeist* has for hundreds of years emphasized the contrary view – that people in other cultures are different from ourselves, and that these differences are basic. Social anthropology in particular has stressed the differences between different peoples in their interpretation of themselves or the universe or their valuations of human life; colonialism made such theories not only respectable but desirable. When I first came to study anthropology it was these differences that I wished to understand and I feel sure that the same goes for much of the fascination of other peoples and their worlds that we feel today, for instance when we watch South American tribesmen on TV, though it is to be hoped that by now we respect them for what they are.

We have seen so far that all men have a common evolutionary history, that they everywhere develop certain kinds of relationships into which they channel their social actions, that every culture has its own range of acceptable and unacceptable ways of doing things, and that tangled in among the culturally-practised actions of men and women there are elements of behaviour patterns that go back to our distant past.

I want now to focus on children. If there is any truth in the idea that behavioural elements exist in human action, shouldn't they be clearest in young children, who haven't yet been well and truly acculturated? Of course, we shouldn't make the mistake of thinking that 'ontogeny recapitulates phylogeny'; it doesn't. We won't find the behaviour of adult apes reflected in human children. We can, however, pose the simple question as to whether young children do or do not show predictable behaviour-patterns, and the answer, judging from the studies made so far – which are lamentably few and mostly non-cross-cultural – is positive.

One of the first ethological studies to be published was made by Blurton Jones on 3–5-year-old children in a nursery school in London. He distinguished between a number of postures, gestures and facial expressions shown by the children; for example, run, jump, hand-slap, wrestle, low frown, fixate, red face, pucker brows, laugh and cry. There were many others – so many that a full list would be tedious. Individual children differed in the extent to which they displayed different units, in their responses to one another and to adults such as their teacher, their parents or the observer. But overall certain patterns emerged. For example, aggression (over who should have objects) involved kicking, pulling, biting, pulling hair, beating, often preceded by fixing the opponent with a frown and lowering of the eyebrows, while shouting with a characteristic low pitch and low explosive quality the words 'No!' or 'Let go!'

As to the child who gets hit or whose property is taken, he may scream, call for help, retaliate or weep, puckering his brows and going red in the face, often staying immobile, sitting down and sucking his thumb.

In the first of what will, I hope, be a large number of cross-cultural studies of child behaviour conducted on ethological lines, Blurton Jones and a colleague from Harvard have recently found many points of similarity between the children they observed in nursery schools in London and those in the Kalahari desert, where they lived for a while with a group of nomadic, hunter–gatherer Bushmen.

Identical or similar kinds of behaviour to those described by Blurton Jones have been found in other groups of 3–5-year-old children. Studies by Grant, for example, have broken down the components of facial expressions to a large extent, distinguishing six different types of frown, eight different kinds of smile, and so on. Plates 7 to 9 show a few of the many expressions distinguished by Grant.

This kind of detailed analysis is not done purely for its own sake. There are medical applications, for example in the understanding of the difficulties and shortcomings of autistic children. There is also reason to suppose that these details really do play a part in our own everyday interactions – that we ourselves, both as children and as adults, are sensitive not just to gross facial patterns but to the precise kinds of smiles and frowns, puckered brows and so on that studies such as these are beginning to reveal. In our signalling to one another we can relay complex information about our feelings that goes along with the verbal and ideational content of what we are saying. Raised eyebrows indicate interest, lowered brows indicate lack of interest, brows drawn down in the centre indicate aggression, brows drawn down at the outer edges indicate submission. Alternatively we can, and in some cultures regularly do, inhibit expression of our feelings by non-verbal means. I think a lot of this is done in Britain, and even more in the U.S.A. This is a fascinating subject which has yet to be investigated.

Does it Matter?

Even if it could be shown that man everywhere had common communicative signals at the non-verbal level, and that all human beings were prone to form certain kinds of social relationships, would it matter? Aren't the important issues elsewhere, in the study of people's beliefs, their systems of categorization, their techniques of government, the distribution of power, and methods of self- and social aggrandizement? Why, of all the possible things to do, poke around among the details of face-to-face behaviour? Is it really worth it?

To look at the problem this way is to look beyond science into the fields of politics and ideology, or even into ethics. Is such looking further necessary? Increasingly, these days, scientists are coming to think that it is, mainly because of continual and flagrant misuse of research findings by governments and other agencies. Ethologists no less than others need to look out that their findings are not misused, and to emphasize positive applications of their science.

It can indeed be well argued that all of science is a social activity, intimately tied up with the power structure which often finances it and expects or hopes to benefit from its results. We all know about Stalin and Lysenko, Hitler and von Braun, and the decisive outcome of the emigration to the U.S.A. of Einstein and a number of other atomic physicists. Again, we all know that nuclear physics can be either misused, to destroy, or put to the public good. Robert Young has argued that the whole of science must be seen as falling within the general fields of ideology, social control, morality and politics. Professor Ziman, the Bristol physicist, opposes this view with the principle that '*Hypotheses non olent*' – 'Theories don't smell'. In other words, politics and ideologies may make use of science but they have no power to validate or invalidate it. I think we definitely have to think of an interaction between science and ideology; they are inseparable and each feeds upon and gives to the other.

This debate is relevant to any study of man, whether ethological, psychological, or sociological. The question always centres around the uses that are, or could be, made of research findings. Ethology is, at the present time, making us more aware of the non-verbal signals we transmit to one another, and forcing us to consider the feelings these signals imply. In particular, the increasingly close coverage of world events by news cameramen and Press photographers is bringing home to us the reality of situations at a face-to-face, non-verbal level, when we might otherwise easily be deceived by words. For instance the public outcry about the My Lai massacre stemmed largely from the publication in *Life* magazine of photographs taken at the scene. Without these, we should have heard nothing but the verbal evidence, which would inevitably have been confused and contradictory. The pictures spoke loud and clear. The reason they did so was that we understood or felt something when we saw certain facial expressions and certain scenes in a certain context. This common response is, I think, a very good thing with great potential, but there is at the same time the danger that it could be misused if governmental agencies were able to impose effective censorship on the publication of pictorial material.

Plates 10 to 12 show some adult human expressions from magazine publications: laughter, hostility, fear and despair. We subjectively understand something of what these pictures are saying. They amuse us or disturb us. How should ethology, the study of these things, proceed? There are many things ethology cannot do. It cannot bring about social change. The vastly complex, exploitative systems of what we call 'Western' societies will not undo themselves and revert to warm, friendly face-to-face groups because of what well-meaning ethologists say; if one day these systems fall apart it will be for other reasons. In the history of social change, what has been the place of the scientist and what ought it to be? Often he wants to contribute to society, to do something humanitarian, to work with those whose concern is the reduction of human misery and suffering. Ethology looks squarely in the face at people in the moment of their actions. It describes with what could be mistaken for callous non-involvement the faces of fear, of anger, of despair as well as those of unhappiness and contentment. Were the ethologist truly uninvolved his activities would be despicable. But such is not, and cannot be, the case; he *is* involved. I want to end with a quotation not from an ethologist but from someone equally or even more involved in the immediacies of human action, Larry Burrows, the English war photographer who was killed in Vietnam in February 1971 at the age of 45. Not long before he died he wrote:

It's not easy to photograph a man dying in the arms of his fellow countryman and later to record the breakdown of his friend. I fought with my conscience. Was I simply capitalizing on other men's grief? But I concluded that what I was doing would penetrate the hearts of those at home who are simply too indifferent. And I felt I was freed to act on that condition.

N. G. Blurton Jones, ed., *Ethological Studies of Child Behaviour* (Cambridge 1972).

N. G. Blurton Jones, 'An Ethological Study of Some Aspects of Social Behaviour of Children in Nursery School', in *Primate Ethology*, ed. D. Morris (London 1967).

I. Eibl-Eibesfeldt, *Ethology, The Biology of Behaviour* (1970). 'Similarities and Differences Between Cultures in Expressive Movements', in *Non-Verbal Communication*, ed. R. A. Hinde (Cambridge 1972).

Jane Goodall, 'Chimpanzees of the Gombe Stream Reserve', in *Primate Behaviour*, ed. I. De Vore (New York 1965).

Ewan Grant, 'Human Facial Expression', in *Man*, Vol. 4, No. 4, December 1969.

Edward T. Hall, *The Silent Language* (New York 1959).
The Hidden Dimension (New York 1969).

Desmond Morris, *The Naked Ape* (London 1969).

Robert M. Young, 'Evolutionary Biology and Ideology: Then and Now', in *Science Studies* 1 (1971), pp. 177–206; and in W. Fuller, ed., *The Social Impact of Modern Biology* (London 1970); also see pp. 235 ff. of the present volume.

Michael R. A. Chance

10 The Dimensions of our Social Behaviour

The rate of technological innovation is now so fast that the implications of one change have hardly been understood and coped with when another is upon us. In these circumstances we may be forgiven for asking whether, if this process continues to accelerate, our ability to handle change will not be overcome by the changes themselves. European culture has accepted change since about the fourteenth century, but the individual has lagged behind. In general, the adjustments made by society to change have come in the subsequent generation of people. It is not too early therefore to ask what changes may be possible in the individual's personality during his lifetime in order to enhance his will-power and our collective competence in social and political life.

Only fragmentary scientific evidence exists on this; but much experiential evidence that it is possible comes from 'psychological cure' and 'religious conversion'. Little weight is attached to this evidence because it is played down by scientific opinion and by the pervasive concept of 'self'. The concept of the self is a powerful integrating force in our culture, but it has become inviolate, self-sufficient and highly intellectualized (if indeed it is not an exclusively intellectual phenomenon), and as a result the individual becomes disengaged from his environment.

To examine our own personality is pejoratively termed 'introspection', implying that this is a dangerous pursuit because it cannot be undertaken without loss of our ability to be objective. Admittedly it is difficult to study the behaviour of another individual without becoming involved with him, but ethology has learnt the techniques essential for human ethology through studying the behaviour of animals.

Ethologists observe behaviour and, by describing individual postures often repeated in the behaviour of a species, have shown that all species of animal possess *fixed action patterns* which provide the shape of much of the behaviour. In the simplest instance, a fixed action pattern is brought into operation by a stimulus and must then be completed. Subsequent stimuli then serve only to orient the action as it proceeds in its fixed manner. This is illustrated by the retrieving movements of a broody goose, which will stretch its neck out to draw in, behind its beak, an egg which has been displaced from the nest. As it pulls its beak in along the ground, the goose moves its head from side to side in order to keep its beak immediately behind the egg as it moves irregularly along the ground. If, after the neck has been stretched out, the egg is taken away, the bird continues to draw its beak in along the ground, but without any adjusting lateral movements. We can distinguish here an inbuilt release component, a set of movements (the withdrawal of the beak along the ground) controlled by stimuli fed back from the environment. These co-ordinate the action of the released component with the object being retrieved.

Some of these fixed action patterns can in many species be rearranged, and thus provide alternative ways of behaving; and some learnt elements are inserted between fixed sequences at specified points, providing some added flexibility. The great apes, the chimpanzee and the gorilla are also capable of constructing their behaviour by direct imitation of ourselves, as when a chimpanzee smokes a cigarette exactly as we do, or behaves in ways which demonstrate that its behaviour is constructed according to the requirements of a situation, as when a mother holds her injured baby so that its wound is protected from contact with her or other objects.

The higher primates, ourselves amongst them, can therefore behave under the dictates of internal sources of information or on information drawn directly from the environment. Whether or not an individual constructs his behaviour in one or other of these ways depends very largely on his social relations, so I shall inquire what the social conditions are which encourage one or other of these two possibilities. This is very much the concern of ethologists who, apart from uncovering the structure of the individual's repertoire in the way described above, study the pattern of social organization by noting how frequently and for how long two or more individuals behave towards one another in specific ways, and how long and how frequently they are found in one another's company.

Recently I have completed a comparative study of the social structure of higher primates[1] and this has revealed a sharp contrast between a society of the great apes on the one hand, and a society of macaques or baboons on the other, as regards the social structure and the structure of the individual's behavioural repertoire. Since these groups are our nearest zoological relatives, we are likely not only to gain insight from studying their social behaviour, but to share the social propensities shown by them; and I shall bring forward evidence that this is so.

Forms of Group Cohesion

Since the war a great deal of interest has been taken in communication between individuals. This has been approached from electronic theory and through linguistics, and much of the interest in ethology has arisen because it has uncovered the forms of communication in animals and of non-verbal communication in man.

We have to bear in mind, however, that communication is not possible between members of a group unless the group coheres. Individuals have to be within earshot, range of vision, or actually in contact, to communicate at all. This cohesion is based on an infrastructure of relationships which has the primary function of enabling the individuals to stay together, and this is what we must now consider, since it is on this basis that the structure of the social behaviour is built.

Every species of sub-human primate has its own unique pattern of social relations which results in a set of sub-groupings within the society as a whole, but, as pointed out in *Social Groups of Monkeys, Apes and Men*,[2] three types can be identified in the majority of groups so far studied. These are (1) the assemblies of adult females and their infants, (2) adult cohorts of males, and (3) clusters of juveniles, consisting of young which are no longer dependent on their mothers but have not yet joined either of the adult groups. For details of these and the idiosyncrasies of each species, see the book.

These sub-groups account for the coherence of their members

over large periods of time; but in addition to them there are two distinct modes in which the society as a whole is brought together. This involves, in both modes, the group members paying attention to a focal individual. One of these, which I have called the *hedonic mode*, based on display as a means of gaining attention, is a recent discovery. Chimpanzee and gorilla societies are constructed in this mode. The *agonistic mode*, by contrast, is based on conflict, and on avoidance of attack from the dominant male. Macaque and baboon societies are constructed in this way.

To argue that these two types of society are constructed on these two modes is to suggest that, for the greater part of their lives, individuals are related to one another in these two different ways. The possibility of being persistently aware of a dominant focus arises in the open terrain inhabited by baboons and the rhesus macaque, but is not possible in the forest conditions usually inhabited by the great apes. Monkeys foraging in open country are potentially under attack by predators and need to keep in sight of the dominant males, whereas gorillas moving on the ground through forest keep in touch by a chain of attention ending up at the focal male. Chimpanzees, on the other hand, moving through the trees, are often separated except by being able to call to one another; and mutual display is used to reunite the group after they have come together again.

We shall now go on to consider the features typical of these two modalities as shown by chimpanzees on the one hand and macaques or baboons on the other. Then we shall show that these two systems by which behaviour is organized have been found in the behaviour structure of two species of macaque. The great apes are exceptional in that they appear not to be able to cohere by agonistic means.

Hedonic Cohesion

First let us consider how the cohesion of the whole group is achieved in an hedonic society through display. Schaller,[3] in his study of the wild gorilla, was the first to point out that when the dominant male was ready to move off again after a rest period he stood in a prominent position and in a characteristic posture: looking ahead of him, legs fully extended, vertical and rigid. After he had adopted this posture for some time, the rest of the group gathered round him and he then moved off. Schaller also pointed out that when an adult male beats his chest and advances towards an intruder (like Schaller himself), this is not only acting as an intimidating display towards the intruder but also indicates his whereabouts to the rest of the group.

Reynolds,[4] in his study of the Budongo Forest chimpanzees, early on found himself witnessing the so-called 'carnivals' in which all the chimpanzees hoot, jump about, beat the resonant bases of trees and wave sticks in the air as they display towards one another in this manner. He noticed that this happened particularly when two groups of chimpanzees met in the forest and that then this mutual displaying was followed by much contact behaviour including touching, kissing, and some pseudosexual behaviour. He and Luscombe[5] found that it was much easier to understand the nature of this mutual display when they studied chimpanzees in a thirty-acre enclosure in New Mexico, at the time when the American Air Force had a research unit there. On my own visit to this place, I noticed that chimpanzees would wander over the enclosure in the early morning, often separated by two hundred yards as they explored in different directions; and then perhaps, as a group clambered into the old trees, they would see another group. Immediately, they moved over towards them and made contact, showing some excitement when they met. On one occasion this led to some old sacking and sticks being thrown into the air. Briefly, what Luscombe and Reynolds found was that at times when the fruit was provided early in the morning a lot of mutual displaying took place. At the same time the chimpanzees gathered into a group.

It was also found that the amount of attention that other individuals paid to any particular chimpanzee depended on his displaying ability, but that the amount of attention did not correlate in any way with the amount of aggressive behaviour shown by any individual. Moreover, an individual's ability to become the focus of attention through displays led him to be the centre of a group of individuals when fruit-sharing took place, and in this way a successful displayer was also successful in getting a large share of the fruit. Subsequently the group broke up into twos and threes, and these pairs and smaller groups moved off in pursuit of different activities.

As I pointed out earlier, the great apes are peculiar in that they do not show any persistent agonism, and this means that, apart from the coherence of small groups, the whole group is brought together only through mutual display binding the individuals' attention from time to time on to one another.

Agonistic Cohesion

The mechanism that holds agonistic-type societies together is of a different kind. As pointed out earlier, the fact that baboons and macaques live largely in open country means that it is possible for them to be aware of the dominant male at all times and for him thereby to be the focus of the group's attention. Although they may be largely preoccupied by foraging and thereby be spread out over quite a large area, they are nevertheless ready at any moment to co-ordinate their own behaviour with that of the dominant male in defence of the group as a whole. As individuals, they do not move out of sight of the centre, so we must assume that they are always attentive to it. This has been demonstrated in the way the hamadryas baboon and the rhesus macaque behave as the troops move away from their sleeping-sites in the morning. Here the direction of the movement of a troop as a whole results from the initiative of sub-adult males moving out in different directions, and from the eventual co-ordination of this initiative of theirs with the direction the dominant male ultimately decides to go.

Kummer's study[6] of the one-male groups of the hamadryas baboon, moreover, makes it clear that this unit is the result of the confinement of the individual's attention within his own group, focused on the male. In this way, baboons move about as a very tightly-packed group. Here their attention is co-ordinated by the infliction of neck bites by the male on the members of his harem if they stray any distance away.

From time to time in semi-captive colonies – and during fairly prolonged episodes in the wild – threatening, chasing and fleeing and various forms of submission are shown in vigorous agonistic encounters between adults of the group, mainly the males. At all times the individual in an agonistic community must be ready to defend his status or avoid being the object of severe attack, and this can only be done by persistent awareness of the dominant focus. The dominant males, having a superfluity of aggressive-ness, may be provoked either accidentally or by transgression of certain spatial and behavioural regularities. Hence an agonistic society is held together by a persistent awareness of the centre, based on a readiness to behave agonistically at any moment. It is not surprising, therefore, that spacing out and status are per-sistent preoccupations of the individuals of such a group. Most interactions within the group (e.g., submission, flight) are de-signed to terminate the conflict inherent in the situation. In this respect, therefore, agonistic behaviour contrasts markedly with hedonic behaviour, as it tends to terminate active interactions whereas hedonic behaviour tends to promote social intercourse.

Comparison of Hedonic and Agonistic Behaviour

In order to make a comparison between the agonistic and hedonic modes it is easier to describe one of them and to contrast this description with the corresponding features of the other, and in doing so I shall attempt to abstract from the information avail-able the characteristic features of the hedonic mode. We shall do this by contrasting the behaviour of the chimpanzee, which exhibits the hedonic mode in its most characteristic form, with the agonistic behaviour shown by baboons and macaques. Until we have as clear an idea as possible about the characteristics of the modes of behaviour in the sub-human primates, we cannot hope to interpret human behaviour.

Undoubtedly the feature that affects most aspects of behaviour is the flexibility of behaviour in the hedonic mode. This leads to an increase in the range of behaviour and the readiness with which a switch in behaviour can take place. In the chimpanzee the range of behaviour is extended by the variety of behaviour which it exhibits in the wild, and also by the readiness with which, in semi-captive situations, it has been found to acquire entirely new forms of behaviour. This may well reflect an enhanced ability to receive rewards for achieving a new skill. This in turn undoubtedly reflects a greater flexibility in the control of attention and the individual control of excitement.

One of the outstanding features of chimpanzee society is the prominence of contact behaviour, and this is well illustrated in Vernon Reynolds's contribution to this series of essays (p. 143).

In the first place, greetings involve contact behaviour in a number of ways: for example, touching hands, touching another's body, kissing and various forms of hugging, and frequently, when greatly excited, some form of sexual behaviour. This is often followed by the group's breaking up into pairs of chimpanzees who move off with their arms round each other, leading to the separation of the various sub-groups of the society and providing the opportunity for a later reunion.

Since the members of an agonistic society are constantly aware of one another and in one another's presence, the opportunities for meeting in the way chimpanzees do does not arise. The meeting between two individuals in an agonistic society always involves a heightening of the latent conflict present, and the individual meets this situation by postural and facial appeasement gestures such as presentation, lip-smacking and 'appeasement face'. If any physical contact is established, this leads to ritual grooming, in which one individual grooms the other, but occasionally mutual grooming takes place. Whereas in the forms of contact shown by the chimpanzee there is a great fluidity in forms of contact, ritual grooming is very stereotyped and consists of a sharp downward and sideways combing movement of the fingers of one hand while the other hand is used for examining and picking at the exposed skin. While pairs or even three sub-adult chimpanzees will be seen moving over fairly large areas in an exploratory fashion with their arms round each other, the sub-adult macaques or baboons have no contact except that the younger sub-adults may jump on the back of elder males in periods of social excitement.

From the work of Mason[7] it is possible to infer that contact in all these instances is a form of reassurance. Undoubtedly, the widespread occurrence of contact in the behaviour of the chimpanzee reduces tension and enables the individual to rapidly control his excitement.

Chimpanzees in the wild are provided with a great variety of ways of using sticks as tools. Sticks or branches are used to hit the ground or to throw at potential predators, and also for poking into termite hills to extract the termites, and in these circumstances awkward projections are broken off. Suitable twigs may be found by the discarding of many until a usable one is found or until one is fashioned in the way described.

Macaques and baboons do not use any instruments in the wild. Hence the whole range of problem-solving behaviour which is open to the chimpanzee (studied by Kohler[8, 9] and Schiller[10] in semi-captivity) is potentially not available to the species in the wild. A startling recent discovery by Menzel[11] has shown that a group of young chimpanzees who had grown up together in semi-captivity were able to develop and jointly exploit a new method of using a pole as a ladder. In all these studies the ability of the chimpanzee to adjust the use of the instrument to the potentiality of the situation – in order not only to reach a set objective but to use an invented skill for more than one purpose – indicates clearly that the chimpanzee is capable of extending its repertoire much closer to that of man than is any other sub-human primate. Groups of chimpanzees can expand their repertoire by invention, whereas groups of baboons and macaques do not.

A notable feature of this expansion of repertoire is the switch of attention from social to non-social aspects of the environment – clearly seen in the mutual inspection of an object by two chimpanzees. Two chimpanzees will sit next to each other and one will watch the other trace the line of a crack in the floor with his finger or a stick, and will momentarily indicate the shared attention between them by running his finger along the crack.

A greater control of attention through an awareness of external features is particularly well illustrated by a mother's awareness of the situation of her young. Both gorilla and chimpanzee mothers are able to anticipate and protect their infants from potentially dangerous situations (see Chance and Jolly[1]). A macaque or baboon mother protects her infant from potential danger only by restricting its activities or responding to its calls.

It seems that, from studies of other species of monkey and baboon, provided thay are withdrawn from their social context they are potentially capable of exhibiting some, if not many, of the problem-solving capabilities of chimpanzees, but only as individuals.[8, 12]

Indeed, many rudimentary elements of problem-solving and inventiveness can be found in some species of basically agonistic societies, as in groups of long-tailed macaques (Angst[13]). Just as the possibilities of problem-solving inherent in the hedonic mode have been extended far beyond the rudimentary elements shown by individuals living in a society intermediate between the two modes (i.e. the long-tailed macaque), so the limitations on individual behaviour inherent in the mechanisms designed to reduce conflict rigidify the behaviour of predominantly agonistic species such as the rhesus macaque and the baboon to an extent which precludes possibilities based on variability. Agonistic societies contain a very large element of conflict, both in the relationships between individuals and the state of the individual's motivation. As a result, spacing out is a way of reducing the impact between two individuals. So also is a 'cut-off' act. This is a deflection, in the simplest instance, of the visual awareness of another individual by diverting the gaze. Very often this means paying attention to something else and not simply closing the eyes, for example. This brings about a continual interruption of attention, so preventing ongoing attention to a single feature of the environment, or the mutual inspection of the same object by two individuals, so typical of the hedonic mode.

In the agonistic mode, displacement of behaviour may take the form of scratching in the ground, for example, but if so, it is of a rigid and repetitive kind, not controlled by an awareness of the environment, as when a chimpanzee moves its fingers along a crack in the ground. The fixity and rigidity of these displacement activities and deflections of attention originate more from the value of these actions in curtailing the conflict between individuals than from an intrinsic interest in the alternative object towards which attention is directed.

Moreover, in this way attention is frequently deflected on to another individual of lower status. This may then be used to displace aggression by threats or actual chasing, as in the following example:

On 10 April 1962, for no apparent reason, 1956-Male-1 attacked an unrelated adult female while she was drinking. Immediately, the dominant male of the group, Old-Male-A, attacked 1956-Male-1, who fled. Old-Male-A chased him round for about half a minute or more; from a bush, up a palm tree and down the other side, round a building and down a trail. Suddenly, out from under another bush 1956-Male-1's parent, Old-Female-I, came running on her hind legs carrying her five day old infant. She ran to stand at her son's side, and together they made violent threat gestures and vocalizations at a part of the area empty of all monkeys and observers, and away from the dominant male. Old-Male-A stopped chasing to look at what they seemed to be threatening, then chased 1956-Male-1 again, who again threatened loudly away from Old-Male-A. Old-Male-A sat down three feet away peering again in the direction in which 1956-Male-1 was threatening. Old-Female-1 climbed to sit between them and her son immediately sidled up to her, sat touching her and groomed her. She walked away and 1956-Male-1 followed her closely, grooming her whenever she stopped, leaving Old-Male-A peering at nothing. Parents often defend their offspring from the attacks of monkeys more dominant than themselves by diverting the attention of the attacker in just the manner described.[14]

Bi-modal Potential in the Macaque Repertoire

So far, we have described the difference between the hedonic and the agonistic mode in terms of the behaviour of species which are organized predominantly in one or other of these two different modes, and we have abstracted the characteristics of each mode. Following the publication of my paper[15] putting forward the hypothesis that rank-ordered behaviour was best understood in terms of the structure of attention, Virgo and Waterhouse have found, from their study of the Bristol Zoo macaque colony,[16] that there were two structures of attention, each focused on a different individual in the colony. They showed that the structure of attention based on agonistic behaviour was focused on an adult female, and the other, based on grooming and affiliative relations (sitting next, etc.), was focused on an adult male. This immediately drew attention to earlier observations of my own at Bristol Zoo, in which changes of the leadership of the colony followed a period of vigorous display by the future dominant male. Hence it became clear that the features of both modalities were present and employed by members of a single species (the rhesus macaque) and therefore the propensities for these two behavioural features were present in the individual rhesus macaque. Current studies under way with Tom Pitcairn and Walter Angst are providing evidence of the same potentials in the behaviour structure of the long-tailed macaque. We are nearing the point, therefore, when we are able to say of the sub-human primates that an individual possesses potential for developing these two modes.

What then are the essential consequences of the understanding of behaviour structure? Since the hedonic mode is alone capable of enabling behaviour to be constructed entirely on the basis of external information, and the stereotypy of the agonistic mode is in such marked contrast to it, we are forced to conclude that the agonistic mode is constructed from fixed action patterns and is therefore programmed from internal sources. We have to distinguish the forms of behaviour that a chimpanzee employed for smoking a cigarette on the one hand and throwing clods of earth at me on the other.

Human Counterparts

In our discussion of the infrastructure of social cohesion and control we have suggested that, depending on the basic modality in which individuals are operating, the type of communication between them will differ. In human relationships, communication of the type we have been discussing is considered 'nonverbal'. By its nature, this type of communication is concerned with the relationship of the communicator with other individuals in a group, or, as I shall call this attribute of an individual, his primary group relations.

The infrastructure of social communication is posture, gesture and facial expression as well as tone of voice, and constitutes the framework of control within which linguistic intercourse takes place.

In an important sense the relationship of an individual who is a member of a group is tacit, and the way the individual becomes competent in this sphere is through practice in social relations. These are the implications of Bernstein's work, about which I am going to speak, for he has discovered that language can be subordinated to, and used only as an extension of, this tacit relationship.

But Michael Argyle,[17] Adam Kendon[18] and Paul Ekman[19] have shown that, in the conversation of literate individuals, eye contact, head and hand gestures are used to control the attention between speaker and listener. This occurs in what we colloquially know as 'talking to one another'. Therefore, language is used in two quite different ways, depending on the way it is related to the infrastructure of interpersonal relations.

Both Bernstein[20] and Jensen,[21] in different ways which are incidental to their main interest, have uncovered the fact that through differentiation in development (ontogeny), different mental faculties can be subordinated to, and come to be part of, this infrastructure controlling relationships within a group.

Both have used class differentiations as a means of studying the operation of 'intelligence', and Bernstein has been specifically interested in uncovering the fact that differences in intelligence of pupils are related to the patterns of social behaviour found in the family and their general social background, but this is only incidental in Jensen's work.

Bernstein suggests that the limitation of intelligence in some classes of pupil arises from the fact that they possess a *restricted code* of language, which, through its own structure, indicates that it is used as an extension of the non-verbal social control system which the individual has grown up to consider the essential framework within which language itself is to be used. As an example, children commenting on a strip cartoon of children playing ball and accidentally kicking it through a window pane, used the pronouns 'you', 'they' and 'we'. 'They' and 'we' indicate out-group and in-group identities and 'you' the speaker's awareness of a single individual within the group.

Nouns describing the objective existence of the components of the cartoon, the ball and the people involved, the window, etc., are not used, and, because of this lack of specification, the language operates only because there is acceptance by the viewer of what is referred to, so that elaboration is redundant. It leaves so much unsaid that it needs the picture to be present in order to make intelligible the meaning of what is said. The picture, in this instance, stands for the shared social situation.

Significantly enough, in this context, the pronoun 'I' is not used, as the person does not see himself as an entity in the total situation, since the situation and the action taking place within it is merely an experience *of his*. He does not see himself as part of an objective situation.

An *elaborated code*, on the other hand, which for us is what we understand by the use of a language, renders explicit what is implicit, and through the use of nouns which can be modified by adjectives, increases the flexibility of the verbal repertoire and leads eventually to the development of a fully syntactic language.

Restricted codes are rigid by virtue of their being clamped on to a social situation. There are hints throughout Bernstein's work that individuals who grow to adolescence with a restricted code form social groups in which strong control is the primary concern of members; that is to say, social identity of those controlled, and the control of a group by a dominant leader. In personal discussion with Bernstein, he admitted that rank-ordered social structure was typical of those using restricted codes. Elaborated codes – because their use of nouns describes objects and persons in terms of their identity rather than their relationship to the speaker – are based on a form of language which is concerned with the assessment of external reality as opposed to social reality of experience within a group. An elaborated code is therefore appropriate to behaviour supported by the hedonic mode and presumably arises out of it. This is consistent with the suggestion in what Bernstein says about the use of the child's imagination as the basis for the construction of an elaborated code. An example of an agonistic human social group would appear to be provided by a social group using restricted codes, since these codes are an extension of the social relationship, which is of a rank-ordered nature.

The social relationships of individuals using a restricted code are therefore essentially similar to the agonistic control structure of a sub-human primate group, and I therefore suggest that it has been already shown that this system can develop into a controlling mechanism in ourselves.

Evidence that an individual's capacity to learn is also related to whether or not he is operating primarily in the context of a social group comes from the work of the psychologist Jensen, who was able to distinguish between individuals who are primarily associative learners and others who are able to develop powers of classification and abstraction.

Jensen is primarily a psychologist, and only really interested in the fact that these two faculties can appear in different individuals, and in what educational situations these occur. Having demonstrated this distinction, however, he *has* noticed that powers of simple deduction go together with competence on the playground and concern with social relations, as against the handling of abstract information. Because he is not primarily concerned with the patterns of behaviour that go with these different powers of learning, the behavioural distinction is not as clear as we would like it, but the fact that there are individuals primarily concerned with social relations and others with these only as a part of their social awareness is a distinction which I confirmed through personal correspondence with him.

It looks very much as if here we have the discovery of different types of learning which may be linked to restricted codes because they are both linked to the development of patterns of behaviour which also restrict the individual to operating within a small or primary group.

The use of language in a restricted code is therefore the subordination of language to an agonistic social structure, in which the information content of the linguistic system is limited, the potential quality of language left undeveloped and the mental faculties not fully developed. If this argument is correct, then it leaves still to be defined the social structure which permits the full realization of the capability of language to convey objective relationships in the sense usually ascribed to scientific statements. Such at least is latent in the hedonic mode, in which social relations are not fixed and therefore are not part of a system specifically functioning to ascribe a role to the individual's behaviour. In such circumstances the individual's attention is free to be guided by interest in external features: an essential requirement for investigating the properties of the external world and the extension of this process into man's pursuit of scientific knowledge.

The extraordinary capacity of man to combine different patterns, components of his behaviour, convention and awareness, and the difficulty of knowing how to obtain valid evidence that specific elements of these are built into a particular pattern, make it difficult to do more than suggest further examples where the basic pattern suggests the operation of agonistic-type cohesion.

One thing we should note before we go on to consider further examples is that an agonistically structured group consists of individuals primarily concerned with their social relations, whereas the hedonic structure permits varying degrees of awareness of the physical environment and the intrinsic nature both of other individuals and of the nature of the physical environment.

Moreover, the experience of the physical environment, as well as of other individuals, is, in the agonistic mode, necessarily an extension of the social experience. Hence if we say that the primary concern of a person in any group is with maintaining the fixity of the social relations and hence the control of others in that group, and that the individual's awareness of objective reality arises out of his or her social relations and not out of concern for the people themselves, we are probably witnessing the operation of the agonistic mode in these individuals. This seems to me to be the basic characteristic of the Hell's Angels brotherhood.

From a report in *The Times* of 31 August 1971, headed 'Pop festival – should have called police sooner'. This was when thirty-nine Hell's Angels terrorized people at Weeley Pop Festival in Essex, for love of their motor cycles, as Colchester magistrates were told. Mr Michael Whatcott, a motor cyclist, said that the gang had not been violent and had threatened no one:

Our boys were given permission to take jobs fighting fires. *The only things we have got in the world are our motor bikes, our fellows and our girls.* We have spent years and every spare penny building up these bikes; they are our one and only life. It hurts to see them damaged, it hurts to see our wounded, but they are used to that and so are our girls.

This statement indicates that their lives centred round their motorbikes and their girls and this is borne out by reading *Buttons: The Making of a President*.[22] The cohesion of the group is their predominant concern and therefore other people are seen as a phenomenon outside the experience of the group, and this leads to frequent confrontations.

One other aspect of the Hell's Angels is their concern for badges and uniforms, which are also seen as extensions of an individual's person. Badges function as a simple method of identifying a group and those outside it, as indeed uniforms do when they assist the definition of social roles. This fixed element helps to define a social position.

Recently a controversy on why children of inner city areas of the U.S.A. show lower academic achievements than the rest of the population was published in the *Atlantic Monthly*. In the issue for June 1972 (Volume 229, pp. 59–67), W. Labov described the differences between the standard English of the classroom and the vernacular language used by members of the street culture. His study, like that of Basil Bernstein, is concerned with the relationship of language culture and social structure, and shows that intellectually poor performance of ghetto children is related to the differences of culture and social experience. They produce evidence incidental to their main concern that shows rank-ordered social relations as the dominant structural influence in the form that the culture takes.

'We see', he writes, 'many speech events which depend on the competitive exhibition of verbal skills, singing, sounding, toasts, rifting, louding – a whole range of activities in which the individual gains status through his use of language. We see the younger child trying to acquire these skills of older children hanging around the outskirts of the older peer groups and imitating their behaviour.'

I am not directly concerned with the nature/nurture controversy, which is wholly wrongly conceived, but evidence is here further provided that peer groups create rank-ordered social relations wherever the culture permits it.

At the beginning, we argued that an infrastructure exists, determining the form of social cohesion in sub-human primate groups, and that this takes two forms, the agonistic and the hedonic. This is not the same as saying that in humans non-verbal means of communication take these two forms, but that the cohesive infrastructure, especially the agonistic, is capable of determining not only the form of the social relations but also the consequent dependent forms of communication at any one level at which the individual relates himself to others. This has been demonstrated in human society because language has been shown to be subordinate to this infrastructure wherever restricted codes are in operation. We must envisage therefore that this same infrastructure will, in the appropriate circumstances, be capable of dominating the form of social relations expressed through convention or the structure of thought. If such occurs, man is not free, but if hedonic-type relations can prevail, the dimensions of man's freedom are as wide as we know they can be.

1 M. R. A. Chance and C. J. Jolly, *Social Groups of Monkeys, Apes and Men* (Jonathan Cape, 1970).
2 Chance and Jolly, op. cit.
3 G. B. Schaller, *The Mountain Gorilla: Ecology and Behaviour* (University of Chicago Press, 1963).

4 V. and F. Reynolds, 'Chimpanzees of the Budongo Forest', in *Primate Behaviour*. ed. DeVore Holt (Rinehart & Winston, New York and London 1965).

5 V. Reynolds and G. Luscombe, *Chimpanzee Rank Order and the Function of Display*. Second Conference of the International Primatological Society Behaviour, Vol. 1, ed. C. R. Carpenter (S. Karger, Basel and New York 1969).

6 H. Kummer, 'Social Organization of Hamadryas Baboons – a Field Study' in *Bibliotheca Primatologica*, No. 6, (S. Karger, Basel and New York 1968).

7 W. A. Mason, 'Determinants of Social Behaviour in Young Chimpanzees', Chapter 9 in *Behaviour of Non-human Primates*, Vol. 2 (Academic Press, New York and London 1965).

8 W. Kohler, *Mentality of Apes*, English translation (Methuen, 1927).

9 M. R. A. Chance, 'Kohler's Chimpanzees – How did they Perform?' in *Man*, Vol. LX, September 1960.

10 P. H. Schiller, in *Instinctive Behaviour*, ed. C. H. Schiller, Int. Univ. Press No. 99, 264–87 (New York 1957).

11 E. Menzel, reporting on spontaneous use of poles as ladders in *Delta Primate Report* (Tulane University 1970).

12 N. Bolwig, 'Observations on the Mental and Manipulative Abilities of a Captive Baboon (Papio droguera)', in *Behaviour* 22, 1, 24–50.

13 W. Angst, *Personal communication* (1971).

14 D. S. Sade, 'Some Aspects of Parent, Offspring and Sibling Relations in a Group of Rhesus Monkeys', in *American Journal of Physical Anthropology*, Vol. 23, No. 1, 1965.

15 M. R. A. Chance, 'Attention Structure as the Basis of Primate Rank Orders', in *Man*, Vol. 2, No. 4, December 1967.

16 H. B. Virgo and M. J. Waterhouse, 'The Emergence of Attention Structure amongst Rhesus Macaques', *Man*, Vol. 4, No. 1, 1969.

17 M. Argyle, 'Non-verbal Communication, in Human Social Interaction', in *Non-verbal Communication*, ed. R. A. Hinde (Cambridge University Press 1972).

18 A. Kendon, 'Some Functions of Gaze Direction in Human Social Interaction', in *Acta Psychologia* 26, 22–63, 1967.

19 P. Ekman, 'Universal and Cultural Differences in Facial Expressions of Emotion', in *Nebraska Symposium on Motivation*, ed. J. Cole (University of Nebraska Press, 1972).

20 B. Bernstein, 'A Socio-linguistic Approach to Social Learning', in *Penguin Survey of the Social Sciences*, ed. Julius Gould (Penguin Books, 1965).

21 A. R. Jensen, 'Patterns of Mental Ability and Socio-economic Status', in *Proceedings of the National Academy of Sciences*, Vol. 60, 1330–7, 1968.

22 J. Mandelkau, *Buttons: The Making of a President* (Sphere Books, 1971).

For further reading

Humphry Knipe and George Maclay, *The Dominant Man* (Delacorte Press, New York 1972).

Liam Hudson

11 The Limits of Human Intelligence

Our collective theme – an excellent one, I believe – concerns the 'limits of human nature'. Or, if I may play with words in what I hope is not a sterile way, 'the nature of human limits'. For, let us not deceive ourselves, there are such limits; I have met them, uncomfortably close, in trying to write this essay. At any given place or time, we are all closely intellectually constrained. There are certain ideas, certain skills, that we can grasp; there are others that float just beyond our reach, tantalizingly; and others still that make no sense to us at all. But – and this is the point – there is ambiguity about the nature of these limits. We do not know why they exist as they do. Nor do we know to what extent, within the lives of individuals or of whole human populations, the sites of these poorly-defined limits can be shifted.

Surprising though this may seem, little research has been done that bears in any very trenchant way on the origins and nature of the intellectual constraints that bind us day by day. On the other hand a great deal of research has been done that trivializes the discussion of such limits, or pre-empts it. A huge literature exists, for example, concerning itself with IQ tests. A substantial though not very satisfactory literature exists dealing with differences in IQ between social classes, and between racial groups. And there also exist, surrounding these literatures, thick clouds of specula-tion, both about causes and about practical implications. But little has been done to link our present preoccupation – the nature of human limits – to hard evidence of any kind. And this strange state of affairs exists, I am now inclined to believe, because we have unwittingly lapsed into a rhetoric of general categories that effectively precludes discovery of any sort at all. We have discussed

Inheritance with a capital 'I', Environment with a capital 'E', Class with a capital 'C', Race with a capital 'R' – all in ways remote from any adequate description of our daily efforts to think. Let us be clear at the start, then, what it is that we are discussing. What, in the real world, is an intellectual constraint? I am not writing about the limits that govern, say, our digit span. It simply does not interest me that I can recall eight digits in a row rather than eighteen or eighty. Let me offer instead an example of what does interest me; one we owe to the Harvard psychologist David McClelland. He tells us, in one of his papers (1963), of a brilliant research student who gave a seminar on a type of research in which he had specialized. His account of the present state of play was, McClelland tells us, masterful. At the end of his piece, McClelland asked the research student what experiments, in his view, ought to be done next. And the student was floored. McClelland repeated his question, pointing out that the student must know as much about this topic as anyone else in the world. He must have some view of where it would be wise to step next. After some prevarication and embarrassment, the student proposed a scheme for further research which was so huge and all-embracing as to be totally impracticable. That student, in a way that is familiar to anyone in research, was constrained. He was stuck. And for reasons that will not, I think, be entirely inscrutable to any of us, he baulked. It was something he would not, or could not, do. He failed to function – or rather he functioned only in a defeated, irrelevant way.

This is the sort of constraint that I want to discuss. There are, of course, others. But having, I hope, established the universe of discourse, using the case of McClelland's student as a sort of reference-point or beacon, I would now like to conduct a brief detour, leading you briskly through areas of the research vineyard where, in my view, the fruit are for the most part misshapen and sour. For it will not have escaped your notice that that dangerous abstraction Intelligence has recently been in the news; and that it has been linked to that other abstraction – equally dangerous – Race. The debate about IQ and race, about nature and nurture, is an object lesson, I believe, in the unconscious exercise of ideology in factual guise. It is also an object lesson in how we may all become besotted with visions: metaphors or models of the human condition that are pregnant with social, moral and even political implication; conceptions of Man that we use, not as examinable, refutable components of our research, but as pre-conditions which inspire research, and bind it all around. The field of intelligence – again it will not have escaped your notice – positively bristles with slippery, slipperily ideological, assumptions. We cannot confront them all in a single essay, but I would like to confront and scotch just one. Namely, the belief that what we inherit – in the intellectual sphere, no less than in any other – is in some useful sense 'fixed' (while, in contrast, what we receive from our environment, from our contact with other people, is always open to change). This pair of beliefs is deeply seductive; and it seduces lay and expert alike. In discussing the issue of racial differences in IQ recently, Professors Jensen and Eysenck have both seemed, in my judgement at least, to fall under their spell. As a postgraduate student I myself accepted them; and I would be a little surprised if a number of people here did not give them, however sneakingly, a little of their allegiance.

Yet they make no sense at all. They are nonsense. It is simply false to believe that qualities we inherit are fixed. No one believes, as far as I know, that our mental abilities – to do arithmetic, to write poems, or to teach, or to run a business – are inherited in the sense that the stickleback inherits his courtship ritual. Our ability to do the world's work, to think straight, is not an instinct in that sense. But those who urge the hereditary view – who offer us neat-looking sums, telling us that intelligence is 80 per cent the product of heredity and 20 per cent of environment – still feel that they have a point. And what they are arguing for is this. They acknowledge that mental skills, unlike sneezes, are not something that just happen: they are operations we learn. They consist in our ability to acquire the symbolic conventions our parents and teachers make available to us. What the hereditarians are urging is that, given the normal state of any given culture at any given time, certain individuals will always achieve higher levels of skill than others; that, in the 'race of life' – to use a metaphor attractive to the hereditary school – some people, the biologically well endowed, will tend to come out on top, and others, the poorly endowed, will lag behind. To put it even more crudely, the claim of the hereditary school is that the same monkey will always get the nuts – irrespective of which tree the nuts are hung on, however high or low, however well they are disguised. And they will do so, because they were born in some general sense superior: they are nature's élite.

Now, there are a number of things to be said about these visions – of monkeys and nuts, and of the race of life, and those who compete in it. The first is to point out that this – the most extreme hereditary view of intelligence, and the most fiercely biologically reductive – itself abandons any idea that inherited qualities are fixed. What is fixed, on this view, is *each person's competitive position*: Smith almost always comes first, Brown arrives somewhere in the middle, Robinson usually comes last, or thereabouts. (I am simplifying, of course; but only to make the logic of this argument plain.) Even those who hold the hereditary view in its most dogmatic form take it for granted that what we are discussing is the individual's ability to benefit from example and instruction; to absorb himself in the intellectual rituals and conventions of the society in which he grows up. And as it is a rank order that we are discussing, there is nothing – in logic, or in practice – to prevent the level of all competitors from shifting (or being shifted) up or down. The causes of such shifts might occasionally prove to be genetic; more frequently and more dramatically, though, they are cultural. The collapse of the Greek civilization in pre-Christian times almost without question shifted downwards the level of intellectual accomplishment that all Greeks displayed; yet no one has suggested that this collapse was the result of a sudden calamity of the genetic code.

The second thing to be said is that, at the descriptive level, the competitive model of society is more plausible in some spheres of human activity than others. At school, and in the exercise of trivial skills among adults – memory games, for example – competitive models do seem to apply tolerably well. With depressing regularity, the same individuals come top, and tend to do so across the board, and others, for whatever reason, remain irredeemably stuck. On the other hand, there can be little doubt that individuals do differ from one sphere to another – even within the terms of the analogy with athletics, which is itself, I think, misleading.

Consider, for a moment, that there are high-jumpers, sprinters, long-distance men, shot-putters. In athletics, as in life, there are qualities that suit us for one form of activity but that may partially disqualify us from success in others. Just as the skills of shot-putting may disqualify the individual concerned from winning races as a sprinter, so in intellectual matters the development of mathematical skills, let us say, may disqualify the individual from thinking comfortably in an allusive, poetic manner; and vice versa. Even at school, one can demonstrate the extent to which some children are already natural specialists. Some excel with numbers, and show little taste for argument in terms of words. For others, the reverse is true. Some show a flair for dealing with patterns and shapes; others still possess a flair for music. And children differ, too, from one year to another. Children who seem stuck suddenly start to move again; children who have been roaring ahead strike plateaux. And both these forms of variability can express themselves even more dramatically once the individual leaves school, and begins to use his brain in earnest. The extent to which such phenomena are matters of native ability and maturation remains an open question. There can be no question, though, that the tendency of recent research has been to suggest that, once the schoolroom has been left behind, temperament and opportunity play an overriding part in determing the use to which our brains are put.

The third point to be made about the 'monkeys and nuts' view is that it is totally speculative, as far as causes are concerned. I do not wish here to delve into the wretchedly inadequate literature that deals with the question of Heredity versus Environment – and of what population geneticists now describe as the 'heritability' of intelligence. But I can say that there is no single piece of evidence I have ever seen that could not quite plausibly be interpreted either from a hereditary or from an environmental point of view. The nearest we come to a test case is that of identical twins reared apart: creatures, so the argument runs, with identical inheritance but different experience. But to confront these cases is to realize how impenetrably complex the patterns of causality are likely to be. Some pairs of twins differ widely; others are quite astonishingly alike – despite having lived almost all their lives apart. The moment we realize that the individual's intellectual growth may be governed by the kinds of relationship he forms with other people – and that identical twins, being so alike, will tend to elicit similar reactions from other people – we are forced to acknowledge how thoroughly the hereditary and environmental accounts of intelligence are confounded.

The same sorts of interpretative quagmire encircle the work on intellectual differences between the races. The moment we realize that the black child's environment – the way people react to him – is governed, at least in part, by the colour of his skin, we must accept how pointless, indeed witless, it is to use differences in average IQ between samples of blacks and samples of whites as evidence of genetic differences between the two. (There is a good deal else that is muddled and mischievous about such research, but, happily, that is not what I have been asked to discuss.)

If there is little to be gained from speculating about possible genetic causes of differences in intelligence between the classes or races, there is little mileage either – and little virtue – in the assertion that all causes are environmental. In a trivial sense, the environmental proposition is obviously true: no environment, no intelligence. But in any sense that is useful, the opposition of hereditary and environmental arguments leads us nowhere. For just as hereditary causes – or organic deficiencies – do not preclude change; (think, for example, of what a gifted teacher did for Helen Keller), so environmental causes do not automatically make change a practical possibility. It seems to me perfectly reasonable to argue, in the case of McClelland's research student, that his refusal to take a risk was, in some way, the result of fears and anxieties that had their root in the experiences of his early childhood. I am not arguing, necessarily, that this is true, merely that it is reasonable. But it does not follow in the least that his reluctance to gamble was something that we could now alter. Like the imprinting of the new-born duckling the predispositions we acquire early in life may be among the most rigidly fixed, and most inexorably constraining, of all the qualities we possess.

I will not labour the point. The debate between the hereditary and environmental schools of thought, and in particular the debate over the question of IQ and race, has generated passion, and will no doubt generate it again. It remains one of those features of academic life that are interesting not for their literal content, but for what they reveal about the nature and circumstances of those taking part. For the conflict is symbolic. It is a verbal war, engaging some of the contestants' least sophisticated passions, between people who differ in temperament, in social and academic identification, and even in political allegiance. Men's lives have been threatened; and all the rhetoric of academic politics has been deployed. Experts have beaten their breasts and proclaimed their own virtue, and the while used every trick they know to undermine the legitimacy of the other side. It has not been an attractive sight. Even so, the tragi-comedy may be one from which lessons can be learned. And I would like to spend some of the rest of my time suggesting what shape those lessons might take.

The chief of these is that in the field of intelligence we have been wasting our time. We have spent fifty years or more constructing a literature of great tedium, and of minimal relevance to the world as it exists outside the schoolroom. More than a decade was spent, for instance, on the inconclusive feud between the American and British schools of factor analysis, over which of two systems for the intercorrelation of IQ scores was the superior. And the while, we have neglected almost totally the study of intelligence as it exists around us: the lives intelligent people lead. Francis Galton, that formidable Victorian patriarch, and founding father of the mental-testing movement, seems to me to bear a considerable share of the blame for our disorientation. The concern of this prodigiously able man for genealogies, for 'blood' – he traced himself back, incidentally, without embarrassment, to Charlemagne – and his acceptance of the analogy between physical excellence and mental excellence, has made it seem reasonable to study human abilities reductively, using the tricks and puzzles which make up intelligence tests to epitomize the more complex skills and judgements on which the exercise of real intelligence depends.

The artifice, the triviality, that work on mental measurement engenders is insidious, and I feel that the moment has come, once again, to reject it with an example. Let us return to the world of flesh and blood, and consider the instance of Miss – later Mrs – X. She brings us back to our senses. At university, a quiet, attractive girl, she was successful, but not outstandingly so. She was what we learn, in English universities, to call a 'solid 2:1': someone who is competent in every way, but less than startling; someone who will bring credit to her teachers, but will not set the town ablaze. Contemporaries saw her as cut out for the fate that in fact befell her: marriage on graduation to a handsome, domineering, successful older man. She bore him children, in substantial numbers; typed his books; bolstered his ego. And after a decade of marriage, it was possible to say that, intellectually speaking, she had reached her limit; that she had gone so far, but would go no further. And that this natural process was one upon which the institution of marriage had set its seal.

There are hundreds of thousands of young women like Mrs X; and the notion of someone reaching her limit or 'ceiling' is one that is acceptable to us in every way – just as it was to Galton a hundred years ago. But Mrs X, after a decade of matrimony, finally threw off what had come to seem onerous, and set out once more on her own. She left her husband, and whilst coping with her children, with her job, and with her husband's outraged hubris, she studied part-time. Brave little woman, we may say – and again, there are thousands, perhaps tens of thousands, like her. But we are in for a surprise. Within a short time, her M.A. had become a Ph.D.; she had made for herself the beginnings of a reputation in a fashionable area of scholarship; and she had found herself a teaching-post at a major American university. No one, I contend, least of all Mrs X, could have foretold this sudden intellectual rebirth. Her story is valuable in itself; but valuable too for its implications.

The case of Mrs X points the obvious moral that our intellectual vitality is closely tied to our emotions; that our intellectual lives and our private lives are intimately interwoven. The point is one that I shall take up in a moment: it is so obvious, and so good, that there is little danger of our losing sight of it. Before expanding upon it, though, I would like to make a number of others that are less obvious, and might be overlooked. The first is that we may give the appearance of having reached our ceiling, our limit, because we have locked ourselves into a situation, a niche, which requires us to behave as though our ceiling has been reached. Marriage for the female graduate is the case I have selected; but equally potent, for both sexes, is 'administrative responsibility'. It is a sad but familiar sight to watch the young Turks of one's own generation settling into their committee-room chairs, and into a system of role expectations that will not demand a single painful thought from them, between now and the grave. It may be that we embrace such responsibilities precisely because we have reached our ceilings, and know it. My own guess is that this is too glib: that the opportunity arises at a point when we are temporarily insecure or tired; that we lapse into the comfort that such jobs offer; and that we rarely muster the strength, as Mrs X mustered it, to make the break, and start to think again.

Before going back to Mrs X, and to my own research-theme – the relation of the intellectual to the personal – I would like to pursue these sociological considerations a little further. (This is, after all, an interdisciplinary occasion, and the topic is too good a one to be left to the sociologists themselves.) Two processes concern me – processes which we take for granted, about which we know little, and which look as though they act in opposite directions. Let me bring back for a moment McClelland's student. He was not born with an exhaustive knowledge of a particular field of research; he was taught how to acquire it. And the excellence he achieved in one sphere of study – his grasp of the literature – seems actively to have blighted his capabilities in another sphere: namely, his ability to form and act upon a hunch. It seems a reasonable surmise that the training he received was one which capitalized upon his likes and dislikes, on his foci of confidence and apprehension. This process of moulding is one that is usually carried through inadvertently: series of curricula are pursued, year after year, and the outcome – as far as the capabilities of individual students are concerned – if not benign, is at least fortuitous. But to say that it is inadvertent is not to deny that it is lawful. In schools and universities, there are systematic relationships to be uncovered between the ways in which students are taught and the range of issues, thereafter, that they can countenance as legitimate. My implication is that much teaching, and much of the best teaching, has the character of an inculcation; an inculcation in which certain prejudices are transmitted about the boundaries of legitimate inquiry.

If I may be autobiographical for a moment, I may say that the education I myself received at Oxford, in philosophy and psychology alike, was of this sort. There, I acquired, from teachers of towering gifts, a range of assumptions that I now regard as misguided. In philosophy, I learned to be impatient with any form of speculation or metaphysics. I acquired a zeal in reducing any proposition to the evidence that could be collected about its truth or falsity; a belief that knowledge consisted of facts that were piled one on top of the other, like building bricks, into patterns; and a willingness to accept trivial arguments – moral arguments, for example, based on what two men might do on a desert island –

as though they were of the same order as more substantial ones. On emerging, I was as a result totally incapable of understanding any contemporary Continental philosophy: Sartre for example, or Merleau-Ponty. And I cannot to this day. For what was valuable had been defined at Oxford as what was clear. Yet it now seems to me that there may well be important propositions that can only be lodged in prose that is obscure – evocative, metaphorical, vague. The same was true of the psychology I was taught: I was, in effect, brainwashed – brainwashed into believing, among other bizarre propositions, that the heartland of psychology lay in examining the powers of shape recognition displayed by the octopus.

You will protest, I am sure, that foolish young men can be persuaded to believe anything; that, within quite wide limits, their characteristic habits of mind, the ways in which they tackle problems, can be shaped for a lifetime. But that is precisely the point I want to make. The intellectual tradition into which our teachers induct us, with all its prejudices and niceties; this acts as a powerful, and at times an overriding, constraint. We think, to an extent that is at times terrifying, within the blinkers that our teachers have lent us; and the better the teacher, the more magnetic his hold on our imaginations, the narrower the effects of this blinkering may prove to be.

This then is my first sociological point: the management of knowledge and belief that teachers daily achieve is a skill that deserves – and I hope will soon receive – the most intimate study. The creation of disciplines, of traditions of thought, may be a necessary and inescapable part of organized thought. Thomas Kuhn, the philosopher of science, has seemed to suggest this. But the cost at which such a demarcation is achieved seems at times an exorbitant one.

My second sociological point runs quite contrary to the first. Many sociologists have written, often with subtlety, about the 'socialization process'; about the ways in which society's agents conspire to squeeze us, putty-like, into our socially defined roles. We are prisoners of circumstance, such theorists imply – whatever that circumstance may happen to be. What they say is all, I am sure, very true and convincing, but I am also sure that it is too simple. Once more, let me resort to an example. Some years ago now I used to do research at a famous boys' school: a place blessed, among its other advantages, with luxurious art facilities, and a quiet, civilized-seeming teacher of painting. A late middle-aged man, he once confided to me that, in his whole career, he had had only one real 'flyer' through his hands. And that he had seen in him nothing out of the ordinary. This was a young man who, near the end of his time at school, decided that he would like to train as a painter; but who, his teacher claimed, had done nothing to suggest that the very considerable risks involved would be justified. Within a very few years, this young man had won for himself a national – indeed international – reputation in the Pop Art style: someone who, if not dazzlingly original, had at the very least interpreted the conventions of Pop Art in a highly accomplished and professional way.

It seems that we tend to look at life, especially institutional life, slice by slice. Because it is difficult, we rarely follow a group of individuals through from school, say, to adult life. Yet when we do, even at the anecdotal or autobiographical level, we find surprise upon surprise. (This, after all, is the principle on which Anthony Powell's series of novels *The Music of Time* turns.) When I was at university, undergraduate life was dominated by a set, or series of sets, of young men who seemed of quite breathtaking brilliance and sophistication. One or two of them have gone on seeming brilliantly sophisticated; but it is fair to say, I think, that by no means all of them have done so. The most unlikely people – the Kenneth Widmerpools of our particular world – have done well for themselves; others, who seemed at the time far more generously endowed, have stopped in their tracks, as if stunned by the success they had already achieved.

Product of my positivistic background, I now feel compelled to draw you back to the last; to round off with some good, puritanical facts. What I have tried to do so far is to resurrect from beneath the pall that mental measurement has cast across this excellent subject, some sense of what the exercise of intelligence is really like, to hint at what sorts of constraint we may expect to find. It now remains for me to give some idea of what happens when you try to explore these constraints empirically, to do some research.

Very briefly, I would like to outline a number of research projects I am myself involved in and which bear in one way or another on the determinants of our capacity to think. The general assumption underlying these projects is simple enough: that if we are to understand why people find it natural to think in the way they do, we must be willing to countenance all of the various sorts of constraint that may act upon them: psychological no less than social, pedagogic, political, cultural. Such an approach I have called, perhaps pedantically, the 'ecology' of human intelligence: it is of its very essence interdisciplinary, and is bound to remain so, I suppose, until we have gathered together sufficient evidence to demarcate a new discipline of our own.

The first study – signed, sealed and published – was designed to test a model, at root Freudian, of the psychic processes that underlie adult work. Here the constraints envisaged are essentially internal to the individual concerned. It was argued, and there is much circumstantial evidence to support this, that those who choose to study the inanimate world – physical scientists and engineers, for example – experience considerable inhibition in matters that are in any sense personal or non-rational. And there exists a fairly simple formal model which relates such inhibition not only to the choice an individual makes of impersonal subject-matter, but to other aspects of his life-style as well. The piece of work I have in mind put this proposition rather neatly to the test. Undergraduates studying history and electrical engineering were subjected to the gothic rigours of the Edinburgh Sleep Laboratory. The study assumed (with Freud) that dreams are the very embodiment of 'primary process' thought – of the non-rational. It was hypothesized that while both groups would dream, physiologically speaking, to roughly the same extent – they would display, that is, the same amount of 'rapid eye movement' sleep – the engineers would recall their dreams on fewer occasions than did the historians. We were assured that this experiment would not work; and that sleep research was a field in which individual differences are relatively sparse and insignificant. But it did work, quite spectacularly. When woken in the midst of periods of rapid eye movement sleep, the arts specialists – in my terms, 'divergers' – almost always recalled what their dreams were about; the engineers quite frequently did not. The implication is that the engineers' inhibition in dealing with 'primary process' thought – with ideas and images that have not been ordered in a conventionally rational way – is not a superficial aspect of their thinking, it is an integral part of the way in which their minds work.

Take a quite different line of attack on the same proposition: on the proposition that our habits of thought are deeply embedded aspects of more general patterns or ways of life. This was a study based on that remarkable document, *Who's Who*. We had hypothesized that members of different academic specialities would differ not only in the subtle aspects of their life-style – in what ways, for example, and on what issues, they talked to their wives – but also in cruder, epidemiological respects as well: their patterns of fertility, for instance, and rates of divorce. We have found – and results from a massive Carnegie study of American academics tend to confirm this – that the marriage patterns of physical scientists are more conventional than are those of specialists in the arts – in age at marriage, in number of children, and in rates of divorce. We also found that arts specialists tend, quite notably, to be infertile. Over 40 per cent, for example, of distinguished British classicists have no children, either because they remain single, or because they have childless marriages. There are a number of interpretations we might hazard here. Our finding about the infertility of arts specialists may be a side-effect of a more general unconventionality; but more obviously psychodynamic possibilities suggest themselves too. One is reminded, for example, of Galton's comment about poets: '. . . a sensuous, erotic race', he called them, 'exceedingly irregular in their way of life'; but, he concluded, not 'founders of families' – their talents being displayed in youth 'when they are first shaken by the tempestuous passion of love'. One thinks, too, of his mistress's comment about the poet Rilke's 'essentially noxious hostility to the body'. It may be, in other words, that the formal exploration of human sentiment and of human affairs that specialists in the arts undertake may represent a displacement – a 'sublimation' – of impulses that other people express in a more forthright and conventional way.

Here, then, we have the constraint of conventionality; and perhaps more subtle, psychic constraints too. Yet neither, though 'psychological', makes much sense if abstracted from the cultural context, the milieu, in which they occur. And our data from *Who's Who* have led us into this context's midst. Two details illustrate the complexities of this ecological relationship of the individual to the cultural environment in which he dwells.

The first concerns rates of divorce. We found that in the British sample, these were particularly high among the creative writers – and among a certain subset of biologists: those born in the first decade of the century, and who went to private schools. On the face of it, this is a meaningless result – uninterpretable. But there is some sense to be made of it, after all. Examining the sample individual by individual, one notices that the biologists who were divorcing were those who, during the 1920s and 1930s, set biology on its feet as an experimental discipline. Here, then, is our interpretative thread: divorce is high, we may hypothesize, among those who take part in a discipline's formative or revolutionary phase. (Rates of divorce among philosophers, though very low, tend to support this: low among neo-Hegelians, higher among those who took part in the Oxford linguistic revolution of the 1930s and 1940s.) A study of marriage and fertility thus leads us to the furthermost shores of the philosophy of science; also to Kuhn's proposition that science proceeds in normal and revolutionary phases, and to his suggestion that those temperamentally suited to one may be systematically unsuited to the other. Ours is doubtless too simple a hypothesis as it stands; but it is compatible with anecdotal evidence, and it is, when you reflect upon it, by no means as far-fetched as it at first may seem.

The second foray into such territory has involved us in evidence of an altogether trickier kind, and I will do no more than lay the facts before you, and hint at an interpretation in broad and tentative terms. In *Who's Who*, we looked at eminent doctors, and classified them in terms of the parts of the body in which they specialize. We also looked at the schools from which they had originally come. What we found is very strange. Specialists who work on the head, as opposed to the lower trunk; who work on the outside of the body, rather than on its innards; who work on male bodies, rather than on female bodies; and who work on living bodies, rather than on dead bodies, are in each case more likely to come from private schools as opposed to State schools, and from schools in England as opposed to schools in Scotland, Wales or Northern Ireland. What is happening in detail, I am not yet quite clear; but, broadly, it seems that the human body possesses symbolic significance, and that some parts are more acceptable to us than others; also, that this system of symbolic values mediates the translation for the young doctor from a system of values governed by social class to a system where values are vested in the kinds of specialized work he undertakes. Such a line of argument leads us to the periphery of the territory of the structural anthropologists – to that of Lévi-Strauss, Mary Douglas and Leach; and the implication is that the symbolic constraints that govern the intellectual life of economically primitive societies may not be entirely irrelevant to events within our own.

The last project I would like to mention – it is very new, and its scale is necessarily more grand – is an inquiry supported by the Nuffield Foundation into an area of sensitivity I have already mentioned: the processes of university teaching, the management of legitimate knowledge, and the control of what students and their teachers believe. We are studying, as participant observers, the ways in which young doctors are taught, explicitly and implicitly, to regard their patients – at one extreme, as people, at the other as lumps of meat. We are also studying the ways in which engineering students are taught to regard the social context in which their professional skills are to be exercised. Soon we hope to tackle arts and social science departments as well. There, as elsewhere, we confront the concept of a 'discipline', and of the ways in which the propositions an individual can entertain are focused and restricted by the establishment in his mind of disciplinary boundaries. For boundaries between disciplines not merely separate one sort of subject-matter from another; they also separate 'us' from 'them', the 'genuine' from the 'bogus'.

We have called this the 'Anabas' project, *anabas* being a genus of fish that from time to time leaves the water and climbs trees. This, symbolically, is what we hope to do too. And in doing so, I hope we will remain sensitive to what I now see as the human scientist's paramount concern: that of pinning his attention to processes of thought as they exist in the real world, rather than drifting off into a rhetoric of abstractions. The morals of recent debates about IQ and race are, as I have said, finally ones about the participants themselves. It is extraordinarily easy, in this field, to elaborate your own personal ideology, believing as you do so that you are an impartial observer, practising Science. In psychology and the social sciences, I would suggest, the impartial observer is a mythical beast. And traditional conceptions of the scientific method, in as much as they apply to one man's attempts to understand his neighbours, form a doctrine that is as remote from us as medieval theology. The first step towards any

rigorous and impartial understanding seems to lie in the acceptance that the psychologist, like the people around him, is fallible.
There is no magic, no special access to the truth. We are not
above the fray, if fray there is; we are in it, and of it. And we are
subject, too, to the special consideration that our own interpretations become part – through the publication of our results – of the
milieu, the cultural brew, on which our own subject-matter is
nourished.

We must find our way back, I believe, into contact with what
Sigmund Koch has called our 'historically constituted subject-
matter'. In the process, there are certain luxuries we will have to
learn to do without: the luxury, for example, of posing as Great
Scientists, whose special techniques lay bare the secrets of mankind; the luxury of indulging unselfconsciously in symbolic warfare – slanging matches with professional rivals who, for whatever reason, we do not like; the luxury, finally, of bandying bold,
fantasy-laden abstractions – Heredity, Environment, Heritability,
IQ, and so on – as though these were anything more than verbal
tokens we use to disperse the fog inside our own heads. Such
conceptual tokens could prove to be the signposts that will lead
us, in the long run, to the path of cumulative understanding. But
used as they are at present, as pillars of personal ideology, they
serve – in a sour phrase of Nabokov's – as little more than 'short
cuts from one area of ignorance to another'.

L. Andreas-Salomé, *The Freud Journal* (Hogarth, 1964).
M. Austin, 'Dream Recall and the Bias of Intellectual Ability', in *Nature*,
    231, 1971, p. 59.
B. Bernstein, 'On the Classification and Framing of Educational Know-
    ledge', in *Knowledge and Control*, ed. M. Young (Collier–Macmillan,
    1972).
F. Galton, *Hereditary Genius* (Macmillan, 1869).
L. Hudson, *The Cult of the Fact* (Jonathan Cape, 1972).
L. Hudson and B. Jacot, 'Marriage and Fertility in Academic Life', in
    Nature, 229, 1971, p. 531.
L. Hudson and B. Jacot, 'Education and Eminence in British Medicine', in
    British Medical Journal, 4, 1971, p. 162.
T. S. Kuhn, *The Structure of Scientific Revolutions* (Chicago University Press,
    1962).
D. C. McClelland, 'The Calculated Risk', in *Scientific Creativity*, ed. C. W.
    Taylor and F. Barron (Wiley, 1963).

Max Clowes

12 Man the Creative Machine:
A Perspective from Artificial Intelligence Research

Mechanism and Behaviour

The view that man is a machine can always be discerned in some corner of contemporary culture. Physiology, psychophysics, molecular biology, brain biochemistry and other branches of modern science are dedicated to some form of the proposition. These sciences provide more or less mechanistic accounts of the behavioural foundations we have in common with life-forms which do not appear to share our capacity for thought, wit and invention. However, mechanisms which exhibit the use of our language or mimic our problem-solving ability – in short, mechanisms which can function as the loom on which the patterns of intelligence are woven – are more difficult to accept as valid representations of human behaviour. My central thesis is that this rejection stems from the extraordinarily impoverished concept of mechanism current in our culture and the extremely superficial grasp of intelligent behaviour afforded by prevalent anthropomorphisms.

The most prolific contemporary source of mechanistic characterizations of complex intelligent behaviour is Artificial Intelligence. My purpose in this essay is to review some of the work in that field and in so doing to portray mechanisms that illuminate, both in their success and their failure, something of the patterns of intelligent behaviour. To provide a concrete feeling for the character of this research, I shall dwell in some detail upon several programmes intended to endow the computer with sight, specifically with the ability to apprehend three-dimensional situations visually presented. The relevance of these programmes to intelligent function centres upon their capacity to use specific categories of knowledge inferentially. The limitations we can point to in that capacity make explicit some features of intelligent functioning that are not easily demonstrated in any other way. This view of programmes – as knowledge manipulators – provides a new medium in which to understand understanding.

Seeing Machines

Imagine we have a television camera whose output can be fed into a computer, and that this camera is viewing the scene shown in Plate 13.

The picture-data fed to the computer are obtained by measurement of the light falling on the camera's photosensitive surface, which is in the position a film would have to be to have taken the photograph above. Measurement of the light intensity is carried out at discrete points arranged regularly over the photosensitive surface to form a sort of retina. The analogy with the retina here is almost complete. Typically the intensity is measured on a scale of zero to fifteen units and the matrix is rectangular with at least 64×64 uniformly-spaced elements, so that the result of 'digitizing' the photograph in Plate 13 is the matrix of numbers in Plate 14.

What are we to do with this neat heap of numbers? In the early days when Pattern Recognition was fashionable the objective would have been to classify the heap: that is, to decide whether it was an 'A' or a 'B', etc., since print recognition was the dominant concern of such studies. Classification could be our objective too, e.g. is it a playblock scene, or cards scattered on a flat surface, or hanging metal rods? – etc. A more significant objective, however – one which does not preclude these global categorizations – is to ask how many blocks there are, what are their shapes and sizes (cubes, wedges, prisms, etc.), how are they juxtaposed – '1' is in front of '2', '3' is supported by '1' and '2', etc. Such a description is the goal of *scene analysis programmes* which like the earlier Pattern Recognition systems adopt the prejudiced, perhaps even blinkered, attitude of making sense out of the heap in terms of *stored information*: about cubes, 'in front of ', 'supported by', 'large', 'small', etc. The application of stored information has much in common with programmes, like that developed by Terry Winograd,[1] for comprehending strings of English words. Here the stored information is a knowledge of English morphology and grammar, as well as a knowledge of the meaning and reference of sentences. In both varieties of programme the interest lies in discovering what kinds of information have to be stored and how it should be accessed.

A presumed playblock world can be relied upon to have objects with reasonably sharp straight edges and pointed corners, and we would expect these features to give rise to local changes of intensity in the TV image which could be detected by comparing the value at each matrix location with the values of the immediately surrounding points. The comparison yields another two-dimensional matrix. Each non-zero number represents a point in the original picture where a local *change* in intensity occurs and the magnitude of the number represents the size of that change (Plate 15).

Table 1

LINE		JUNCTION			REGION	
Name	*End-points*	*Name*	*Line members*	*Type*	*Name*	*Lines and junction*
a	4, 1; 4, 4	A	fgl	ARROW	1	A1BmEnCg
b	4, 1; 5, 2	B	lm	ELL	2	AfDcF, etc.
c	5, 2; 5, 2·5	C	hng	FORK		etc.
d	5, 2·5; 5, 5	D	cdf	TEE		
	etc.		etc.			

We would expect such points to have non-zero neighbours arranged in linear patterns corresponding to the straight edges we believe to be present in the picture. These neighbours can be collected together into line-groups which can be represented simply by their end-points. Thus the *line diagram* (Fig. 1) to which the original picture has now been reduced can be described by giving a list of lines (Table 1) and for each line the co-ordinates (x, y) of its end-points relative to an origin of measurement O at the centre of the diagram.

It is difficult to realize that the line diagram portrayed here is not the end-product we are seeking. We can begin to understand it by concentrating upon this line list (cover over the diagram it refers to). How many objects does it describe? That is, how many sub-groups of lines are there where each sub-group refers to a single object? (For the present we shall ignore lines corresponding to shadow edges.) To answer this it helps to list the ways these particular lines are interrelated topologically. Two types of information are needed: the junctions that lines belong to, and the regions that lines and junctions belong to. Adolfo Guzman[2] noticed that the *shape* of a junction was a pretty reliable indicator

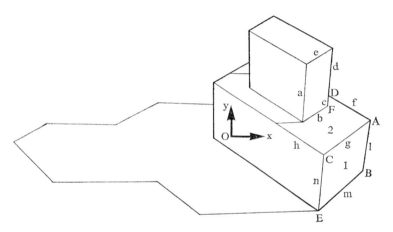

Figure 1 A complete line diagram of the simple 'blocks' scene, Plate 13

of its three-dimensional significance, and formulated some simple rules for collecting together the sub-groups of regions which plausibly form bodies. Thus a three-line junction which looks like an ARROW (see Fig. 1 and Table 1) is usually a corner where only two out of the three surfaces of the body are visible. The two 'barb' regions of the junction belong to the same body but the 'outer' region of the junction does not. Three-line junctions that have two of the lines collinear – 'TEE' junctions – almost always arise because one body is obscuring another and so no local associations are provided here. Junctions in the shape of a Y or FORK usually correspond to convex or concave corners with all three surfaces visible, and therefore provide evidence for linking all three regions together as a body. By counting up the links between regions promoted by rules of this general type, it is possible to partition region-lists, derived from very complicated scenes, into intuitively plausible bodies (Fig. 2 and Table 2).

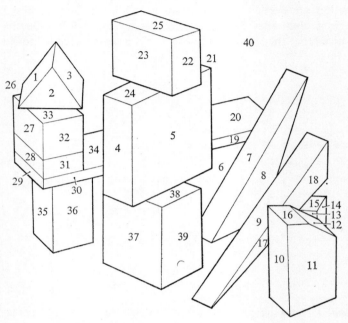

Figure 2   A complex 'blocks' scene

Table 2

(BODY 1.	*is*	:3:2:1)
(BODY 2.	*is*	:32:33:27:26)
(BODY 3.	*is*	:28:31)
(BODY 4.	*is*	:19:20:34:30:29)
(BODY 5.	*is*	:36:35)
(BODY 6.	*is*	:24:5:21:4)
(BODY 7.	*is*	:25:23:22)
(BODY 8.	*is*	:14:13:15)
(BODY 9.	*is*	:10:16:11:12)
(BODY 10.	*is*	:18:9:17)
(BODY 11.	*is*	:7:8)
(BODY 12.	*is*	:38:37:39)

The analysis tells us nothing, however, about the *shape* of these bodies: we can rectify this by replacing the rules for *linking regions* by rules for *describing these junctions*. For example: label all the lines of a FORK *convex*, the shaft of an ARROW *convex* and its two barbs *convex-occluded*, and the collinear lines of a TEE *convex-occluded*, taking care to put the *occluded* label on 'the right way round' so as to show which region the line 'belongs' to. Now, every junction in the picture shares a line with one other junction so that we cannot assign descriptions independently to junctions: we must take account of context so as to make the different descriptions *agree*. With appropriate rules for the different possible descriptions of ELLS, TEES and ARROWS we can achieve an analysis of the picture that does what Guzman's does *and* tells us quite a lot about the shape of the objects in terms of the concave/convex distinctions, and about inter- and intra-object occlusion. The analysis also correctly picks out holes, which Guzman's analysis concludes are separate objects.

This kind of analysis also throws light on a particular kind of 'impossible object'. It turns out that different areas of the picture promote different and therefore incompatible labellings of the lines which link the two regions together. Thus in Fig. 3 AB is labelled *convex* in the foreground and *convex-occluded* in the background.

'Funny' pictures of this type are a good test for picture-analysis schemes – they function somewhat as 'anomalous' sentences (e.g. 'Colourless green ideas sleep furiously') do in the formulation of linguistic theories.

But this type of description still leaves a lot to be desired – for example we cannot from it derive anything about the form of the picture which would have been obtained from a *viewpoint* just to the left of the one which yielded this picture; or say anything about where the light is coming from, i.e. account for the shadow-lines – both of which are essential though unconscious components of the sense *we* make of such data.

A characterization of the relation between an object and its faithful picture portrayal is familiar to every student of perspective. Dürer's famous woodcut illustrates it perfectly (Plate 16). The picture plane and viewpoint completely determine the *geometrical* form that the scene will take on in the picture. We, however, have only the picture and there is an infinite number of object-geometries and associated viewpoints that *could* have given rise to the geometry of the picture-lines. The task is as it were to enrich the labelling we have thus far been able to assign, so as to make explicit all the spatial relationships in the scene. One way to accomplish this is to assume we know what objects can occur but not how big they are nor how they are arranged. L. G. Roberts[3] devised a programme which used the *crude* shapes (triangle, quadrilateral, etc.) of picture-regions surrounding a

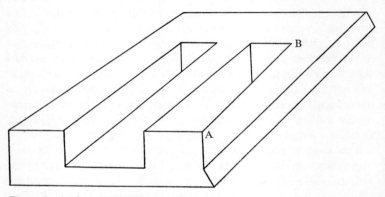

Figure 3   An impossible 'blocks' scene

picture-junction as a pattern with which to search over a wide range of stored three-dimensional models to find a possible fit. Whenever a possible candidate is found, an algebraic version of the laws of perspective-projection is used to test whether the *precise* shape and position of the selected picture-regions is consistent with one view of the candidate model. To do this the programme generates a 'predicted picture' which can be compared line by line, junction by junction, with the selected picture-regions. If its prediction is confirmed, the programme passes on to other parts of the picture; otherwise it tries another model, and so on.

More recently Falk[4] has described a refinement of this 'search-over-models' procedure which uses a version of Guzman's analysis to break up the picture into plausible 'bodies' followed by reasoning based on the need for objects to be *supported*. He is able to determine quite a lot of the three-dimensional shape of the Guzman 'bodies' as the basis for searching over the models, rather than just using crude topological features as did Roberts. The use of support early in the analysis contrasts markedly with Roberts's use of it *after* identification has been achieved, as a means of determining absolute size of the objects.

What Do These Machines Tell us?

The various schemes I have described all have in common that they can be thought of as a search over preconceived labelling of a line as *convex* or *concave*, or preconceived patterns of spatial co-ordinates. There is a considerable similarity with the language-understanding programme that Terry Winograd has described (see pp. 208 ff.) which conducts a search over sentence-models (its knowledge of English grammar), over rules which specify meaningful combinations of the actions and objects designated by the words of a sentence (its semantic models), and over an actual situation in a simple 'blocks world'. The order of this search varies according to the actual sentence being processed, because the routines concerned with grammar can call upon those concerned with semantics (and vice versa), to help decide between alternative grammatical models. Thus, the familiar *hierarchical descriptions* of language – syntax, semantics, pragmatics – are supplemented by a much richer *heterarchical functioning*. It is the absence, to date, of such a functional organization in vision programmes that gives rise to perhaps their greatest single weakness: the detection of picture-lines is extremely susceptible to error. That this should be so is hardly surprising. On the one hand, illumination is rarely constant across the whole of a surface; on the other hand, pairs of adjacent surfaces are often equally inclined to the light so that the edge which relates them cannot give rise to a change in illumination across it. There are numerous cases of 'non-existent edges' in Plate 13. Only with very careful lighting could such scenes be converted successfully to line diagrams by the differentiation method described earlier. ('Natural' objects of course are usually coloured functionally. The scenes described here are rather heavily camouflaged. Work on coloured scenes[5] has been described but is irrelevant to the main point: we are not seriously discommoded by non-existent edges in these 'camouflaged' scenes.) It seems that to decide whether a picture-fragment is an edge or not, we – and the programme – must appeal to 'higher order' knowledge (i.e. does it make 3-D sense?). Conversely a decision to search for a contrast step in a specified area of the picture may stem from the three-dimensional sense that is emerging from the analysis. This is precisely the pattern of heterarchical functioning that Winograd's work delineates.

The vision programmes I have described fall short of human ability, in that they need to find lines in order to make sense of the scene, whereas we don't. But in other respects they bear out the psychological investigations of Adelbert Ames, James Gibson, Richard Gregory and others.[6] These have shown how the sense we make of scenes is determined by our expectations: that rooms should have walls perpendicular to the floor (Ames's room demonstration), that physical objects should be supported (Gibson), that physical objects occlude one another in a systematic pattern (Gregory). The programmes I have described exhibit just these characteristics and they would be 'fooled' by the Ames room and these other demonstrations just as we are. Both programme and eye function so as to project their prejudices (models) upon the world; devising programmes helps to clarify what is needed for the successful functioning of a 'prejudice machine'. The weakness we have identified is but the tip of an iceberg whose extent we can now dimly discern, and it is with the delineation of this iceberg that I am mainly concerned here.

I shall identify three main issues:

(1) Heterarchical function

The fundamental requirement for successful functioning is that the prejudices be so organized that they can be deployed heterarchically. The programmes I described capture various kinds of knowledge about scenes and pictures of scenes – prejudices – in forms which mediate the application of that knowledge, mainly in an *hierarchic* fashion. Roberts finds lines in a picture in a fixed way, using only the grey-level information present in the retinal array; in the photograph of blocks (Plate 13) this would work well for most of the edges, but not so well that subsequent model-searching would find the block 'prejudice'. Rather a programme should try also to understand how the scene was lit (where the light is coming from) so as to provide a *wider context* from which to

3 A very simple 'blocks' scene　　　　　*　.　.　.　.　portion digitized　.　.　.　.　.　.　.　*

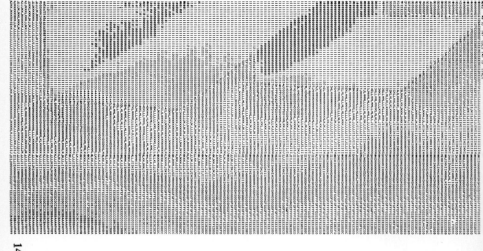

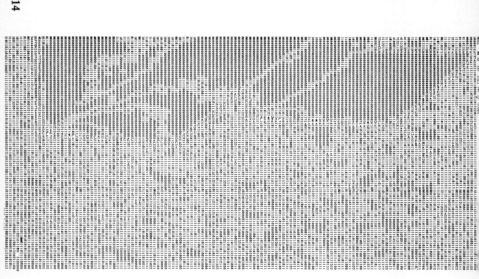

14 A digital representation of part of the scene in Plate 13. Sixty-four distinct levels of brightness are measured and displayed here with the characters 0, 1-9, A, B-Z (0 being black)

15 Measures of local changes of intensity in Plate 14

6 Dürer's graphic portrayal of the logic of picture formation

17 'My hoop looks funny . . .'

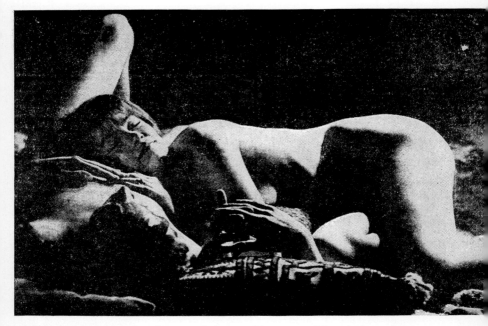

18 A knowledge of anatomy is a great help in making sense of the raised
objects in the foreground. (A still from *Sunday, Bloody Sunday*)

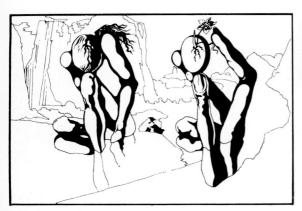

19 The similarity of pictorial format is no
barrier to the different percepts occasioned
by these two forms. (Based upon an
original by Salvador Dali)

20 A mechanical turtle designed
for use in educational
experiments

infer the *pictorial form* that certain edges would take, i.e. that they would be absent. Hypotheses (prejudices) about the way the scene is lit can be used so as to infer the shapes of objects from the distribution of light in the picture, and hypotheses about objects can be used in conjunction with the distribution of light in the picture to infer how the scene is lit. A similar symmetry arises in respect of hypotheses about objects and support, and support 'interacts' with a knowledge of lighting too. The programmes we have discussed lack the sort of knowledge of lighting I refer to here, but overshadowing the need to rectify that omission is the requirement *to make that knowledge usable in different combinations with the other varieties of knowledge (of viewpoint, object-models, support) that the system has.*

The order and the context in which one will want to make use of lighting knowledge cannot be determined in advance – it will vary from picture to picture and with the details of object-knowledge. We might for example want to use it at a point in the interpretation where a body has been partially identified but we suspect a 'missing' edge. Again we might have an edge shadowed on to a known support-plane from which we would like to infer something about the location of the light-source relative to both support-plane and that edge. (Analysis of shadows has been almost completely ignored save for a programme written by Orban, a colleague of Guzman, which successfully deletes the shadow-lines from diagrams such as Fig. 1, using a logic rather similar to that devised by Guzman.)

These different contexts arise partly from the picture-data and partly from the knowledge which has already been applied to the interpretation of the picture. A fundamental control-issue in the design of heterarchical systems is that of seeing the relevance of a particular type of knowledge in the current context, in the context indeed of all other knowledge which has been applied or could be applied. The problem is familiar to us in the guise of conscious problem-solving (proving theorems in geometry, for example). The extent to which it occurs in relatively mundane acts of perception and comprehension emphasizes the homogeneity of intelligent functioning. It was precisely this homogeneity that Helmholtz had in mind when he described perception as 'unconscious inference'. Programming perception discloses something of the reality behind the slogan. The achievement of heterarchical functioning makes demands upon the ways in which knowledge must be wedded to know-how, so that relevance when perceived can be acted upon. The innovations called for lead away from contemporary programming-languages – which assume that the programmer can always specify in advance which sub-programme will be appropriate – to languages where the programmer can create *programmes capable of taking that decision* (and undoing it too if necessary) at the particular stage of ongoing comprehension that has been reached. Winograd's programme is written in just such a language, a version of Hewitt's 'PLANNER'.

(2) Varieties of knowledge

The varieties of knowledge I have discussed thus far are limited and more or less amenable to algebraic treatment. The varieties of knowledge which support perception seem much more extensive and less amenable to contemporary mathematical formalisms. We have no difficulty in seeing the elliptical form in Plate 17 as a *circular* hoop, an inference strongly supported by the requirement that it be in the boy's palm in an orientation constrained by the hand's anatomy. The boy *could* be holding a buckled hoop – complaining about it too – but then the way in which his hand would be oriented would almost certainly be different. The knowledge we are tapping here is part of the immensely rich semantics of the human body, its morphology, its postures, its meaningful relation to other entities in the scene. We can be made aware of the unconscious inferences that such a knowledge will support by studying 'puzzle pictures' such as Plate 18, a scene from a recent film. Are both his hands on his chest? Where is her right hand? Where is his? How might they be related? Is this a situation in which their hands could be intertwined? *We* can use rich social and anatomical knowledge to answer these questions and so to guide and motivate decisions about ambiguous portions of the photograph; we can in short use the *meaning* of the situation as the context for unconscious (or on occasion conscious) inference. What we mean by 'meaning' is just this web of inferences: at present much richer and more extensive than anything we have been able to give a procedural embodiment to. The semantics of contemporary vision-programmes is limited to a knowledge of occlusion, support and perspective projections; but it would be very surprising if a knowledge of lighting and of socio-anatomical situations were not added very soon.

(3) Matching or meaning?

Making sense of a picture may mean pursuing a number of possibilities many of which will need to be abandoned. The issues here are illuminated in part by the search-strategies I have already described, but one feature of those strategies is extremely misleading. The criteria for accepting an interpretation are in effect that there be a complete perfect match between the prejudice and the picture. In Roberts's case this match is spelt out in detailed metrical terms: the geometry of the picture predicted from the model must fit the geometry of the picture–fragment used to retrieve that model, to within a specified tolerance. But what should that tolerance be? What sort of considerations and contexts go into inferring its form and magnitude? The logic underlying this rhetoric can be illustrated by considering yet another puzzle-picture. Dali's *The Metamorphosis of Narcissus* – of which Plate 19 is a free schematization – provides an example rich in the varieties of knowledge we have already discussed – support, anatomy, lighting – as well as having yet deeper meanings which make the picture more than just a puzzle.

The two forms – a seated figure with head resting on upraised knee and a hand holding the unfolding flower – have a remarkably similar pictorial form. In each instance there is a great deal of detail, especially the patterns of highlights and shadows, which does not contribute to the interpretation and has to be ignored. The underlying patterns of inference concern, in one respect, anatomical posture – what the human figure is doing with bowed head upon knee. On the other hand, the inference from the way in which the egg is being held supports the implication that the viewer is looking at his own hand both because of the anatomical possibility (turn the hand around and this implication wouldn't hold up) and for the detailed visual inspection or self-love that Narcissism connotes in our culture. The important point is that it is the patterns of inference that have been aroused which constitute the sense of the picture and which define *what fragments of the picture are important to that pattern of inference as well as those fragments which are not*. The concept of exactly matching one's models and prejudices is inappropriate. The sense of a picture is that web of knowledge-based relations between objects and situations, including the viewer, which is maximally supported by the picture. Rorschach blots, pictures with cleverly hidden incongruities or 'secondary' interpretations, all testify to the role of the picture (and to 'sense-data' more generally) as a litmus paper by which to judge the plausibility of a knowledge-based pattern of inference, rather than as a neat heap of numbers seeking total explication according to quantitative numerical criteria. The point I am making here has been made more clearly and at greater length by the art historian Ernst Gombrich in his book *Art and Illusion*. It is, briefly, that all comprehension is essentially metaphorical; what we mean by 'literal' is merely that the sense is consistent with the *total* context of the act of perception and not unrelated to, or at variance with, it. It is hard to see how comprehension or perception could have this character in the absence of heterarchical function. Unlimited metaphor could only be apprehended within a system able to judge the relevance of any part of its knowledge to the context given by the sensory impression and its contemporaneous setting, and then to apply that knowledge appropriately. Limitations on the 'accessibility' of spheres of knowledge will manifest themselves as perceptual rigidity – a fact which Rorschach capitalized on for diagnostic purposes. The converse – the poet's eye – must involve a capacity for heterarchic functioning beyond the norm. But the *creative quality* of the poetic vision is surely invoked in smaller measure in countless encounters on the plane of workaday existence.

Knowledge, Inference and Programmes

A view of perception as a process involving inference is not especially new, although the aggressively experimental paradigms of some branches of contemporary psychology would seem to have abandoned it. Nor is the realization that the inferences involved draw upon varieties of knowledge co-extensive with our understanding of such diverse topics as the psychology of interpersonal relationships and how objects can be held. The essentially novel content of this work is the idea that knowledge and the inference schema that it supports can be represented by programmes. M. Minsky points out that this idea requires us to discard the view:

that computers are nothing but assemblies of flip-flops; that their programs are really nothing but sequences of operations upon binary numbers ... It is equally correct to say that the computer is nothing but an assembly of symbol-association and process-controlling elements and that the programs are nothing but networks of interlocking goal-formulating and means-ends evaluating processes.[7]

The vision programmes I have described are rich illustrations of knowledge and inference. An example is Guzman's method of inferring the body membership of picture-regions from the geometries of picture-junctions. The consistency of junction descriptions (convex, concave, occluded) is an inference-scheme based upon a knowledge of what it is to be a plane surface (i.e. an edge cannot change from convex to concave along its length). The inferences we can draw from the requirement that a body be supported achieves a procedural embodiment both in Roberts's work and that of Falk.

Some of the deficiences I have noted in these various schemes, especially the lack of heterarchical functioning, enrich our understanding of the character of inference-making machines. They are much more labile in their mode of operation than the usual connotations of the word 'inference' would lead us to suspect. From this standpoint, the whole of computing science begins to take on a different quality. From Minsky again:

Before computation, the community of ideas about the nature of thought was too feeble to support an effective theory of learning and development ... Now we have a flood of such ideas (from general systems programming, Artificial Intelligence, computer hardware ...), well defined and implemented, for thinking about thinking; only a fraction are represented in traditional psychology.[8]

Could the importation of computational metaphors into the understanding of human intelligence achieve that degradation of the personal life that behaviourism seems to suggest? Could it for example explain away artistic achievement? I believe not. Indeed, quite the opposite, it opens our eyes to the ways in which the unique experience of the individual has entered into the artist's product. Knowledge in the sense that I have used it is not distinguishable from organized experience, and it is in the unique use to which each of us puts that experience that the concept of an individual arises. Artificial Intelligence research is for the first

time providing us with a rigorously unassailable account of how
all that is possible. In so far as this rigour rests upon the elementary binary operations of the digital computer, such interesting
behaviour as Artificial Intelligence programmes achieve can be dis-
missed as mere machinery (cf. Minsky above). But then one can
dismiss the intricacies of human behaviour as nothing but neurophysiology. There is no doubt in my mind that we are moving
inexorably towards a reinstatement of mind viewed as a computational system. The structure of these systems will increasingly come
to support and illuminate our intuitive concepts of consciousness,
imagination, purpose and thought.

Understanding Understanding

The possibility that a deep understanding of intelligence is emerging from what Minsky calls 'the curious and intricate craft of
programming' is to me an exciting prospect, to others perhaps an
extremely frightening one. My optimism derives in large part from
the fact that this 'deep understanding' will not have many of the
characteristics we have come to associate with science and technology. The facts which shape the design of a programme for
seeing things are not the reaction-times, confusion matrices and
exposure-times of the experimental psychologist, but the 'impos-
sibility' of a portrayed object or the visually-structured metaphor
of Dali's *Narcissus*. Form, meaning, reference, denotation are the
facts to be 'explained' in the design of a programme to understand sentences: the functioning of Terry Winograd's remarkable
programme nowhere illustrates the conviction referred to earlier
that 'all comprehension is essentially metaphorical'. Increasingly
the pattern that Artificial Intelligence research reveals is one where
the traditional barriers between art and science, philosophy and
psychology, mathematics and literature are seen as obfuscatory.
It is no accident that it is Minsky's colleague Seymour Papert
who is teaching school children physics, music, linguistics and
juggling by having them acquire the 'curious and intricate craft of
programming'.

We should view programmes which manipulate knowledge, not
as robots (although there are hostile environments like coal-
mines where such devices are long overdue), but as a medium in
which we can work out the possible forms of intelligence. It is one

way to arrive at an understanding of what it is to be human, perhaps at an integration of many aspects of human nature separately exposed in the traditions of the visual arts, literature, mathematics and psychology – traditions that at present seem to have little in common. We are accustomed to think of the appreciation of art, literature and mathematics as esoteric, calling for highly-developed skills cultivated by long schooling. One thing that is apparent from the little we have so far accomplished in Artificial Intelligence is that even the most mundane acts – balancing, speaking, recognizing a familiar face – are marvels of intelligent functioning which deploy all those abilities we have thought characteristic of the sophisticate. And not least among these is the creative act of making use of what is relevant and ignoring that which is not.

1 T. Winograd, *Understanding Natural Language* (Academic Press, 1972).
2 A. Guzman, 'Decomposition of a Visual Scene into Three-dimensional Bodies', in *Automatic Interpretation and Classification of Images*, ed. Grasselli (Academic Press, 1969), pp. 243–76.
3. L. G. Roberts, 'Machine Perception of Three-dimensional Solids', in *Optical and Electro-optical Information Processing*, ed. Tippet *et al.* (M.I.T. Press, Cambridge, Massachusetts 1965), pp. 159–97.
4 G. Falk, 'Interpretation of Imperfect Line Data as a Three-dimensional Scene', in *Artificial Intelligence*, 3, in press.
5 See J. Feldman *et al.*, 'The Use of Vision and Manipulation to Solve the "Instant Insanity" Puzzle', in *Proceedings of the Second International Joint Conference on Artificial Intelligence* (British Computer Society, pp. 359–64.
6 For the work of Ames, see R. L. Gregory, *Eye and Brain* (Weidenfeld & Nicolson, 1966).
7 M. Minsky, *Semantic Information Processing* (M.I.T. Press, 1968), p. 11.
8 M. Minsky, 'Form and content in computer science', in *Journal of the Association for Computer Machinery*, **17**, 2, pp. 197–215.

Terry Winograd

13   The Processes of Language Understanding[1]

The title of this series of essays was, clearly, designed by intrepid philosophers. As a visitor from the scientific side of the fence, I don't have the courage to venture into theories on the limits of human nature. Instead I want to describe some of the things being done in the field of Artificial Intelligence to extend the limits of what we understand about human nature.

First, I want to dispel any uncomfortable feelings that you (and I as well) have about the name 'Artificial Intelligence'. The word 'artificial' brings to mind all the synthetic, unnatural technical marvels which form so much of our daily existence. Combining it with 'intelligence' gives a ring of ominous science fiction. I want to emphasize in this essay the degree to which our field is as much a study of the natural as the artificial. It is concerned with understanding intelligence in whatever form we can give that word meaning, and it has goals which are quite separate from practical tasks of building robots, chess-playing programmes, and other beasts of the future. There is a strong tradition among us (if it can be called a tradition in a subject under twenty years old) of thinking very hard about the processes which go on in the human mind. At the centre of our study lies a desire to understand how the tools of computing, the ideas and metaphors which arise in programming computers, can be used in the study of the mind. Our reach extends into territory claimed by a variety of traditional subjects, such as psychology, philosophy, and linguistics, and I hope to convey some feeling for the concepts which are beginning to be used in those fields.

I want to exclude from the beginning the kind of computer use that first comes to mind for most people. This is the image of the super-fast, super-accurate adding-machine, grinding through mountains of data in seconds, doing arithmetic, printing forms, and storing masses of information. These technical abilities of computers are indeed impressive, but I am much more interested in the computer as an active metaphor – a way of looking at the world which is different from the more familiar paradigms of physics and mathematics.

What do I mean by 'active metaphor'? Primarily the computer gives us a way of thinking about processes. A computer pro-gramme is a representation for a dynamic process, unfolding over time and exhibiting behaviour. In studying it, we are concerned

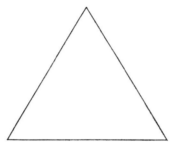

Figure 4 A geometrical design

not with a static pattern, but with the intricacies of continuing behaviour. What is more, we study these complexities of behaviour by looking for the simplicity of the programmes which underlie it.

As an elementary example of a procedural viewpoint, I want to present some ideas being developed by Seymour Papert at the Massachusetts Institute of Technology.[2] He is interested in the problem of teaching children about thinking, and one exercise involves simple geometric designs such as the one in Figure 4.

Consider how you would go about describing this figure to someone who couldn't see it. Digging back into plane geometry, you can think of a number of ways. It is an equilateral triangle with sides of a certain length, sitting on a base. It is a set of three points with certain Cartesian co-ordinates, connected in pairs by line segments. It is made up of three lines whose equations could be described. There is little difficulty in coming up with a variety of ways to specify in a few words exactly what is there. Contrast this with the more complex designs of Figure 5. Faced with the task of describing these, you would be at a loss to provide a simple

Figure 5   a–d More complex geometrical designs

geometric description or to list the sets of lines and points involved. There are no obvious ways to describe them as combinations of simpler figures whose form and relationships are easily characterized in a few words.

Let us take a slightly different point of view. Let us look not at the finished figure, but at the drawing of the figure as an active process. In a very concrete form, we can imagine a mechanical turtle like the one in Plate 20 (which was designed for use in the education experiments).

It has a pen which projects beneath it and draws a trail on the ground as it moves. It understands a simple language (named LOGO) whose commands tell it to do things like going forward a given distance, or turning right a given angle. By giving it an appropriate sequence of these basic instructions, we can get it to draw designs. The triangle of Figure 4 can be produced by the sequence:

```
FORWARD 100
LEFT 120
FORWARD 100
LEFT 120
FORWARD 100
LEFT 120
```

Imagine the turtle starting at the lower left corner of the triangle, facing towards the right. The first FORWARD command moves it along the base line, a distance of 100 (the distances are in terms of arbitrary small 'turtle steps'). It then turns 120 degrees to the left, leaving it heading along the right-hand side towards the apex. After it has drawn that side, the next turn sets it back towards the origin, and the final turn leaves it in its original position and heading.

One of the first things we want to do is give this procedure a name, so that we can get the turtle to do it without typing all of the steps each time. We can name it TRIANGLE and tell the turtle how to do it by typing:

```
TO TRIANGLE
FORWARD 100
LEFT 120
FORWARD 100
LEFT 120
FORWARD 100
LEFT 120
```

Now whenever we give the command TRIANGLE, the turtle

will draw the triangle for us. But there is something unsatisfactory about the description. It doesn't capture the essence of the procedure, which is highly repetitive. The same sequence of actions (FORWARD 100, LEFT 120) takes place over and over. There is an elementary programming concept to describe such activity, called *recursion*. We can redefine TRIANGLE using recursion:

```
TO TRIANGLE
    FORWARD 100
    LEFT 120
    TRIANGLE
```

If we now tell the turtle to TRIANGLE, it begins the same way by walking forward 100 steps, then turning left 120 degrees, but then there is a trick. As the third instruction we have told it to TRIANGLE from its new position. It starts anew into the procedure TRIANGLE by walking forward another 100, left another 120, and then beginning all over again, *ad infinitum*. This particular programme leaves the poor beast wandering around the triangle for ever, but we needn't worry, as there are many simple ways to make him stop.

Instead let us look at what we have described. We have specified a particular triangle with a side of length 100, and could do the same thing for any other size. But it seems silly to have a separate programme for every size we want, when the procedures are all really the same. A basic programming tool is the use of *variables*, which allow us to give procedures *inputs* specifying the details of their task. We can rewrite our programme:

```
TO TRIANGLE :SIDE
    FORWARD :SIDE
    LEFT 120
    TRIANGLE :SIDE
```

The procedure now expects an input which will tell it the value for the variable SIDE, which replaces 100 in our more general procedure. Instead of saying 'TRIANGLE' we now say 'TRIANGLE 100' to get the same drawing. If we say 'TRIANGLE 200', it will draw one twice as large, while 'TRIANGLE 10' produces a miniature.

Sharp-eyed readers will immediately chime in – 'Why stop there?' 'Why not make the angle a variable too?' Indeed, we can write a new procedure (let us call it POLY since it really is no longer a specialist in triangles) which expects two inputs:

```
TO POLY :SIDE :ANGLE
    FORWARD :SIDE
    LEFT :ANGLE
    POLY :SIDE :ANGLE
```

We now get our original triangle by ordering 'POLY 100 120'. What have we gained? Certainly all this is at least as complicated as the other ways of describing a triangle. But now the procedure does all sorts of other things too. If we say 'POLY 100 90', it will draw a square, since after each side, it will make a 90-degree turn before beginning the next. After four repetitions, it will be back where it started. A quick bit of calculation shows that we can give POLY any angle which divides 360 evenly, and it will draw a regular polygon whose number of sides is the quotient. But what if we specify some other angle, like 144? A little mental turtle-simulation will show that this is exactly the way to produce the star of Figure 5a. Each FORWARD brings the turtle to a point of the star, and each LEFT turns it back towards the centre, ready to continue across to a point on the opposite side. It is an interesting exercise to decide just what a POLY will look like for a given angle (and it gives children new motivation to learn the skills of arithmetic when faced with this problem).

Let us carry it one step further. Instead of making all the sides the same length, we can specify that each time the recursion takes place, the length should be increased. Our new procedure (called POLYSPI) is:

```
TO POLYSPI :SIDE :ANGLE :INCREASE
    FORWARD :SIDE
    LEFT :ANGLE
    POLYSPI :SIDE + :INCREASE :ANGLE :INCREASE
```

Now when we tell the turtle to 'POLYSPI 100 60 10', it draws Figure 5b. After each side, the new POLYSPI command has an increased SIDE length. 'POLYSPI 20 90 5' gives the 'squiral' of Figure 5c, and the pyrotechnics of Figure 5d are just the result of asking for 'POLYSPI 40 173 6'.

There is a moral lurking in all this geometry. By now it should seem plausible that something which appears complex at first glance may be generated by a simple process which can be described in a few lines. We call this description the *algorithm* for the process, and in specifying the algorithm fully, we capture the essence of the behaviour. Our active metaphor provides the tools for distilling this essence.

My own research has concentrated on the processes involved in using human language. That is a long way from what we have just been looking at. Geometrical shapes have an intrinsic simplicity, and in any event it seems that their mathematical nature should lend itself to computer description. It is easy to see how a few simple rules can handle a polygon, but language is in a different world of complexity. What I hope to persuade you is that a direct attempt to understand the processes of language is the key to untangling that complexity.

There is no magic formula, and we must not fall into the '1, 2, 3, infinity' fallacy. There is a kind of defeatism which says: 'If I can't describe what is going on in two or three basic underlying rules, then it must be un-understandable: it must be indescribable, infinite in a way which we can never fill in or model on a computer.' But maybe there are just a large number of rules – fifty or a hundred or a thousand, with that many more exceptions – but not infinite, not unimaginable. How can we handle a system like that? How can we investigate and understand the interactions between such a set of processes? Here our computer is 'active' in another sense – as an active partner in exploring the consequences of a theory. We are dealing with processes which don't have a simple set of Newton's laws or Maxwell's equations. There is no quintessence which can be reduced to a few equations, whose application explains everything. Not only is there no simple set of axioms, there is no simple way to break the system down into independent parts.

These same sorts of complexity are characteristic of computer systems, and we can use computer-simulations as an analogue of the process under study, to test our theories. We can put our descriptions into a programme and see what it really does: whether it acts as we would expect a person to, and in what ways the similarities and differences reveal essential properties of the process. The interactions it explores are all implicit in the description, but they are not accessible to direct study, even by their author.

To give some substance to this description, I will explain in some detail the research I have done in creating a system of programmes to carry out simple language behaviour.

One important tenet of the approach is that language must be viewed as a process of communication between intelligent beings. We cannot reduce it to independent elements of 'syntax', 'semantics', etc. There is a strong trend in modern linguistics to take some particular aspect, such as syntax, and study it without direct concern for the part it plays in the communication process. There is an implicit belief that such separate components will be relatively easy to stick together in understanding the broader phenomena.

I have begun instead from the viewpoint of considering the entire range of knowledge which goes into understanding language. It does involve syntax, but it also involves semantics – the way we get the meaning from a sentence – and it also involves in a very real way the pragmatics of meaning. A language is not just a set of symbols, an arbitrary string of formulae, but is a system for conveying meaning between people in real-world situations. The emphasis of study was in integrating the structure of language with its meaning.

You may be aware of earlier projects involving computer handling of natural language, in particular the effort in machine translation. Translation was seen from the beginning as a potential use of computers. As early as 1948, a famous memorandum by Warren Weaver suggested the possibility, and a tremendous effort was made in the hope that machine translation could ease the problems of international communication. After fifteen years of working on translation, the people in the field came to the sad conclusion that their studies had been a flop. There were beneficial side-effects in computer technology and linguistics, but the original goal was not achieved. Nobody could present a computer with a piece of text and come out with anything close to a satisfactory translation.

Why did this happen? What is being done today that is different? The answer lies in the problem of meaning. The machine translators felt that translation could be accomplished without making explicit connections between syntax and meaning. The translation was divided into separate activities of looking for meanings of words, and converting structures from one language to another according to syntactic rules.

Let us look at a typical sort of problem. We are translating from an American newspaper into French, and come across one of the two sentences below:

(a) *The city councilmen refused to give the women a permit for a demonstration because they feared violence.*

(b) *The city councilmen refused to give the women a permit for a demonstration because they advocated revolution.*

The translator must translate 'they' into either the masculine or feminine pronoun in French, 'ils' or 'elles'. He cannot keep the ambiguity of the English, and his choice determines the basic meaning of the translated sentence. Knowledge of the language and of linguistics gives no clue. Is it the demonstrators who fear violence, or the councilmen? Who is revolutionary? A human translator may well not even be aware of the problem. In reading the sentence, his knowledge of current American politics guides him into seeing only the interpretation in which the demonstrators are troublemakers seeking change, while the councilmen are pillars of the system, concerned with 'law and order'. How can a translating-machine handle this sentence? Somehow it must have a knowledge of politics and be able to apply it in understanding the sentence. It needs a whole body of knowledge which would not be found in a dictionary or even an encyclopedia.

This example may sound a little contrived, because it tries to illustrate how subtle the necessary knowledge may be, without making use of a context outside the sentence. Within normal discourse a tremendous amount of context is shared between speaker and hearer, and similar problems arise in nearly every sentence. It involves not just pronouns, but the choice of meanings for words and the analysis of the syntactic structures as well. Let us compare the sentences:

(a) *His shoes were scorched by the fire.*

(b) *His shoes were stored by the fire.*

These are two quite different constructions. In translating into a language which did not have a passive voice as does English, the first would be translated into something corresponding to *The fire scorched his shoes*. But *The fire stored his shoes* completely misrepresents the second. Our understanding of meaning is necessary to decide on the syntactic analysis of each sentence.

Faced with this realization, many people were pessimistic about whether computers could ever handle natural language at all. The problem of translation turned out to need a prior solution to the problem of understanding and of applying a wide variety of knowledge about the world.

My solution to this dilemma has been to accept the fact that language, meaning, and thought cannot be separated, and to attack them by limiting the size of the relevant 'world'. Rather than simplifying language to a set of isolated sentences, out of context, and without a real meaning, I chose to work within a discourse in a real situation of communication. But it was a situation which was so severely limited that the computer could be given the equivalent of knowledge about the political predilections of local politicians. The hope was that by simplifying in this direction we could avoid unnatural simplifications in our theories of language and language-use, and could attempt to integrate syntactic theories with semantics and pragmatics.

The topic chosen was the world of a simple robot with a mechanical hand, which manipulates a set of toy objects on a table. There was no actual robot used, even though such a robot is being developed for studying vision and problem-solving in our laboratory. Instead, a person converses (via teletypewriter) with a simulated robot on a television screen attached to the computer. On the screen, the robot moves about a set of simple coloured blocks and pyramids, obeying commands to do such things as building stacks and putting them into a box. Figure 6 shows a typical scene.

The programme also answers questions about what is on the screen, and about what it is doing, as well as accepting information for use in its reasoning. It understands many of the devices which occur in language based on the use of context. This includes things like pronouns which refer to previously-mentioned objects and events, substitute phrases like 'the one', adverbs like 'then' and 'there', and a variety of other mechanisms which depend on the fact that the person being addressed is involved in the same situation and has a memory of what has gone on previously in the conversation. These are interwoven with the more local problems of syntax and semantics in deciding what structure underlies a sentence and what meaning it conveys. Figure 7 shows excerpts from an extended dialogue with the system.[3] The lines in capital

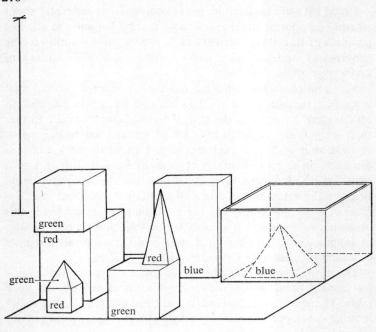

Figure 6 **Building stacks**

letters were the responses by the computer, while the others are the human side of the conversation. At the same time, actions were being carried out on the screen, as described in the italicized text. The dialogue begins with the situation as shown in Figure 6.

Given the initial command '*Pick up a big red block*', the system must interpret the intent of the speaker, and must also recognize that the big red block cannot be picked up without first moving away the green cube which it supports. Part of the system embodies the sort of pragmatic knowledge needed to plan a series of actions for achieving the desired goal.

The second command, '*Grasp the pyramid*', illustrates a typical place where the situation enters into understanding. A definite noun-phrase like '*the pyramid*' is used to indicate a pyramid which the hearer is already aware of. If there is no particular one already in mind, the speaker will use an indefinite phrase like '*a big red block*' in Sentence 1. In this case, there are three pyramids in the scene none of which has been mentioned or otherwise distinguished. The only appropriate response is to complain that the description is senseless in this context.

Sentence 3 shows some of the complexity of the grammar, involving relative clauses, use of the pronoun '*it*', and use of the phrase '*the one you are holding*', which refers to '*block*'. The special '*I assume . . .*' message is printed because '*it*' was potentially ambiguous. It could refer to '*the one you are holding*' as well as '*a block which is taller than the one you are holding*'. The system has a set of *heuristics* (rules of thumb) for choosing interpretations in such cases.

In order to answer the question in Sentence 4, the system must generate the appropriate English phrases to describe the objects. We give it an initial full description of the scene, so it knows what is in the box. It keeps track of the sentences typed into it and the ones it produces, so when in Sentence 5 it sees the phrase '*the pyramid*', it deduces that it must refer to the one just mentioned in the previous answer, and does not reject the phrase as it did earlier.

Semantic knowledge enables it to answer simple hypothetical questions like those of Sentences 6 to 8. The dictionary entry for '*pick up*' includes the fact that the subject must be 'animate'. Since a table is inanimate, the answer to '*Can the table pick up blocks?*' is 'No'. '*Can a pyramid be supported by a block?*' gets

Figure 7 Excerpts from a dialogue with the programme

1. Pick up a big red block.
   OK.
   There is a green cube on top of the only big red block. The system first moves the green cube to a place on the table, then grasps the red block and raises its hand.

2. Grasp the pyramid.
   I DON'T UNDERSTAND WHICH PYRAMID YOU MEAN.

3. Find a block which is taller than the one you are holding and put it into the box.
   The system puts the red block down on the table, picks up the tall blue block, and puts it into the box next to the blue pyramid.
   BY 'IT', I ASSUME YOU MEAN THE BLOCK WHICH IS TALLER THAN THE ONE I AM HOLDING.
   OK.

4. What does the box contain?
   THE BLUE PYRAMID AND THE BLUE BLOCK.

5. What is the pyramid supported by?
   THE BOX.

6. Can the table pick up blocks?
   NO.

7. Can a pyramid be supported by a block?
   YES.

8. Can a pyramid support a pyramid?
   I DON'T KNOW.

9. Stack up two pyramids.
   I CAN'T.

10. Will you please stack up both of the red blocks and either a green cube or a pyramid?
    OK.
    The system first takes the green cube which has nothing on it and puts it on to the large red block. It then clears off the small red cube by finding a place on the table for the green pyramid and putting it there. It then puts the red cube on top of the stack containing the other red block and the green cube.

11. How many things are on top of green cubes?
    I'M NOT SURE WHAT YOU MEAN BY 'ON TOP OF' IN THE PHRASE 'ON TOP OF GREEN CUBES'.
    DO YOU MEAN:
    1 – DIRECTLY ON THE SURFACE
    2 – ANYWHERE ON TOP OF?
    THREE OF THEM.

12. Had you touched any pyramid before you put the green one on the little cube?

YES, THE GREEN ONE.

13. When did you pick it up?

WHILE I WAS STACKING UP THE RED CUBE, A LARGE RED BLOCK AND A LARGE GREEN CUBE.

14. Why?

TO GET RID OF IT.

15. Why did you do that?

TO CLEAR OFF THE RED CUBE.

16. Why did you clear off that cube?

TO PUT IT ON A LARGE GREEN CUBE.

17. Why did you do that?

TO STACK UP THE RED CUBE, A LARGE RED BLOCK AND A LARGE GREEN CUBE.

18. Why did you do that?

BECAUSE YOU ASKED ME TO.

19. How did you do it?

BY PUTTING A LARGE RED BLOCK ON THE TABLE; THEN LETTING GO OF IT; THEN PUTTING A LARGE GREEN CUBE ON IT; THEN LETTING GO OF THAT CUBE; THEN PUTTING THE RED CUBE ON THAT CUBE; THEN LETTING GO OF THAT CUBE.

20. Put the blue pyramid on the block in the box.

The system takes the blue pyramid and puts it on to the large blue block which is in the box.

OK.

21. Does a steeple

SORRY, I DON'T KNOW THE WORD 'STEEPLE'.

The system interrupts immediately when it sees a word it can't figure out.

22. A 'steeple' is a stack which contains two green cubes and a pyramid.

I UNDERSTAND.

23. Are there any steeples now?

NO.

24. Build one.

OK.

One of the large green cubes is cleared off by removing the red cube and two pyramids. Then the two green cubes and the tall red pyramid are stacked up to fit the description.

an easy affirmative answer since there is an example in the scene. '*Can a pyramid support a pyramid?*' is harder, since there are no examples and no immediate way of knowing whether this is just happenstance. The command '*Stack up two pyramids*' leads the system to try planning a sequence of actions to achieve it, which fails.

The sequence of actions produced by Sentence 10 converts the scene of Figure 8 to that of Figure 9. Given a choice of '*either a green cube or a pyramid*', the system uses various heuristics to decide which object will involve the least work. In order to get '*both of the red blocks*', it needs the small red cube in the front left-hand corner. To be picked up, it must be cleared off by getting rid of the green pyramid which is on top of it. Part of the analysis involves choosing an appropriate sequence of motions and positions to carry out the stacking operation, and the system remembers the structure of this planning, as well as the actual motions carried out.

Sentence 11 (which occurs after several other motions have taken place in the original dialogue) involves a phrase with two potential meanings. The system does not have sufficient reason to know whether '*on top of*' involves actual contact of the surfaces or a more general notion of support. Both meanings are in the dictionary, along with their paraphrases, enabling the system to query the user for further information.

Sentences 12 to 19 involve the actions carried out in obeying Sentence 10. A '*When?*' question provokes a description of the top-level action being carried out at the time; '*Why?*' causes an examination of the planning which was done; and '*How?*' causes a listing of the immediate goals needed to carry out the action. Knowledge of discourse structure enables it to understand such sentences as '*How did you do that?*' or simply '*Why*'?

Faced with potential ambiguity, the system can also use knowledge of the situation, as in Sentence 20. There are two interpretations to '*Put the blue pyramid on the block in the box.*' One is analogous to '*Put the blue pyramid on to the block which is in the box.*' The other is '*Put the blue pyramid which is on the block into the box.*' In this case the system recognizes that only the first interpretation is possible, since '*the blue pyramid on the block*' has no referent in the scene.

New words can be defined in terms of old ones, as in Sentence

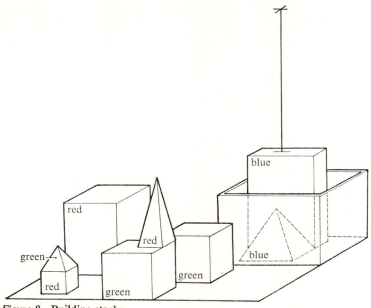

Figure 8 **Building stacks**

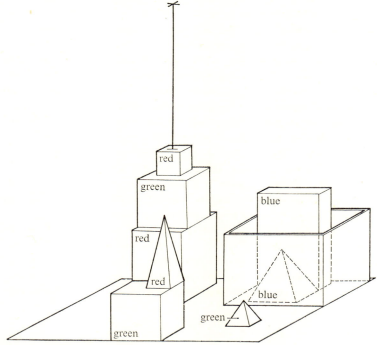

Figure 9 **Building stacks**

22. '*Steeple*' is not in the dictionary, so the system rejects it in Sentence 21. By saying '*A "steeple" is a stack which contains two green cubes and a pyramid*' we attach a syntactic and a semantic description to the word '*steeple*'. We can then use this description in recognizing steeples, as in '*Are there any steeples now?*', and as a blueprint in the command '*Build one.*'

Other capabilities include accepting simple facts like '*I own the red block*' and using them in deductions; attaching proper names to objects; answering questions about past situations; choosing an answer depending on what the speaker already knows (as indicated by the words he uses in describing an object); and a variety of more complex discourse-mechanisms.

What does this all lead to? It is all very nice to be able to converse with a robot about its toys, and it might even lead to practical applications. But what does it have to do with human nature, or even human language? If a programme is just a series of tricks which produce a specialized set of phrases, it may tell us very little about what goes on in real language-use. In the rest of this essay I want to give you some feeling for the type of knowledge that is involved in these procedures, and how the different parts of language-understanding are interrelated in the programme. These will be of interest to the degree that they seem plausible as metaphors for our own processes of language.

Language is traditionally divided into three aspects – syntax, semantics, and pragmatics. This is a useful distinction for some purposes, but it is important to remember that it is not a simple reduction of a complex system into simpler parts. If we divide our study into segments we must be all the more aware of the interactions among them. There is no simple hierarchy in which one aspect commands or feeds another, but a 'heterarchy', with independent parts communicating in a variety of ways.

Let us begin with the problem of representing simple facts: of how the system knows, for example, that a particular block is red. As a basis it has an internal 'model' of the world, containing objects, properties, and relationships. It is not a model in the strict mathematical sense, nor in the sense of a small but complete replica. Rather it is a symbolic description which abstracts the significant aspects of the world and describes them in symbol-structures. We will not discuss here the philosophical implications and problems of such models, but will be more concerned with their use in the language-process. The symbols do not represent any set of pure theoretically unanalysable primitives, but rather are based on the loose sets of categories which an intelligent system uses in trying to deal with its world. 'Chair' may be an atomic symbol, not because it is irreducible in any strict logical way, but because it represents a category which people find useful to have in dealing with the everyday world. The ultimate meaning of such symbols lies in the set of relationships they have with the other symbols, objects and procedures in the model.

Figure 10 shows some simple assertions in a formalism like the one used by the programme.[4] The words appearing in the formulae

(BLOCK1 IS–A BLOCK)
(BLOCK2 IS–A PYRAMID)
(BLOCK1 IS–AT (LOCATION 100 100 0))
(BLOCK1 SUPPORTS BLOCK2)
(CLEARTOP BLOCK1)
(MANIPULABLE BLOCK1)
(BOX1 CONTAINS BLOCK4)
(COLOUR–OF BLOCK1 RED)
(BLUE IS–A COLOUR)
(EVENT23 CAUSED EVENT24)

Figure 10 Representation of simple facts

are not equivalent to the corresponding English words, but are symbols in the internal model. A word like 'block' may have several interpretations, only one of which is represented here, and a concept like 'CLEARTOP' may have no single English representation, being represented by a variety of phrases. In the actual programmes, care is taken to distinguish the internal symbols from the English words, and to distinguish the symbols for specific objects (like BLOCK1 in this example) from names of properties and relations. The detailed form of the expressions is unimportant. What matters is that they are built consistently, that they can express the range of concepts we need, and, most importantly, that there is a set of procedures which can use them.

A concept like CLEARTOP is defined operationally by a procedure like the one diagrammed in Figure 11. It shows the steps in clearing an object it calls x. It begins by seeing if x supports any object (which it will call y). If so, it calls as a goal 'GET–RID–OF y' and when this succeeds it loops back to the beginning. As long as x supports anything it circles around the loop. When nothing is left, it asserts that x is CLEARTOP. GET–RID–OF, in turn, is defined by a procedure which involves trying to PUT the

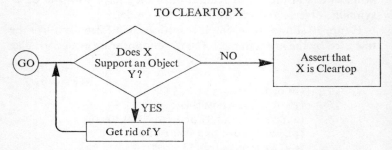

Figure 11   Operational procedure with the CLEARTOP concept

object on the table. PUT in turn calls GRASP to grasp the object, then FINDSPACE, then MOVE. Note that the procedure for GRASP may in turn call CLEARTOP on an object before grasping it. The definitions are constructively circular, allowing recursion in a natural way.

In an appropriate higher-level programming language, we might express the CLEARTOP programme as in Figure 12.[5]

```
(CONSEQUENT (CLEARTOP ?X)
   START
   (IF (?X SUPPORTS ?Y)
      THEN (GET-RID-OF ?Y) (GO START)
      ELSE (ASSERT (CLEARTOP ?X))))
```

Figure 12   Programme for CLEARTOP

To see how such procedures would operate, consider the problem of grasping BLOCK1 when the robot is initially holding

BLOCK2. The command 'GRASP BLOCK1' will set up as its initial subgoal 'GET-RID-OF BLOCK2'. This will set up a goal of 'PUTON BLOCK2 TABLE' which in turn will find a space, then call PUT with the chosen location. At one instance during that process, the current goal stack would look like Figure 13. This is remembered by the programme, and a little thought will show how it can be used to answer questions involving *Why's* and *How's*. If BLOCK2 is the red block and BLOCK1 is green, a question like '*Why did you put the red block on the table?*' would be answered by taking a step up the stack and saying '*To get rid of it*'. '*Why did you do that?*' takes another step to answer '*To grasp a green block*', and the response when it reaches the top is the obvious '*Because you told me to*'.

The procedural representation of meanings seems at first to be specifically suited for handling imperatives. What would it

---

```
(GRASP BLOCK1)
    (GET–RID–OF BLOCK2)
        (PUTON BLOCK2 TABLE1)
            (PUT BLOCK2 (LOCATION 453 201 0))
                (MOVEHAND (LOCATION 553 301 100))
```

Figure 13 Snapshot of a goal stack

mean to make a statement or a description into a procedure? One of the unifying principles of the system is that all meanings can be thought of as procedures. A person says something to another person in order to cause a process to go on, whether that involves actions in the physical world, verbal actions in giving a response, or mental actions in searching for a bit of knowledge or storing one away. We can think of a description of an object like '*a red block which supports a pyramid*' as a command to find a particular object in the situation, or a programme for recognizing such an object. For each phrase of the input sentences, an appropriate procedure is produced.

In order to do this, there must be connections between the English words and the concepts used in the internal model. There is a dictionary containing the meanings of each word, and information about when they apply. A simple word like '*cube*' can be defined as shown in Figure 14. This says that when '*cube*' is used as a noun, it represents an object which is manipulable and rectangular, i.e. a block, and has equal dimensions in all dimensions. There may be several meanings for a word, applied according to context. For example, an adjective may have different meanings depending on the type of object it modifies.

But things aren't so simple for all words. Words like '*it*', '*one*', and '*the*' don't have meanings which can be stated directly in terms of the world-model. They convey facts about the message being sent, and the way it is to be interpreted. If I say '*the block*', I am indicating that I expect the addressee to be aware of which block I am referring to. Some phrases, like '*the sun*' clearly refer

---

```
(CUBE
    ((NOUN (OBJECT
            ((MANIPULABLE RECTANGULAR)
             ((IS ? BLOCK)
              (EQUIDIMENSIONAL ?)))))))
```

Figure 14 Dictionary definition for '*cube*'

to unique objects our models share. Others, like '*the queen*', may have a unique meaning within a particular discussion, depending on what country and era we are discussing. In Sentence 5 of the dialogue, an understanding of the phrase '*the pyramid*' involves consideration of what has been mentioned recently in the discussion. The programme must account for this interaction of world knowledge, shared experience, and linguistic context in interpreting the meaning of '*the*'.

Actually, the situation is even more complicated. '*The*' can also be used to convey an impression of uniqueness for a previously unmentioned object. If I say '*The reason I wrote the programme was* ...' it implies there was a single primary reason, while '*A reason I wrote the programme was* ...' implies that there were several. A person's knowledge of the language allows him to make the right implications, and as our language-understander gets smarter it will need to do so as well.

In order to relate this semantic analysis to the sentence, we want first to break it into meaningful chunks and determine their relationship to one another. A sentence like '*Every musician likes long romantic sonatas'* can be parsed as shown in Figure 15. There are many different theories of syntax and methods for parsing, and the one used in my system is based on a theory, called systemic grammar, particularly suited for the analysis of meaning. Its constituent analysis involves breaking the structure into chunks which are relevant to conveying meaning. In the example, noun-phrases are used to describe objects, clauses express relationships and events. Our semantic programmes use this natural grouping to build up the meanings. Each word is associated with a procedure representing its meaning, and this procedure is called as a part

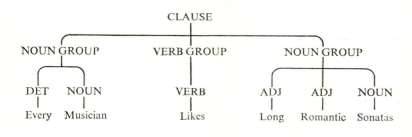

Figure 15 The parsing of a sentence

of putting together the meaning of a basic chunk. The procedure described above for '*the*' is called while working on the description of an entire phrase like '*the big red block*', and involves actions like looking in the model for items fitting the description. Notice that our description of the behaviour of '*the*' really isn't peculiar to that word, but applies to other *definite* noun-phrases like those beginning with a possessive. '*Carol's reason for writing the programme was . . .*' implies just as surely that there was a single reason, and talking about '*Carol's exam*' implies that the hearer knows about a particular exam. One of the fundamental observations of systemic grammar is that the behaviour of syntactic constituents, both in entering into structures and in conveying meaning, can be classified into highly-structured categories. We can describe a constituent by assigning *features* like '*definite*', and make use of them in carrying out the understanding process.

Parsing not only involves building a tree showing the structure, but also involves analysing the features of each constituent and the functions it plays in the larger structures.

The features can be organized into *system-networks*, like the fragment shown in Figure 16. Here we see that a clause can be either MAJOR (able to stand alone as a sentence) or SECONDARY (like '*which is on the table*' in '*the block which is on the table*'). Each MAJOR clause is either IMPERATIVE, DECLARATIVE, or INTERROGATIVE, and if the latter, then a further choice must be made between the *wh-* form (as in '*When did she go?*' or '*Who went?*') or the YES-NO form (as in '*Did she go?*'). Each of the features shown leads to further sets of choices which indicate the

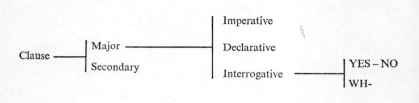

Figure 16   System-networks

structure of the clause in more and more detail. It is important to note that these features are syntactic, not semantic. A clause is interrogative because it has a particular form like '*Will you shut the door*', even if it is being used as a command. A further part of the theory relates the features describing each constituent to the different syntactic and semantic functions it can play in any larger constituent, either within the sentence or within the discourse.

Systemic grammar provides a framework for describing structures, which form an integral part (along with the definitions of the words used) of the input to the semantic analysis programmes. It does not, however, describe how one is to arrive at such a description for a particular sentence. Grammars of natural language are inherently complex, and any formalism for syntax faces deep problems of controlling the interactions between large numbers of rules. Transformational grammar does this by devising an abstract generation-process, which goes through various stages in a controlled way, regulating the sequence of the rules according to a variety of constraints. This procedural character gives it the ability to describe many of the facts about syntax in a compact way, but it is not oriented towards the actual interpretation or generation processes people use, and it is very difficult to explain how the syntactic operations interact with meaning.

I feel that it is more natural to think in terms of the actual process of interpreting sentences, expressing the flow of the process explicitly in the form of a procedure. The grammar is a programme, written in a language called PROGRAMMAR whose primitive actions are those for building systemic descriptions. It allows semantic and deductive programmes to be called at any point in the process, making their interactions with the syntax more explicit and understandable. The process of understanding is not divided into separate phases for the different aspects of analysis. As soon as a potentially meaningful chunk is parsed, semantic programmes are 'called' to see if it makes sense, and how it fits with other parts of the meaning and the context. If no sense can be made of it, the parser is redirected to find another possible structure. Thus, syntax directs the understanding, while understanding guides syntactic analysis.

In this brief description, it is not possible to flesh in the details of the system. What is more important is a general feeling for the way that its basic orientation allows it to handle the complex and difficult interactions involved in a process like language-understanding. The ability to relate its understanding of the world to its knowledge of language-structure and context depends critically on the organization of knowledge as procedures.

This same orientation is being used in other areas of understanding thought-processes. Workers in Artificial Intelligence have attacked problems like vision, learning, and abstract problem-solving from this same viewpoint of looking for the underlying procedures. They have come up with a number of fascinating and suggestive results.

Our understanding of human thought-processes is in a primitive state. It is far too early to answer questions like 'Does the brain really work like that?' We cannot examine its programmes in detail, and do not even understand the basic principles of its organization. But it does seem undeniable that an activity like language-understanding must involve the interaction of dynamic processes. The computer, as active metaphor, can give us new ways of looking at those processes, moving forward the limits of our understanding of human nature.

1 An earlier version of this essay was presented as the Computers and Thought Lecture at the International Joint Conference on Artificial Intelligence at Imperial College, London, 2 September 1971.

2. See S. Papert and C. Solomon, 'Twenty things to do with a computer', in *Educational Technology*, March 1971.

3 For the full dialogue, and a complete description of the programme and the underlying theories, see Terry Winograd, *Understanding Natural Language* (Edinburgh University Press and Academic Press, New York 1972).

4 This is not identical in detail to the formalism used in the actual programmes. The syntax has been simplified for easy understanding. But there is no basic difference at any point in either what can be expressed or how it works. For more detail see Winograd, op. cit.

5 The programmes are written in a language called Micro-Planner, which is a partial implementation of Carl Hewitt's PLANNER language. For more detail see Carl Hewitt, 'Procedural Embedding of Knowledge in PLANNER', Papers of the Second International Joint Conference on Artificial Intelligence, British Computer Society, 1971; and G. Sussman, T. Winograd and E. Charniak, 'Micro-Planner Reference Manual', AI Memo No. 203, Artificial Intelligence Laboratory, Massachusetts Institute of Technology, 1971.

Part Three

Criticism

Robert M. Young

14 The Human Limits of Nature

I

I find it worrying that an Institute for Contemporary Arts is turning deferentially to science for social and cultural wisdom and guidance. Presumably the people to whom these essays are addressed believe that this is a project worth pursuing. It seems to me that the contributors and their audience are gathered in the name of science, but that we are at the same time gathered as symptoms of some sort of social, cultural, political and indeed ideological malaise. We seek a basis in science for our goals and for the ordering of society. Scientists and other related experts are becoming secular priests, who are supposed to help us order our conduct, our work and the world that we live in.

I would like to begin by discussing the phrase 'human nature' and to attempt a critical examination of the moral, political and ideological positions which are bound up with that concept. My first point is to suggest that we scrutinize the phrase. The juxtaposition of the term 'human' with that of 'nature' is part of common language. We all mean something by 'human nature'. We do not think it is silly, or deeply problematic, to combine the two words. But the commonsensical juxtaposition of humanity with nature, if we reflect on it, conceals very deep issues. Its usual meaning is in the area of 'What is man like? What is characteristic of man? What regularities of what people do, think and feel can we employ as guides in our relations with our fellow men?' That is all fairly clear, although imprecise. But the juxtaposition of humanity with nature is not really so straightforward. In many ways, we think of our humanity as something different from, as over against, the concept of nature. This 'over-against-ness' is one of the pervasive trends in the Western and other intellectual traditions. Humanity, we like to think, is not merely a natural phenomenon. Yet we believe deeply, if we take science seriously, that there is nothing about man which is not, at least in principle, explainable by the concepts and methods of the natural sciences.

This assumption that scientific naturalism applies to man and to all of his works is fundamental; it is the *sine qua non* of psychology and of the social – or some would say the 'behavioural', and others would say the 'human' – sciences. The assumption has become fundamental as a result of four interrelated phases in the history of thought, at least since the eighteenth century. The first phase was the attempt to take the corpuscular and mechanical physics of the Mechanical Philosophy, deriving from the Scientific Revolution, and apply it to the mind: the development of the so-called 'association psychology'.[1] Then this psychology interacted in complicated ways with the development of the modern theory of evolution.[2] Then associationism and evolutionism and related neurological conceptions combined with ideas from romantic philosophy to produce the psychoanalytic theory in the work of Sigmund Freud.[3] I think the vogue of psychoanalysis as a cultural philosophy is past, and we are now in a period in which many people are seeing these naturalistic assumptions in terms of the disciplines of ethology and genetics. These, of course, are related to other aspects of the social and human sciences, and indeed to demography, social statistics, and other disciplines. They are all founded on the further assumption that the aspects of man which are most significantly human, that is, his mental functions, are based ultimately on natural processes: to put it in its simplest form, that the brain, as a physiological system, is the organ of the mind.

II

I want to spend a bit of time considering the gap between this general principle of scientific naturalism as applied to man – i.e., scientific naturalism and determinism – on the one hand, and particular specifications of it on the other. One of the themes which I shall develop concerns the ways in which our acknowledgement of determinism as applied to man plays a socio-political role in inducing a kind of fatalism. That is to say, I intend to examine the project of searching for the limits of human nature, and to attempt to lay bare what seem to me to be some of its goals and some of its latent functions. In doing this I hope to bring moral and political criteria to bear on that project. In the end, I shall stand it on its head, or perhaps turn it inside out, and suggest that we might just as fruitfully search for the human limits of nature as for the limits of human nature. I am not just playing with words in suggesting that the project of searching for the limits of human nature is itself problematic. In conducting this critique, I shall touch briefly on ethology and talk quite a bit about biology and psychology and the sociology of knowledge from a marxist perspective. My aims are to show that there is an implied fatalism in the project itself, that it plays a role in treating men like things (i.e., that it reifies men), and that it is an important aspect of our alienation from our own belief that we can shape the world – or at least that we can try to shape the world – as we wish.

Now to consider the project itself: the limits of human nature are presumed to be natural. That is, according to the theory of evolution, man's origins and his nature are the results of, and are controlled by, the uniform laws which govern all natural processes. To fly in the face of these laws in setting goals for ourselves and for society is at one level quixotic and at another strictly impossible. So, if we would know how men should live, it is certainly prudent to inquire about the constraints on how they can live. Since nothing transcends the laws of nature, the relevant scientific findings and generalizations will show us how men must live. The limits of human nature are, once again, presumed to be natural. The investigation of natural processes is the domain of science. Therefore science will, if anything can, teach us how men should, can, and must live. Science is done by scientists, men who are highly-trained experts. It is to them that we must turn for sciences of behaviour, of ethics, of society and of politics.

This may sound crude. I think it is. But I also think it conveys the assumptions underlying this series of essays. If we look at the Prospectus to the original ICA lecture series we are told that the series 'aims to ask what are the irreducible foundations of human nature on which culture builds, and whether there are limits within which human nature develops or evolves'. Four specifications of this project are spelled out: first, 'in what sense is it meaningful to talk of "constraints" or "limits" on human nature'; second, 'what limits have been defined in the past'; third, 'what such limits could be suggested in the light of modern science'; and fourth, 'what are the ideological implications of differing theories about human nature'. My contribution falls under the last heading, the ideological implications of differing theories about human nature, but I intend it to reflect back on the other specifications.

First, I want to notice two features of these formulations. Our attention is drawn to the ideological '*implications*' of differing theories about human nature, and it is elsewhere said that 'Science is often pressed into service to justify models of political and economic behaviour'. It is often pointed out that power lies with the person who defines the situation or the question. These formulations, it seems to me, tacitly assume that science is one thing and its ideological implications quite another, and that the findings and theories of science are neutral. Particular interest groups then come along and use or abuse them – they 'press them into service' to justify models of political and economic behaviour. If we accept these formulations our task is very clear: be vigilant in preventing the employment of scientific ideas as justifications for models of political and economic behaviour. If we do this, the argument runs, science will have *no* ideological implications. The reason is that the same view which separates science from ideology, defines ideology as 'an inverted, truncated, distorted reflection of reality'.[4]

It seems worth while to spend a little time looking at the concept of ideology, and in doing so I shall be guided by Lefebvre's useful essay, 'Ideology and the Sociology of Knowledge'. 'Ideologies', by this account, 'come down to false representations of history or to abstractions from history. Every ideology, then, is a collection of errors, illusions, mystifications, which can be accounted for by reference to the historical reality it distorts and transposes.'[5] 'Ideologies operate by extrapolating the reality they interpret and transpose.'[6] This is not to say that ideologies reflect *no* reality, but that they attempt to represent *all* of reality in terms which reflect the interests of *particular* groups. Ideologies generalize 'special interests – class interests – by such means as abstraction, incomplete or distorted representations, appeals to fetishism'.[7] 'Once ideology is related to the real conditions that gave rise to it, it ceases to be completely illusory, entirely false.'[8]

The reality it conveys is real, but partial. 'Ideological representations invariably serve as instruments in the struggle between groups (peoples, nations) and classes (and fractions of classes). But their intervention in such struggles takes the form of masking the true interests and aspirations of the groups involved, universalizing the particular and mistaking the part for the whole.'[9] 'In setting out to answer all questions, all problems, they create a comprehensive view of the world. At the same time they reinforce specific ways of life, specific behaviour patterns, "values".'[10] 'Thus every ideology represents a vision or conception of the world, a Weltanschauung based on extrapolations and interpretations.'[11] Ideologies 'refract (rather than reflect) reality via pre-existing representations, selected by dominant groups and acceptable to them'.[12]

This analysis of ideology, and indeed the modern conception of the term, is derived from arguments which Marx and Engels developed in their work, *The German Ideology*.[13] The basic assumption is that 'Those who wield material (economic and political) power within the established social and juridical order also wield "spiritual" power. The representations, i.e., the consciousness of society, are elaborated into a systematic idealizing of existing conditions, those conditions which make possible the economic, social and political primacy of a given group or class.' Individual theorists and activists 'play an important part in forming the general consciousness and in excluding representations contrary to the interests of the ruling group. As a result, "their ideas are the dominant ideas of their epoch".'[14] This is not to say that such people are self-consciously deceptive. On the contrary, the strength of ideological representations lies very much in the extent to which people reflect and propagate views which they may not themselves self-consciously or self-critically hold. The analogy to psychology is a good one. 'From everyday experience we know that ideas serve often enough to furnish our actions with justifying motives in place of the real ones. What is called rationalization at this level is called ideology at the level of collective action. In both cases the manifest content of statements is falsified by consciousness' unreflected tie to interests, despite its illusion of autonomy.'[15] Attempts to analyse ideologies seek to replace the alleged whole with a clear and demystified picture of the part of society whose interests are being served.

Now, let us recall how this discussion of the concept of ideology began – with the assertion that science can have *no* ideological *implications*. The relationship between science and ideology is said to be that between truth and error, or, more accurately, between partial truths and special pleading. We must simply unmask the attempts to press the findings and theories of science to the service of particular social and political theories.

Unfortunately, the situation is not so simple. The problems with which we are concerned exist in two sorts of conceptual space where the terrain and boundaries are very uncertain indeed. There are two extremely important gaps which reveal our problem. The first lies between the general principle of scientific naturalism – as specified in the theory of organic evolution – and particular findings which may or may not be relevant to man in complex societies. Thus, for example, in the nineteenth century when Herbert Spencer attempted to generalize the theory of evolution as a justification for his own *laissez-faire* economic theories, Thomas Henry Huxley was able to come along and say, 'That's all very nice, but the general theory of evolution does not imply that – or any other – *specific* interpretation.'[16] The second gap lies between our very limited knowledge of animal behaviour and the very complex issues which arise because of human communication by language and by other cultural artefacts. We know that man is an animal and that he has a great deal in common with other organisms, but we cannot with any confidence directly apply findings from apes or rhesus monkeys – much less from pigeons and rats – to human social situations. These are the reasons why one must treat the arguments of people like Desmond Morris and B. F. Skinner with extreme caution – not that they have no relevance, but that we are in no position to assess their relevance.

These gaps – between the general principles and particular findings and between other organisms and man – do not merely define our ignorance. They also indicate a wide area within which speculation and ideological extrapolations can and do operate. But the problem does not end here. It is relatively – I should say *only* relatively – simple to guard against extrapolations from science in the service of particular ideological positions. What is not so easy is the assessment of the role of ideology in the assumptions and substance of perfectly reputable and cautious findings and theories in science. If we take seriously the assertion that all thought is highly constrained by the social and political context in which it occurs and that it *is*, in fundamental ways, a mediation of that context, then why make an exception of scientific thought? If we dig our heels in and make relative exceptions of some aspects of science – for example physics and chemistry – we are still faced with a continuum of disciplines whose fundamental concepts are more or less impregnated with social and political assumptions. And if we are as cautious as we can be about reading in such assumptions, we will still have to grant that the concept of human nature – of all concepts – is a happy hunting ground for social and political preconceptions, especially in the hands of eminent biologists.

Thus, our problems lie in three domains: the relationship between particular findings and the general principle of scientific naturalism, the relationship between other organisms and man, and the foundations of particular scientific findings and theories *about* other organisms and man. The nearer we get to what really interests us as men in society, the more our debates – both as scientists and as laymen – reflect our social and political contexts and assumptions, whether or not we are aware of those influences.[17]

What I am saying is not only that science is pressed into service to justify models of political and economic behaviour, but that these models are constitutive of the project of inquiring into human nature and society. Furthermore, the models deeply influence the more basic biological sciences to which we turn for guidance. When the participants in social and political debates turn to ethology, to genetics or to psychology or evolutionary theory for guidance, what they hear is, to a considerable extent, the echoes of their own debate, mediated and mystified in the form of science.

As we attempt to find our way through this sparsely-charted territory, we are uncertain about the boundaries, the landmarks and the possibility of the mapmaker's being disinterested. This is not a fact about his intentions, but about the relationship between thought and society, the relationship between knowledge and interest. One of the most cautious and eminent of men who have reflected on biology, Professor René Dubos, says this about scientific objectivity:

Despite our pathetic attempt at objectivity, we as scientists are in fact highly subjective in the selection of our activities, and we have goals

in mind when we plan our work. We make *a priori* decisions concerning
the kinds of facts worth looking for; we arrange these facts according
to certain patterns of thought which we find congenial; and we develop
them in such a manner as to promote social purposes which we deem
important[18]

If this can be said of the goals and purposes of which scientists
are aware, it is likely to be even more relevant to the ones which
they hold without self-conscious awareness.

III

I have deliberately dwelt at length on the general problems of
science and human nature before turning to particular examples.
I want now to consider some historical and current cases in the
light of the approach which I have outlined, beginning with some
examples from this series of essays. Alan Ryan said in his discussion 'The Nature of Human Nature in Hobbes and Rousseau',
the concept of human nature sets 'a limit to political possibility'.[19] The sort of approach which I am proposing would say
that it is just as likely to be the case that political and ideological
perspectives set definitions to the limits of human nature – definitions which then lead men to despair of certain political possibilities. In 'The Limits of Man and his Predicament', Arthur
Koestler argued that the trouble with our species is not what the
ethologists say – aggression or territoriality – but, rather, an
excess of devotion to words, beliefs and groups. He also pointed
out the bad effects of language on our social and political lives,
and touched on the poverty of our perceptual apparatus and the
split in evolution between the thinking and the feeling parts of
the brain.[20] Once again, it is just as arguable that our problems
are due in no small measure to an excess of deference to science
in its extrapolated form of scientism, alienating us from the belief
that we can achieve a just society. The alienation takes the form
of saying that it's not on, because of our brain structure, because
of our language, because of the poverty of our perceptual apparatus.

Turning now very briefly to ethology – which I will not discuss
in detail, because I want to treat it by analogy to another argument I am mounting – Michael Chance discussed the concept of
instinct, the role of fixed action patterns, patterns of social

organization. He offered us an analysis which is presumed to be relevant to man, because it was included under the title 'The Dimensions of our Social Behaviour'. He discussed 'hedonic' versus 'agonistic' bases for group cohesion among primates. (Lest it be forgotten, we are primates.)[21] We have already got four terms, four conceptions, which set some kinds of limits on what seems possible in man. The first is the concept of instinct, the second that of aggression, which has wide currency in popular literature, the third that of territoriality, and finally there is that of the hierarchical organization of biological and bio-social systems. I want to address these putative limits of human nature by considering a related concept, the analysis of which will shed light on the others: that is, the psychoanalytic concept of the unconscious, which is based on a theory of human instincts. If there were space, I would like also to go deeper into the biological sciences and discuss some more fundamental ideas – the concept of function, the concept of adaptation, the concept of equilibrium – three conceptions which are alleged to be non-controversial, and which are seen as the coinage of discourse in the discipline. All of these conceptions fall under a certain approach to the study of human nature.

The limits of human nature are, once again, the limits of nature. But the way that we approach those limits is in terms of refractoriness – the refractoriness of nature, in spite of man's best efforts, compounded by the refractoriness of man's own nature. In the period which gave rise to the modern versions of the conceptions with which we are working and with which we have been conjuring in this series, there also arose a continuous tradition of using science as a rationalization of existing economic and social relations in society. This tradition extends from Adam Smith and Robert Malthus to the present, all in the name of the relations between nature and human nature. I will not have time to consider Adam Smith, but his own 'scientific' analysis of the economy was a justification of *laissez-faire* and of the hierarchical division of labour.[22] If we turn to Thomas Robert Malthus, and if we read a late edition of his work, as Darwin did, we find that the clear ideological assumptions behind his argument are overlaid by ever-growing masses of statistical data. (It is one of those books which accreted as it went through editions.) But if one looks at the first edition, one finds that it was a polemic, and avowedly so, against revolutionary utopian and anarchist views, addressed specifically to Rousseau, Condorcet and Godwin.

I want to quote a few passages towards the end of his argument, just to give some idea. Malthus's *Essay on the Principle of Population* is supposed to be the foundation of the modern mathematical treatment of man's relationship to nature. Malthus says that 'The savage would slumber for ever under his tree unless he were roused from his torpor by the cravings of hunger or the pinchings of cold, and the exertions that he makes to avoid these evils, by procuring food, and building himself a covering, are the exercises which form and keep in motion his faculties, which otherwise would sink into listless inactivity.' 'Necessity has with great truth been called the mother of invention'.[23] A little later, he says:

> As the reasons, therefore, for the constancy of the laws of nature seem, even to our understandings, obvious and striking; if we return to the principle of population [the principle that population will grow geometrically while man's ability to feed himself can only grow arithmetically] and consider man as he really is, inert, sluggish, and averse from labour, unless compelled by necessity (and it is surely the height of folly to talk of man, according to our crude fancies of what he might be), we may pronounce with certainty that the world would not have been peopled, but for the superiority of the power of population to the means of subsistence. ... Had population and food increased in the same ratio, it is probable that man might never have emerged from the savage state.[24]

He says on the next page that 'If no man could hope to rise or fear to fall, in society, if industry did not bring with it its own reward and idleness its punishment, the middle parts [i.e., the middle class] would not certainly be what they now are.'[25]

I have quoted Malthus at length, because I think that his argument is a watershed for conceptions of man in nature, and I think that we still live in that watershed. It is a century and three-quarters since Malthus penned those words about the middle class. I venture to suggest that many would still accept his assertions about the middle class, but with heavy irony. Malthus's analysis set in train a double history, a history of science inextricably bound up with ideology, which embraced man as a part of nature and subject to natural laws, at the same time that the findings and laws of the scientific study of man were interpreted in a reconciling and rationalizing way, bringing men to accept the existing order of society as part of the immutable order of nature.

There are two points to be made about this: a general one about the relations between scientific naturalism as applied to man in general and the uniformity of nature on the one hand, and particular laws about particular societies on the other; and a second, deeper point which raises the problem of how much the ideological perspective is determinate in the formation of particular reputable scientific laws. Since Malthus, it has been increasingly assumed that the hopes of man for a better society are faced with two insurmountable mundane obstacles: the limits of his own nature and the niggardliness of a hostile environment. He lacks resources sufficient to exploit nature to yield plenty, and his own sloth and his own cravings produce inevitable suffering. The Malthusian argument, I stated a moment ago, is a watershed. I mean this in a general sense – that, as someone said, it cast gloom over the whole nineteenth century,[26] and I think we can find that gloom still spread over our newspapers. But, more particularly, it was a direct and specific influence in the development of the theories of evolution, on which our own interest in the biological limits of human nature depends. Thus, for example, Darwin specifically and avowedly derived his own mechanism of natural selection from Malthus. Darwin was stuck for an answer and he picked up Malthus one day in 1838 and had a proper 'Eureka!' experience.[27] Having gained respectability in biology, the same theory, now in a scientific form, emerges again as a social theory in the ideas of Walter Bagehot and in the whole development of Social Darwinism – the theories of the group of writers discussed by Raymond Williams.[28] The general conception which was put forward was the promise of progress at the cost of struggle, a conception which Malthus was offering as a modification of the belief in inevitable and relatively painless progress towards utopia. His was a more painful process of progress through struggle.

In the course of the nineteenth century the concept of progress came to depend on the theory of organic evolution. Condorcet, Benjamin Franklin, William Godwin and others had written on progress as a theoretical possibility and placed their hopes for it in the future developments of science. But, as Dubos reminds us, it was the doctrine of organic evolution – the mechanism which

Darwin developed on the basis of Malthus's theory – 'which eventually provided the theoretical basis for the concept of progressive historical change. The doctrine of evolution therefore provides one of the most striking examples of the influence of scientific knowledge on modern culture', an influence which is now almost universal.[29] Theoretical biology has introduced into human thought a new element – guaranteed progress – which pervades all aspects of traditional culture.[30] But – and this is one of the themes I wish to stress – at a price. It is a double-edged theory: progress through struggle. We must reconcile ourselves to the 'necessary' inequalities and suffering as the 'inevitable' price which we must pay for that progress.

IV

You can buy a book called *Marx and Engels on Malthus*. That is, Marx and Engels spent so much time fulminating against Malthus that somebody thought that it was worth the trouble to collect it all together in one book.[31] And the reason they did so was that the Malthusian conception – and the other ideas of classical economics which were intimately related to it – took existing social and political relations and called them natural relations. Existing social relations were rooted in the conventions of the existing power-structure, but they came to be seen as manifestations of unalterable laws of nature. Marx and Engels were utterly opposed to the claim that it is unnatural that other kinds of society might come to be. This was not only the nineteenth-century critique of Marx and Engels: if you are following the current debate, you will find that it is the same critique mounted by Georg Lukács in *History and Class Consciousness*. The same critique was mounted by Lucien Goldmann, by István Mészáros, by Wilhelm Reich, by Herbert Marcuse and by Jürgen Habermas.[32] But it is neither a new debate nor one confined to marxist circles. In the nineteenth century, the argument took place within the biological and critical literature. For example, the co-discoverer of the theory of organic evolution was Alfred Russel Wallace. Just six years after he had discovered the theory independently from Darwin, he came to consider its relationship to his own socialist beliefs. In that tussle the Malthusian aspect of evolution lost, and Wallace's socialism won out. Similarly, Henry George juxtaposed the conceptions of *Progress and Poverty*, and produced for the nineteenth century the alarming thesis that progress *produced* poverty.[33] And finally, as Raymond Williams has mentioned, Prince Kropotkin tried to say, 'Yes, of course we must base our social theory on biological theory, but let us look again at biological theory.' He found that mutual aid and co-operation were extremely important factors in evolution, balancing the role of struggle for existence.[34]

All of these views in the biological and social sphere were explicitly anti-Malthusian. One of the things I am trying to support is the claim that we are still living according to a conception of human nature which is fundamentally Malthusian. This conception lies at the bottom of our interest in ethology and psychology and genetics as potential keys to the limits of human nature. But instead of turning directly to these disciplines, I want to conduct my argument as a critique of some aspects of psychoanalysis, a discipline which depends on the same assumptions about the limits of human nature. Before doing that, however, lest you think that I am creating straw men, I should like to refer you to the arguments of Professor C. D. Darlington, which have recently been erected on the basis of genetics: that the existing order of society is as it is and as it must be because genetics says so. I have discussed this elsewhere and do not want to go into it here.[35] But I have found a new piece of evidence which I should like to share with you. This is a recent Friday Evening Discourse at the Royal Institution in London by Sir Hans Krebs, Nobel Prize Winner in Physiology and Medicine, and Professor of Biochemistry at Oxford: 'Some Facts of Life – Biology and Politics'.[36] It begins by suggesting that we take a biological approach to social problems:

My approach is based on my training as a physician and a biologist, and the thesis which I shall put forward argues that one of the roots of many troubles is an inadequate appreciation of basic biological principles – of the facts of life – which govern the conduct and well-being of *homo sapiens*.[37]

Fact No. 1: unless life is constantly renewed by hard effort, it runs down. The individual must eat and drink, and through clothing and shelter he must protect himself against the inclement environment. In a highly developed society he has to earn so that he can buy food and shelter; and to earn means that he must render some service for which somebody is willing to pay. He who does not render such service to society fails to contribute to life and has to be carried by others.[38]

Fact No. 2: is the fact that the lives of societies, such as nations, are, in principle, subject to the same laws as the lives of individuals. A nation, like an individual, has to earn its living in the face of tough competition.[39]

Fact No. 3: is the fact that *homo sapiens*, like all other species, does not by nature work unless he has an incentive. Effective incentives are the need for food and shelter, and a desire for pleasure. In the last resort these are all to be had for money, and for the great majority of *homo sapiens* (there are of course exceptions) money is the greatest single incentive for overcoming natural laziness. . . . If productive work is one of the bases on which the well-being and strength of society rests, the laws of social organization should do everything to encourage work.[40]

Successive governments, by their tax laws, have deterred people from making the optimal contribution to the welfare of the country and, indeed, unions have done the same thing by their restrictive practices. 'Let me emphasize that this is a mistake of successive governments irrespective of party. I am not concerned with party politics but with biology; the need for incentives is a biological phenomenon.'[41]

. . . a continued decrease in working hours is an unrealistic and utopian dream. The survival of nations, alas, is a matter of ruthless competition with other nations. An ineffectual or lazy nation is weak in competing in world trade because the goods that it produces are liable to be expensive. It's also slow in making weapons to defend itself against harder working nations. It may thus be starved out or destroyed by them.[42]

A strong society, then, is one where constructive work – and this of course includes the unpaid labour of the housewife and voluntary social work and creative hobbies – is planned to be healthy and efficient.[43]

(I am sure that, having read this argument, the supporters of Women's Liberation will cease forthwith to fly in the face of these 'facts of life'.)

Sir Hans Krebs goes on to talk about 'the beast in man', the genetic basis of criminality, and the failure of the law to protect society. In short, he assumes that inequality, private property and deviant behaviour are the result of unalterable laws of nature.

He also thinks that it is extremely important that society – for biological reasons, of course – should not change too rapidly because man cannot adapt to the welfare state, trade union protection, the restraining influences of competition, or changes in customs such as the new permissiveness. It is 'the responsibility of society to keep a constant watch on the consequences of any change which it introduces . . .'.[44] We must keep society in 'equilibrium' – one of the concepts which I said I wished there was space to discuss.[45] His account is also said to explain 'anti-foreigner and the anti-racial feeling and the religious strife which we at present witness in Northern Ireland'. All these attitudes have a deep biological root.[46] Krebs says we must 'face the facts' and orient our lives accordingly. All this follows 'logically', he claims, from what he has stated before, such as the biological basis of the evil-doer.[47] What we need, he concludes, is a 'spiritual revival', new 'inspiring leadership' and close attention to the 'facts of life'.[48]

Now, of course, I have chosen this because it is an easy target. But I have also chosen it because of the position which Sir Hans Krebs occupies as a professor, as a Nobel Laureate (every medical student – I had to do it when I was a medical student – has to learn the Krebs Sugar Cycle). It is the relationship between that eminence and these arguments to which I wish to draw attention. The eminence provides a licence to mount these arguments. When Richard Nixon elicits deference by extolling the 'work ethic' or national security, we are at least clear that he is talking politics; when eminent biologists do so we are increasingly finding ourselves deferring on the basis of respect for science. I take it that this is why the series of talks on 'The Limits of Human Nature' was organized, and why the latter may sell a lot of paperbacks. But I also chose to discuss Krebs's arguments, because they so neatly echo the passages from Malthus which I was quoting earlier. Malthus, Krebs and Nixon have a considerable amount in common, aside from being winners in the struggle for existence. Have we no alternative but to defer to them?

V

I think we do have an alternative and I now want to spell it out by considering a version of neo-Malthusianism. The current analogy to the dismal science of classical economics – i.e., to the arguments of Adam Smith, Malthus and Ricardo – is, I think it fair to say, the psychoanalytic view of man, one which is slowly being reinforced by and integrated with ethology. The arguments which I shall review are, in principle, based on the same sort of approach. A critique of some of the assumptions of psychoanalysis can thus lead to a general critique of science and scientism. You will recall that Freud strove mightily to formulate his theory in terms of the physico-chemical sciences. Indeed, in 1895 he engaged on a project which he wrote out and later ordered to be torn up (it wasn't), in which he tried to express his new and odd findings in strictly neurophysiological terms.[49] He later moved on to a metaphorical representation of the same conception, so that we have in the psychoanalytic theory 'mental forces', 'mental energies', 'mental structures' – that is, terms borrowed from the physical and chemical sciences and expressed metaphorically. We also have the biological conception of 'instinct'.[50] The theory of instincts provides the basic structure of psychoanalytic theory.[51]

Freud developed his views of man in society in an essay, 'Civilization and its Discontents',[52] and it is these views, as explicitly expressed there and as contained throughout his mature writings, which I wish to review through the perspectives of two theorists, Wilhelm Reich and Herbert Marcuse. I am using this approach as an analytic tool to give us some conception of what it is like to get underneath the 'givenness' of these theories of instincts, of territory, of hierarchy, or of any other theory which claims man must be like this or that and there is nothing we can do about it. As Reich points out,

> Freud's cultural and philosophical standpoint was always that culture owes its existence to instinctual repression and renunciation. The basic idea is that cultural achievements are the result of sublimated sexual energy; from this it follows logically that sexual suppression and repression are an indispensable factor in the cultural process.

This is the 'reality principle' on which civilization depends.[53] Reich argues that 'What is correct in this theory is only that sexual suppression forms the mass psychological basis for a *certain* culture, namely, the *patriarchal authoritarian* one in all its forms. What is incorrect', he says, 'is the formulation that sexual suppression is the basis of culture in general.'[54]

It is a basic error of official psychoanalysis to think of the impulses as absolute biologically given facts; true, this is not inherent in psychoanalysis but in the mechanistic thinking of the analysts which, as is always the case with mechanistic thinking, is supplemented with metaphysical theses. Impulses also develop, change and subside.[55]

Reich also argues that anti-social impulses 'result from social repression of normal sexuality', and that 'they have to be repressed because society – rightly – does not allow them to be satisfied'.

. . . these impulses are considered *biological* facts by psychoanalysts. . . . This naïve mechanistic biologism is so difficult to unmask because it serves a definite function in our society: that of shifting the problem from the sociological to the biological realm where nothing can be done about it.[56]

Reich argues, on the other hand, that 'There is such a thing as the *sociology of the unconscious* and of antisocial sexuality, that is, a social history of the unconscious impulses with regard to their intensity as well as their contents. Not only is repression a sociological phenomenon, but also that which causes the repression.'[57]

The fact that this reality principle is *itself relative*, that it is determined by an authoritarian society and serves its purposes, this decisive fact goes carefully unmentioned; to mention this, they say, is 'politics' and science has nothing to do with politics. They refuse to see the fact that not to mention it is also politics.[58]

When psychoanalysis does not dare to accept the consequences of its findings, it points to the allegedly non-political (unpragmatic) character of the science, while, in fact, every step of the psychoanalytic theory and of the practice deals with political (pragmatic) issues.[59]

The compulsive moral point of view of the political reaction is that of an absolute antithesis between biological impulse and social interest. Based on this antithesis, the reaction points to the necessity of moral regulation; for, they say, were one to 'eliminate morals', the 'animal instincts' would gain the upper hand and this would 'lead to chaos'. It is evident that the formula of the threatening social chaos is nothing but the fear of human instincts.[60]

'What is meant by social order', he argues, is the particular, and in his view 'the *reactionary* social order, and by personality development is meant the development of a personality which is capable of *adjusting* to *that* order'.[61] He talks in particular about the role of the family. One of the conceptions which lies at the root of psychoanalytic assumptions is that the psychoanalytic drama is worked out within the family. In a similar way the studies in ethology, e.g., the studies of rearing of monkeys, take particular sorts of family relationship as basic. Reich wants to offer a critique of the family, a critique of the concept of work, and of all the things which are taken as fixed and unalterable in the project of research on the limits of human nature. He points out that the role of the family has changed in the development of modern society from a primarily economic to a political function.

Its cardinal function, that for which it is mostly supported and defended by conservative science and law, is that of serving as *a factory for authoritarian ideologies* and conservative structures. It forms the educational apparatus through which practically every individual of our society, from the moment of drawing his first breath, has to pass. It influences the child in the sense of a reactionary ideology not only as an authoritarian institution, but also on the strength of its own structure; it is the conveyor belt between the economic structure of conservative society and its ideological superstructure; its reactionary atmosphere must needs become inextricably implanted in every one of its members. Through its own form, and through direct influencing, it conveys not only conservative ideologies and conservative attitudes towards the existing social order; in addition, on the basis of the sexual structure to which it owes its existence and which it procreates, it exerts an immediate influence on the sexual structure of the children in the conservative sense.[62]

The basis of the middle class family is the relationship of the patriarchal father to wife and children. He is as it were the exponent and representative of the authority of the state in the family. Because of the contradiction between his position in the production process (subordinate) and his family function (boss) he is a top-sergeant type; he kowtows to those above, absorbs the prevailing attitudes (hence his tendency to imitation) and dominates those below; he transmits the government and social concepts and enforces them.[63]

'The anchoring of sexual morality and the changes it brings about in the organism, create specific psychic structures which form', Reich argues, 'the mass psychological basis for an authoritarian social order.' He concludes that 'the evaluation of the family thus becomes the keystone for the evaluation of the general nature of different kinds of social order'.[64]

I am not asking you to agree with this point of view, but only to notice that he has adopted a critical attitude to what is taken as biologically fixed in the orthodoxy of psychoanalysis, of ethological studies, and, *a fortiori*, to the belief that you can mount very general social and political arguments on the basis of genetics or any branch of the biological sciences. Let me take an example which makes criticisms of Reich's work based on ethology. In his disappointing book on Reich, Charles Rycroft argues: 'His whole political, social and sexual stance can indeed be interpreted as a massive rejection or dismissal of the problem of dominance in human relationships. It was, he believed, possible to conceive of a world in which nobody dominated anybody in any way whatsoever.' I said that I was going to attempt to illuminate assertions about ethology by discussing psychoanalysis. Rycroft goes on: 'One again wonders what he would have made of the recent ethological work which suggests that the establishment of hierarchies, in which each member of a group has and knows his place, is one of the basic biological mechanisms for maintaining peace and cohesion within groups.'[65] Thus, Reich's arguments are decisively refuted by the pecking-order in any farmer's henyard.

This cryptic dismissal of Reich's views on dominance and hierarchies should not be taken lightly. There is a developing alliance between orthodox psychoanalysis and the rapidly-growing field of speculation based on the study of animal behaviour, ethology. For our purposes, this marriage of ideological convenience begins with certain speculations (*On Aggression*) which Konrad Lorenz, the father of much of both scientific and 'pop' ethology, developed while working with American psychoanalysts.[66] On the particular question of dominance, my own fleeting reference to the pecking-order in a farmer's henyard refers to the beginnings of the modern ethological investigation of one organism's keeping another in check by threatening behaviour. This competitiveness had been justified on economic and then biological grounds throughout the nineteenth century.[67] But since the observations of domestic fowls by the Norwegian zoologist Thorlief Schjelderup-Ebbe in 1913, the alleged biological basis for the hierarchical division of labour has received renewed support from the study of animal behaviour.[68] The generalizations and extrapolations which have been based on this and on other studies are now much disputed. For example, one recent critical reviewer of the shortcomings of social dominance theory remarks:

There remains the problem of why social dominance came to be accepted as the normal structuring mechanism of primate societies. There is a great deal of evidence indicating that the early studies which contributed so much towards the establishment of the concept as a normal structuring mechanism, were in fact studies of populations under severe social stress.[69]

But the caution with which these concepts are treated in the professional literature has not inhibited popularizers of ethology from making the sorts of remarks which give critics of the critics of orthodox psychoanalysis – e.g., Rycroft – a confident air. For example, in one of the most widely-read works in this genre, Desmond Morris says of us 'naked apes', 'As primates we were already loaded with the hierarchy system. This is the basic way of primate life.'[70] More recently, two South African authors have devoted an entire book to the issue: *The Dominant Man: The Mystique of Personality and Prestige.* Here are some representative passages from their chapters 'Animal Dominance' and 'The Submissive Personality': 'History and anthropology demonstrate that all human societies are organized around some kind of dominance hierarchy . . .'. But, they say, this must be seen in the light of 'the animal background against which human dominance must be viewed if we want to keep it in its proper biological perspective . . .'.[71]

In a matter of two or three decades, the ethologists have brought about a revolution in man's understanding of his social behaviour. . . . In particular, we now know that a type of dominance that can scarcely be distinguished from human dominance is characteristic of all socially organized birds and mammals.[72]

In fact, the dominance hierarchy, of which the chicken-yard pecking order is an elementary example, has since been shown to be the basic form of social organization in all vertebrate species.[73]

So, biology proves that society cannot be fundamentally changed, and human history reflects this 'basic form'.

Frequent reference to dominance and subordination in our day-to-day language, as well as man's long-standing dependence on the division of large communities into caste hierarchies, clearly shows the extent to which the dominance order system continues to play a central part in human affairs. In fact, the anthropologist Lionel Tiger has referred to the dominance order as the universal spinal cord of a human community. Throughout history, certain basic social patterns along pecking order lines have recurred time and again with little variation. Human communities have displayed an overwhelming tendency to stay in the well-worn grooves of dominance and submission. Political revolutions break out with brilliant new social ideas. One or two new ideas may stay, but for the most part the hierarchy system reasserts itself in a new disguise and the egalitarian movement disintegrates.[74]

Lionel Tiger and his collaborator, Robin Fox, have indeed combined anthropological, sociological and ethological arguments in support of this conclusion,[75] and it has been further supported by a recent historical and political analysis of ten modern revolutions, none of which resulted in the elimination of an hierarchical social order but which – whatever their other achievements – only produced 'the circulation of élites' in politics and society.[76] The author of *Modern Revolutions* would be the last to appeal to biology in support of his conclusions, but biologists and social scientists seem only too willing to lend a pessimistic basis to the dismal failure to transcend authoritarian structures which history does indeed indicate. We are assured in *The Dominant Man* that pre-history, history *and* genetics say that it must be so.

The result of many millions of years' development in a social direction is that every hierarchical animal now possesses the ability to abandon its competitive feelings in the presence of an acknowledged superior – a special arrangement of psychological equipment which allows a weaker animal to accept the domination of a worthy leader.[77]

The exact way in which a subordinate submits to authority will obviously vary from one species to another. The various psychological and physiological processes that contribute to the deferential behaviour of a human being will presumably be more amenable than most to cultural conditioning. Nevertheless, the presence of an underlying genetic foundation is beyond question.[78]

Man, like every other successful vertebrate, has evidently inherited a well-developed capacity for deference which checks his dominance ambitions at appropriate moments. . . . Since everybody must settle for a unique interpersonal position relative to everybody else's, we are left with a society of unequals.[79]

I have quoted this book at length as a parallel to my treatment of Sir Hans Krebs's 'Facts of Life' and for the same reasons. I have done so before concluding my remarks on Reich's critique of psychoanalysis, in order to help us to see what we are up against in attempting to take a critical approach to various forms of biologism. Reich was deeply critical of Freudian biologism, 'the tendency to treat as universal and biologically inevitable attitudes and impulses' which can be equally argued to be determined by cultural conditions. He rejected biologism and accepted Freud's early view 'that neurosis is basically the result of the conflict between instinctual needs and the reality which frustrates them', but he felt that the outcome of this conflict was not biologically predetermined. The problem was one of altering the social reality rather than of succumbing to Freud's pessimistic cultural philosophy, with its roots in biologistic fatalism. Rather than seeing society as the result of a biologically-based psychic structure, he saw character-structure as the result of a certain kind of society.[80] 'As soon as an ideology has taken root in the structure of people and has altered it, it has become a material social power.'[81] His advocacy of psychoanalysis was combined with a critical approach to its implicit support for authoritarian society. He argued that bourgeois society produces the character structure it requires by means of the mediation of social institutions.

His criticisms of authoritarianism in the family, the school and in religion were based on an attempt to integrate his marxism with his psychoanalytic work. Where Freud saw a contradiction between marxism and psychoanalysis, Reich used aspects of each to provide illumination and evaluation of the other. He was as critical of official communist orthodoxy as he was of the orthodox Freudians, and was also an early explorer of the parallels between Hitler's fascism and Stalin's. All three orthodoxies reviled him: he was expelled from Freud's circle as well as from the Communist Party, he had to flee from Hitler's Germany, and his works were banned by the Gestapo.

Nearly four decades have elapsed since his early work, which is now being separated from the eccentricities of his later ideas, his bizarre theories and his tragic end in an American prison.[82] If we want to learn about the role of ideology in our definitions of 'the limits of human nature', a critical reading of Reich's work is of great potential benefit, especially *The Mass Psychology of*

Fascism, The Sexual Revolution and his pamphlets 'What is Class Consciousness?' and 'Dialectical Materialism and Psychoanalysis'.[83]

VI

Now I want to discuss Marcuse for a while. I am lumping Marcuse and Reich together, rather than splitting them, although there are important differences between them.[84] For example, Marcuse argued that Reich failed to make any essential distinction between repressive and non-repressive sublimation, and that Reich's sociological insights involve what Marcuse calls 'a sweeping primitivism'. He agreed with Reich's emphasis on instinctual repression as the root cause of authoritarianism and deference to it but disagreed with Reich's belief that it could be overcome by concentrating on sexual liberation.[85] Marcuse raises the same sorts of issues that I have been discussing but in a slightly more precise and systematic (and therefore less personally resonant) form. He grants that there is such a thing as the reality to which man must adapt, but he wants to distinguish the inescapable aspects of that reality from those aspects which are peculiar to the existing social order. That is, he wants to make a distinction between the Freudian reality principle and the extra requirements of existing societies which he calls the 'performance principle'.[86] Similarly, he wants to make a distinction between the legitimate domain of repression and that extra or 'surplus' repression which is attributable to specific social orders.[87] And finally, he wants to note that 'sublimation' is not easily put aside, in the sense that one can come along and say, 'Oh! we now have a permissive society'. Society can and does offer that kind of permissiveness in a repressive form which he calls 'repressive de-sublimation'.[88] He makes an analogous argument at the straightforward political level about the concept of tolerance – that you can let tolerance flower in a way which is objectively repressive, just as you can de-sublimate in a way which is objectively repressive.[89] Like Reich, Marcuse argues that psychoanalysis – which represents itself as based on biology – is fundamentally social and historical. He turns psychoanalysis against itself, and claims that the Freudian theory of instincts makes it possible to understand the hidden nature of certain decisive tendencies in current politics. He points out that the basic psycho-analytic concepts are social and political. They 'do not have to be "related" to social and political conditions – they are themselves social and political categories'. Thus, he argues that Freud 'discovered the mechanisms of social and political control in the depth dimension of instinctual drives and satisfactions'.[90] In the Freudian account of socialization, the superego absorbs the authoritarian models of 'the father and his representatives, and makes their commands and prohibitions its own laws, the individual's conscience'.[91] Thus, 'The individual reproduces on the deepest level, in his instinctual structure, the values and behaviour patterns that serve to maintain domination. . . .'[92] This occurs within the family, which reflects the dominant patterns in the society. He goes further and claims that society has proceeded to take some of these functions out of the hands of the family and place them in the schools, in the mass media, and in other public forms.[93]

Marcuse maintains that if we take seriously the possibilities of liberation, we must acknowledge that our struggles will fly in the face of conceptions of 'the biologically given', and transcend 'the laws of nature' as now conceived. His argument rests on two assertions. The first is that science has created the means to overcome the scarcities, the struggle for existence, on which the pessimistic and repressive social extrapolations from biology depend. This point is related to a deeper one – that all human needs have an *historical* character. They are not merely fixed by inheritance. They 'lie beyond the animal world. They are historically determined and historically mutable.'[94]

When Marcuse was asked point-blank if he meant quite literally that this would involve a 'qualitative transformation of the physiological structure of man' he said yes, but added that human nature is not merely physiological. It is historically determined and develops in history. Man does not thereby cease to have a natural history, but he can be freed from its character of struggle for existence, and authoritarianism and alienation, by our placing the techniques of advanced technology in the service of democracy rather than domination.[95] Elsewhere, in his *Essay on Liberation*, Marcuse equivocates on this point, and says that he does not use the terms 'biological' and 'biology' in the scientific sense.[96] But he turns around about ten pages later and writes about changing the instinctual nature of man.[97] I make this point about his equivocation, because I do not want it to be thought that the Right has a monopoly on biologization. Both Reich and Marcuse – and indeed Reich to an absurd extent in his later life – attempted to base their claims about the social changes they wanted, on exactly the kinds of biological assumptions which they are criticizing in the works of traditional theorists.[98]

What I want to emphasize about these arguments, however, is that they are deeply anti-Malthusian – or perhaps I should say post-Malthusian. That is, Malthus and Freud argued that 'Progress is only possible through the transformation of instinctual energy into the socially useful energy of labour, that is, progress is only possible as sublimation.[99] Culture, according to Freud, '*is* sublimation: postponed, methodically controlled satisfaction which presupposes unhappiness. The "struggle for existence", "scarcity", and co-operation all compel renunciation and repression in the interests of security, order, and living together.'[100] But the very achievements of Malthusian and Freudian sublimation have opened the way to its transcendence. The repressive reality principle becomes superfluous to the extent that civilization is no longer oppressed by the kinds of scarcity, the struggle for existence, which have led to our seeing them as absolute laws of nature. So the achievements of repressive progress can 'herald the abolition of the repressive principle of progress itself'.[101] 'What on more primitive cultural levels was – perhaps – not only a social but also a biological necessity for the further development of the species has become, at the height of civilization, a merely social, political "necessity" for maintaining the status quo.'[102] We have here an analogy to Reich's views on the family. The reality principle has changed functions, from that of necessity in the biological sense to that of necessity in the political and ideological sense. Marcuse claims that '... at the present stage of civilization, much of the toil, renunciation, and regulation imposed upon men is no longer justified by scarcity, the struggle for existence, poverty, and weakness'.[103]

As I said, I have stressed the similarities between Reich and Marcuse, but there are important differences. Reich considered Freud's essay 'Civilization and its Discontents' an unmitigated disaster, and he rejected the Freudian antithesis between life and death instincts, between love and aggression, Eros and Thanatos. Marcuse accepted the distinction but wanted to modify it. But if we look at their respective later works, we find Reich moving (as he became more paranoid) towards an antithesis between basic energies – good and bad (there was the bad orgone for those who are connoisseurs of Reich) – while Marcuse (I think under a certain amount of pressure from the student movement) became more overtly libertarian. Marcuse advocated some forms of sublimation, but Reich went much further and stressed the genuinely liberating potential of unqualified desublimation. Thus we find them on some kind of continuum extending from Freud's conventional Malthusian pessimism, in which civilization depends on repression; to Marcuse's modified view, in which you divide between a natural and a conventional aspect (that is, between proper repression and surplus repression, between a reality-principle and a performance-principle) and in which the role of the second aspect of these was particular to existing societies as distinct from possible ones; and finally to Reich's nearly pure libertarianism, which led ultimately to arguments for sexual revolution which concentrated on what might be called 'the politics of intimacy' at the expense of more traditional radical strategies. Achieving orgiastic release was increasingly seen by Reich as prior to attempts to change social and political structures in the public world.

Marcuse and Reich have in common a critique of what Freud takes to be 'given' and 'natural', fixed and inevitable. They consider man's alleged instinctual limitations to be problematic and historical. They may be 'given' for the individual, but they are not assimilable to the immutable laws of nature. Rather, they are reflections of a particular historical conjuncture, and different men with a different consciousness, not fettered with Malthusian, Freudian, ethological, and/or genetic pessimism, might try to bring about a different world.

I hope that I have laid the groundwork for making comprehensible one of Marcuse's more abstract passages on the need to transcend present views of science, of nature and of human nature:

In Nature as well as in History, the struggle for existence is the token of scarcity, suffering and want. They are the qualities of blind matter, of the realm of immediacy in which life passively suffers its existence. This realm is gradually mediated in the course of the historical transformation of Nature; it becomes part of the human world, and to this extent, the qualities of Nature are historical qualities. In the process of civilization, Nature ceases to be mere Nature to the degree to which the struggle of blind forces is comprehended and mastered in the light of freedom.

And, to the degree to which Reason succeeds in subjecting matter to rational standards and aims, all sub-rational existence appears to be want and privation, and their reduction becomes the historical task. Suffering, violence, and destruction are categories of the natural as well as human reality, of a helpless and heartless universe. The terrible notion that the sub-rational life of nature is destined forever to remain such a universe, is neither a philosophic nor a scientific one. . . .[104]

Rather, its role is political in the widest sense: 'Glorification of the natural is part of the ideology which protects an unnatural society in its struggle against liberation.'[105]

VII

I want, finally, to consider some of the wider implications of this critique. Marcuse points out that if we are going to take a transcending view of human nature, then we must also take a transcending view of science. Once we have unmasked the political character of much which passes for the 'given' in nature and human nature, then we have to go on to see that there is an intimate relationship between our scientific views and our political views. Marcuse says: 'But this development confronts science with the unpleasant task of becoming *political* – of recognizing scientific consciousness as political consciousness, and the scientific enterprise as political enterprise.'[106]

Much depends on the way one asks the questions and what one is prepared to accept as answers. Of course one would find limits to an ideological approach to science and nature, as anybody who was wanting to have some wheat in the Soviet Union during the Lysenko period could tell you.[107] At the same time, to be naïve about the role of political assumptions in science is to acquiesce in a particular representation of man, one which is in the service of a particular social order.

We can generalize the discussion in the light of the views of Lukács, Marcuse and Habermas. One of Habermas's disciples, Trent Schroyer, argues that 'Contemporary science and technology

serve as a new strategy for legitimating power and privilege.'
'Insofar as the practice of the scientific establishment is held to
be neutral' and applicable to all aspects of society 'while actually
justifying the extension of repressive control systems, we can
assert that the contemporary self-image of science functions as
an all-embracing 'technocratic ideology'.[108] The gap of which I
spoke before, between the general principles of scientific naturalism and particular problems of man in society, has been filled by
the scientistic self-image of science. Where knowledge is absent,
extrapolation fills the domain of the moral and political debate
about the conflicting goals and interests of men. '"Scientism"
means science's belief in itself: that is, the conviction that we can
no longer understand science as *one* form of possible knowledge,
but rather must identify [all] knowledge with science.'[109] Indeed,
Schroyer claims that 'the scientistic image of science has become
a dominant legitimating system of advanced industrial society'.[110]
More and more spheres of decision-making are being seen in a
technological and scientific way, requiring information and
instrumental strategies formulated by experts, and are therefore
removed from political and moral debate.[111]

Now, I want to cast us back to Marx. He was able to formulate
his critique against a particular set of economic doctrines – the
classical economics of Smith, Malthus and Ricardo. We are
forced to broaden ours in the face of this kind of generalization
of science, to the whole 'scientistic' theory of science itself, an
approach which Schroyer sees as 'the fundamental false consciousness of our epoch'.[112] If we are going to begin to free ourselves from this defeatist approach; it seems to me that we have to
take a critical view of science, one which demystifies the treatment
of men as things, completely assimilable to the laws of the natural
sciences as now understood and as illegitimately generalized.
This is the project which we are engaged upon when we criti-
cize the belief that we can find the limits of human nature.
And if we fail to seek the human limits of nature we will find ourselves in the position where the distinction between deliberate,
reasoned, debated social action and adaptive, technological
deferential action breaks down.[113] That is, the distinction is
becoming meaningless without the kinds of critical reflection in
which I think Reich and Marcuse, for all their undoubted faults,
have been engaged. If we do not take this kind of approach, we

shall find ourselves in the curious position of freeing man from the tyranny of nature, of transcending the struggle for existence, but replacing that freedom with a perfectly assimilated social coercion, again in the name of nature and of science. Science therefore becomes the ideology of power, a totalized world view which produces a fatalism on the one hand, and amenability to technological manipulation on the other. The alternative is a critical and transcending view of science, one which looks hard at its reifications, its fetishisms, its role in alienation, and, indeed, at the whole scientistic programme.

I am not suggesting that science is merely ideology, but that it is ideology as well. This is especially true of debates about human nature. Our concepts of nature and human nature are to a considerable extent mediations of our social, economic, political and ideological preconceptions. When we turn to experts for knowledge of the limits of human nature we are engaged in more far-reaching and fundamental forms of deference than we realize. Marx taught us that exchange relationships, commodities, even the means of production, are only the social relations and the labour of men in an intransigent, fetishized, reified and alienated disguise. We should ask ourselves the extent to which our ideas of nature and human nature are exactly the same thing. Ideology is an all-pervasive material force, penetrating into our most intimate and subjective relationships as well as into our putatively disinterested inquiries in the biological and human sciences. We must recover our right to define our own nature through our struggles to overcome our limitations. One component of this is the need to demystify the limits of human nature. As Reich said, 'We must get into the habit of subjecting every fetishised matter to the glaring light of naïve questions, which are notoriously the most testing, the most promising and the most far-reaching.'[114]

This is not, of course, an entirely new view of science. In earlier periods there were rich and deep criticisms of science which juxtaposed its presumption with human moral values. They are worth re-reading: Marlowe's *Doctor Faustus*, Swift's *Gulliver's Travels*, Mary Shelley's *Frankenstein*, Zamiatin's *We*. Then, perhaps, we can approach B. F. Skinner's *Walden Two* and *Beyond Freedom and Dignity*, and some other works which I have mentioned, with less deferential attitudes. We might even begin to see the need to

264   *Criticism*

move on from interpreting the world in various fatalistic ways, to changing it.

1 Robert M. Young, 'Association of Ideas', in Philip P. Wiener, ed., *Dictionary of the History of Ideas* (Scribner's, New York: in press).
2 R. M. Young, *Mind, Brain and Adaptation in the Nineteenth Century* (Oxford University Press, 1970); 'The Role of Psychology in the Nineteenth-Century Evolutionary Debate', in Mary Henle *et al.*, eds., *Contribution to the History of Psychology* (Springer, New York: in press).
3 Henri F. Ellenberger, *The Discovery of the Unconscious: The History and Evolution of Dynamic Psychiatry* (Allen Lane The Penguin Press, 1970, esp. Chs. 4, 5, 7).
4 Henri Lefebvre, *The Sociology of Marx* (1966); trans. Norbert Guterman (Allen Lane, 1968; also paperback), ch. 3, p. 64.
5 ibid.
6 ibid., p. 70.
7 ibid., pp. 65–6.
8 ibid., p. 65.
9 ibid., p. 71.
10 ibid., p. 70.
11 ibid., p. 80.
12 ibid., p. 69.
13 Karl Marx and Frederick Engels, *The German Ideology* (1845–7); trans. Clemens Dutt *et al.* (Progress, Moscow 1964); there are a number of paperback editions of selections, for example the one edited, with an Introduction, by C. J. Arthur (Lawrence & Wishart, 1970).
14 Lefebvre, op. cit., p. 68. The internal quotation is from the classical passage in *The German Ideology* (Progress edition), p. 61.
15 Jürgen Habermas, *Knowledge and Human Interests* (1968), Appendix: 'Knowledge and Human Interests: A General Perspective' (1965), trans. Jeremy J. Shapiro (Heinemann, 1972; also paperback), p. 311.
16 For a representative selection of Herbert Spencer's views, see *The Man versus the State, with Four Essays on Politics and Society*, edited, with an Introduction, by Donald MacRae (Penguin Books, Harmondsworth 1969). For Huxley's criticisms, see Thomas H. Huxley, *Evolution and Ethics and Other Essays* (1886–94), *Collected Essays*, vol. 9 (Macmillan, 1894).
17 Liam Hudson has made a promising beginning to an analysis of the role of ideology in psychology in *The Cult of the Fact* (Cape, 1972), esp. ch. 11; cf. David Ingleby, 'Ideology and the Human Sciences: Some Comments on the Role of Reification in Psychology and Psychiatry', in *Counter Course: A Handbook for Course Criticism*, ed. Trevor Pateman (Penguin Books, Harmondsworth 1972), pp. 51–81.
18 René Dubos, 'Science and Man's Nature', in *Science and Culture*, ed. Gerald Holton (Beacon paperback, Boston 1967), pp. 251–72, esp. pp. 259–60.

19 See p. 13.
20 See p. 49 ff.
21 See p. 158 ff.
22 See Adam Smith, *An Inquiry into the Nature and Causes of the Wealth of Nations* (1776). A convenient edition is the Everyman, 2 vols. (Dent, 1910, etc; and Dutton, New York). Cf. R. M. Young, 'Darwinism and the Division of Labour' (a sketch from Smith to the present), in *Listener* 88, No. 2264 (17 August 1972), pp. 202–5.
23 Thomas Robert Malthus, *An Essay on the Principle of Population, as it Affects the Future Improvement of Society with Remarks on the Speculations of Mr. Godwin, M. Condorcet, and Other Writers* (1798); a convenient reprint of the first edition, from which these passages are quoted, is edited, with an introduction, by Antony Flew (Penguin Books, Harmondsworth 1970), p. 203.
24 ibid., pp. 205–6.
25 ibid., p. 207.
26 Humphrey House, 'The Mood of Doubt', in *Ideas and Beliefs of the Victorians* (Dutton paperback, New York 1966), pp. 71–7.
27 R. M. Young, 'Malthus and the Evolutionists: The Common Context of Biological and Social Theory', *Past and Present* No. 43 (May 1969), pp. 109–45, esp. pp. 128–9.
28 See p. 115 ff.
29 Dubos, op. cit., pp. 253–4. Strictly speaking, the theory was jointly discovered by Charles Darwin and Alfred Russel Wallace, and its popularization as the basis for a theory of social progress owed more to Herbert Spencer than to Darwin and Wallace. However, it is 'Darwinism' which gave scientific respectability to the general conception. For a discussion of the public debate and its relations with the idea of progress, see R. M. Young, 'The Impact of Darwin on Conventional Thought', in *The Victorian Crisis of Faith*, ed. Anthony Symondson (S.P.C.K., 1970), pp. 13–35.
30 Dubos, op. cit.
31 *Marx and Engels on Malthus*, ed. Ronald L. Meek, trans. Dorothea L. and R. L. Meek (International, New York 1954; also paperback).
32 In a general essay of this kind it would be tedious and pointless to cite much of the relevant literature, so I shall only mention certain key works. I have attempted to provide a general overview of science and its history from a radical perspective – with particular reference to the nineteenth-century debate – in 'The Historiographic and Ideological Contexts of the Nineteenth-Century Debate on Man's Place in Nature', *Changing Perspectives in the History of Science*, ed. Mikuláš Teich and R. M. Young (Heinemann, 1973), pp. 344–438. These issues are related to the current debate in an earlier paper 'Evolutionary Biology and Ideology: Then and Now', in *Science Studies* 1 (1971), pp. 177–206. Both of these papers are extensively annotated. The present essay is in some ways an extension of those articles while at the same time it is intended to be both more accessible to the general reader and a more particular application of the issues raised therein, concentrating as it does on the relations

266   *Criticism*

between biology and psychology. See Georg Lukács, *History and Class Consciousness* (1923); new edn (1967) with Preface, trans. Rodney Livingstone (Merlin, 1971); Lucien Goldmann, *The Human Sciences and Philosophy* (1966), trans. Hadden V. White and R. Anchor (Cape, 1969; also paperback); István Mészáros, *Marx's Theory of Alienation*, 2nd edn (Merlin, 1970; also paperback); Wilhelm Reich, *The Mass Psychology of Fascism* (1933), 3rd edn, revised and enlarged, trans. Vincent R. Carfagno (Farrar, Straus & Giroux, New York 1969; also paperback); Herbert Marcuse, *One Dimensional Man: the Ideology of Industrial Society* (Routledge & Kegan Paul, 1964; also paperback); Jürgen Habermas, *Toward a Rational Society: Student Protest, Science, and Politics* (1968–9), trans. Jeremy J. Shapiro (Heinemann, 1971; also paperback), esp. ch. 6; see also above, note 15 and below notes 51, 53, 80–86, 88–90, 96, 98.

33 See R. M. Young, '"Non-Scientific" Factors in the Darwinian Debate', *Actes du XIIᵉ Congrès International d'Histoire des Sciences* (Blanchard, Paris 1971), vol. 8, pp. 221–6.

34 Peter Kropotkin, *Mutual Aid: a Factor of Evolution* (1902; Allen Lane The Penguin Press, 1972); see also p. 125.

35 C. D. Darlington, *The Evolution of Man and Society* (Allen & Unwin, 1969); R. M. Young, 'Understanding It All', *New Statesman* 78 (26 September 1969), pp. 417–18; cf. 'Evolutionary Biology and Ideology: Then and Now', op. cit. (note 32), pp. 188, 205.

36 *Proceedings of the Royal Institution of Great Britain* 44 (1971), pp. 169–184; reprinted in *Perspectives in Biology and Medicine* 15 (1972), pp. 491–506.

37 ibid., pp. 170–1.

38 ibid., pp. 171–2.

39 ibid., p. 172.

40 Loc. cit.

41 ibid., p. 173.

42 ibid., pp. 173–4.

43 ibid., p. 174.

44 ibid., p. 179.

45 The ideological use of the concepts of adaptation and equilibrium have been touched upon in Cynthia E. Russett, *The Concept of Equilibrium in American Social Thought* (Yale, New Haven 1966), and Barbara Heyl, 'The Harvard "Pareto Circle"', *J. Hist. Behav. Sci.* 4 (1968), pp. 316–334.

46 Krebs, 'Some Facts of Life', op. cit. (note 36), p. 180.

47 ibid., p. 181.

48 ibid., pp. 180, 181, 183.

49 Sigmund Freud, 'Project for a Scientific Psychology' (1895), in *The Standard Edition of the Complete Psychological Works of Sigmund Freud* (Hogarth, 1966), vol. 1, pp. 283–346; M. Peter Amacher, *Freud's Neurological Education and its Influence on Psychoanalytic Theory* (International Universities, New York 1965); Karl H. Pribram, 'The Neuropsychology of Sigmund Freud', in *Experimental Foundations of Clinical Psychology*,

ed. Arthur J. Bachrach (Basic Books, New York 1962), pp. 442–68; 'The Foundation of Psychoanalytic Theory: Freud's Neuropsychological Model', in *Adaptation: Selected Readings*, ed. K. H. Pribram (Penguin Books, Harmondsworth 1969), pp. 395–432.

50 Sigmund Freud, *The Interpretation of Dreams* (1900), in *Standard Edition*, vols. IV–V, esp. ch. vii; 'Instincts and their Vicissitudes' (1915) and 'The Unconscious' (1915), ibid., vol. XIV, pp. 109–40, 159–215; *The Ego and the Id* (1923), ibid., vol. XIX, pp. 3–66; *New Introductory Lectures on Psycho-analysis* (1933), lecture xxxi: 'The Dissection of the Psychical Personality', ibid., vol. XXII; Siegfried Bernfield, 'Freud's Earliest Theories and the School of Helmholtz' in *Psychoanalytic Quarterly* 13 (1944), pp. 341–62; 'Freud's Scientific Beginnings', *Amer. Imago* 6 (1949), pp. 3–36; 'Sigmund Freud, M.D., 1882–1885', *International Journal of Psycho-analysis* 32 (1951), pp. 204–17; David Rapaport and Merton M. Gill, 'The Points of View and Assumptions of Metapsychology', ibid., 40 (1959), pp. 153–62; David Rapaport, *The Structure of Psychoanalytic Theory: A Systematizing Attempt* (International Universities, New York 1960) – both of these are reprinted in *The Collected Papers of David Rapaport*, ed. M. M. Gill (Basic Books, New York 1967), along with other pertinent articles. The physical and physiological aspects of Freud's approach are also discussed at length in the first volume of Ernest Jones, *The Life and Work of Sigmund Freud*, 3 vols. (Basic Books, New York 1953–7).

51 Although many aspects of the psychoanalytic movement – and in particular the school known as 'ego psychology' – have played down the role of instinct, it would be difficult to convince a serious reader of Freud's own work that his views were not fundamentally based on a theory of instincts as the biological basis for the individual's personality and for social behaviour. Whatever reservations might be held about the relations between Freud's views and those of Wilhelm Reich, Reich's exposition of Freud's fundamental theories makes this point convincingly. See W. Reich, *Dialectical Materialism and Psychoanalysis* (1929), trans. anon. (Socialist Reproduction pamphlet, 1972), pp. 20 ff.

52 Sigmund Freud, 'Civilization and its Discontents' (1930), *Standard Edition*, vol. XXI, pp. 59–145; cf. *The Future of An Illusion* (1927), ibid., pp. 3–56 and *Beyond the Pleasure Principle* (1920), ibid., vol. XVIII, pp. 3–64. The following works provide useful short introductions to Freud's thought: Charles Brenner, *An Elementary Textbook of Psychoanalysis* (International Universities, New York 1955; also Anchor paperback); Richard Wollheim, *Freud* (Fontana paperback, 1971).

53 Wilhelm Reich, *The Sexual Revolution: Toward a Self-Governing Character Structure* (1930), trans. Theodore P. Wolfe, 4th edn (1949), revised (Vision, 1969; also paperback), p. 10.

54 ibid.
55 ibid., p. xxx.
56 ibid., p. 17.
57 ibid., p. 18.
58 ibid., p. 19.

59 ibid., p. 20.
60 ibid., p. 22.
61 ibid., pp. 40–1.
62 ibid., p. 72.
63 ibid., p. 73.
64 ibid., p. 79.
65 Charles Rycroft, *Reich* (Fontana paperback, 1971), p. 56.
66 Konrad Lorenz, *On Aggression* (1963), trans. Marjorie Latzke (Methuen, 1966; also paperback), pp. ix–xiii. When Lorenz spoke about his growing belief that the findings of ethology could be integrated with those of psychoanalysis, at a meeting of experimental ethologists in Cambridge in the early 1960s, he was met with a scepticism which was very prescient in the light of subsequent further popularizations and speculations. This scientific caution has since been united with a political critique of the ideological role of both psychoanalysis and 'pop' ethology. For an example of the liaison between ethology and psychoanalysis as seen from the psychoanalytic side, see Anthony Storr, *Human Aggression* (Allen Lane, 1968), dedicated to Lorenz, who on the dust-jacket praises the book as 'a real synthesis of psychoanalytical and ethological thought'.
67 See p. 265, note 22.
68 T. Schjelderup-Ebbe, 'Social Behavior of Birds' in *Handbook of Social Psychology*, ed. Carl Murchison (Clark, Worcester, Massachusetts 1935), pp. 947–72.
69 J. S. Gartlan, 'Structure and Function in Primate Society', in *Folia Primat.* 8 (1968), pp. 89–120, esp. p. 115; cf. T. E. Rowell, 'Hierarchy in the Organization of a Captive Baboon Group', in *Animal Behaviour* 14 (1966), pp. 430–43; Irwin S. Bernstein, 'Primate Status Hierarchies', in *Primate Behavior: Developments in Field Laboratory Research*, ed. Leonard A. Rosenblum (Academic, New York 1970), pp. 71–109. For a balanced, liberal critique of social generalizations in popular works on ethology, written by a professional physical anthropologist, see Alexander Alland, Jr, *The Human Imperative* (Columbia paperback, New York 1972).

A professional ethologist, Dr Patrick Bateson (of the Sub-Department of Animal Behaviour, University of Cambridge), points out that proponents of the view that dominance is a fundamental feature of animal and human social organization could reply that animal data are all the more relevant to the study of man *because* most human populations are 'under severe social stress'. (See Desmond Morris, *The Human Zoo* [Cape, 1969; also Corgi paperback].) Therefore, the argument runs, hierarchies are inevitable (and even desirable) in this context, and to attempt to break them down would be to treat symptoms rather than causes. A radical critique of this defence has two components. First, one should emphasize that the 'severe social stress' of human societies (especially advanced technocratic ones) is a *social* and *historical* phenomenon, and therefore amenable to alteration if one ceases to see social conventions in biologically reductionist terms. Second, to attempt to break down hierarchies without attacking their structural basis in the anti-democratic order of such societies would indeed be to treat symptoms rather than causes. This is part of the essential point of overcoming biological fatalism: as a prerequisite to believing that fundamental structural change in the social order and the resulting social relations is possible.

Turning once again to the dominance concept in ethology, Bateson argues that its inadequacy is that it provides such a partial description of social organization and has very little explanatory power. If it is observed that one individual displaces another in a particular context, the chances of predicting which one will displace the other in a different context are pretty poor. Furthermore, while dominance hierarchies are found throughout the animal kingdom (including cockroaches!), the distribution is spotty, and the available evidence supports the hypothesis that what we call 'dominance' behaviour has evolved for all sorts of disparate reasons. These reasons make the extrapolation from animal data to the layman's conception of dominance in the human hierarchical division of labour far too facile. Sophisticated ethologists are currently very wary of genetic reductionist explanations and are increasingly employing richer interpretations of behaviour which is characteristic of a given species. They are also granting a very important role to historical factors in understanding the antecedents and characteristics of human behaviour.

70 Desmond Morris, *The Naked Ape* (Cape, 1967; also paperback). The quotation is taken from the 7th (!) Canadian printing of the Bantam Books paperback edition (New York 1969) of 'The Runaway Bestseller in England and America', p. 128.

71 Humphry Knipe and George Maclay, *The Dominant Man: The Mystique of Personality and Prestige* (Souvenir, 1972), p. 2.

72 ibid., pp. 2–3.

73 ibid., p. 5.

74 ibid., p. 13.

75 Lionel Tiger, *Men in Groups* (Nelson, 1969; also paperback); Lionel Tiger and Robin Fox, 'The Zoological Perspective in Social Science', *Man* n.s. 1 (1966), pp. 74–81; *The Imperial Animal* (Secker & Warburg, 1972).

76 John M. Dunn, *Modern Revolutions: An Introduction to the Analysis of a Political Phenomenon* (Cambridge University Press, 1972; also paperback).

77 Knipe and Maclay, *The Dominant Man*, p. 21 (see note 71).

78 ibid., p. 29.

79 ibid., p. 32.

80 Paul Edwards, 'Wilhelm Reich', in *The Encyclopedia of Philosophy*, ed. P. Edwards, (Macmillan & Free Press, New York 1967), vol. 7, pp. 104–15, esp. pp. 109–10. This article is a very clear short account of Reich's ideas. A longer, though less incisive, account is: Michel Catter, *The Life and Work of Wilhelm Reich*, trans. Ghislaine Boulanger (Horizon, New York 1971).

81 Reich, *The Sexual Revolution*, p. xxvi (see note 53).

82 For a sympathetic treatment of Reich's later life, see Ilse Ollendorff Reich, *Wilhelm Reich: A Personal Biography* (St. Martin's, New York 1969; also Avon paperback).

83 See above, notes 32, 51 and 53; Wilhelm Reich, 'What is Class Consciousness?' (1933), trans. anon. (Socialist Reproduction pamphlet, 1971). The only work of Reich's which remains acceptable in orthodox psychoanalytic circles is his *Character Analysis* (1933), 3rd edn, trans. Theodore P. Wolfe (Farrar, Straus & Giroux, New York 1949; also Noonday paperback). On Reich's relationship with Freud, see *Reich Speaks of Freud*, ed. Mary Higgins and C. M. Raphael (Farrar, Straus & Giroux, New York 1967; also Noonday paperback). Reich's essays, written in the period before he emigrated to the United States, are becoming more readily available. See 'The Sexual Struggle of Youth' (Socialist Reproduction pamphlet, 1972); *Sex-Pol: Essays, 1929–1934*, ed. Lee Baxandall, with an Introduction by Bertell Ollman (Random House, New York 1972; also Vintage paperback). For related views of psychoanalysis and Marxism, see Erich Fromm, 'The Method and Function of an Analytic Social Psychology: Notes on Psychoanalysis and Historical Materialism' (1932), in Fromm, *The Crisis of Psychoanalysis: Essays on Freud, Marx and Social Psychology* (Cape, 1971), pp. 135–62. Fromm later became a socialist humanist, but this early essay is very sharply argued, while chapters 1 and 2, on the current state of psychoanalytic orthodoxy and on a social view of Freud's model of man, are illuminating.

84 For useful expositions of the ideas of Reich and Marcuse, see Paul A. Robinson, *The Freudian Left: Wilhelm Reich, Geza Roheim, Herbert Marcuse* (Harper paperback, New York 1969), published in Britain as *The Sexual Radicals* (Temple Smith, 1970; also paperback). For a political analysis of the implications of Reich's work, see Maurice Brinton, 'The Irrational in Politics' (Solidarity pamphlet No. 33, 1970). One of the most widely-available short accounts of Marcuse's work is so bad-tempered and nit-picking as to be worse than useless: Alasdair MacIntyre, *Marcuse* (Fontana paperback, 1970).

85 Rycroft, *Reich*, p. 45; Herbert Marcuse, *Counter-revolution and Revolt* (Allen Lane The Penguin Press, 1972), p. 130.

86 Herbert Marcuse, *Eros and Civilisation: A Philosophical Inquiry into Freud* (1955), with a Political Preface (1966) (Allen Lane, 1969; also Abacus paperback); Abacus edn, pp. 42, 47–52, 66–7, 158–9 and ch. 6.

87 ibid., pp. 31–4, 42.

88 Marcuse, *One Dimensional Man*, pp. 69–76. For a discussion of the history and political role of popular music which develops a critique of it in terms of repressive de-sublimation, see R. M. Young, 'A New Nation?', Bath Festival of Blues and Progressive Music, Programme June 1970, pp. 29–34. The festival was held in the heady atmosphere of libertarian hopes which were, however briefly, raised by the Woodstock Festival. The article was reprinted with reflections on the festival as 'The Functions of Rock', in *New Edinburgh Review* No. 10 (December 1970), pp. 4–14; cf. Herbert Marcuse, *Negations: Essays in Critical Theory*,

trans. Jeremy J. Shapiro (Beacon, Boston 1968; also paperback), p. 239; *Counter-revolution and Revolt*, p. 115.

89 Herbert Marcuse, 'Repressive Tolerance', in Robert P. Wolff *et al.*, *A Critique of Pure Tolerance* (Cape paperback, 1969), pp. 93–137.

90 Herbert Marcuse, *Five Lectures: Psychoanalysis, Politics and Utopia*, trans. Jeremy J. Shapiro and Shierry M. Weber (Allen Lane The Penguin Press, 1970), p. 44.

91 ibid., p. 2.

92 ibid., p. 3.

93 ibid., p. 47.

94 ibid., pp. 62, 63, 65.

95 ibid., pp. 71–2, 80–1.

96 Herbert Marcuse, *An Essay on Liberation* (Beacon paperback, Boston 1969), p. 10 n.

97 ibid., p. 21; cf. pp. 16, 17, 51, 63, 88, 91. The chapter in which these issues are mainly discussed is entitled 'A Biological Basis for Socialism?' Marcuse has returned to this issue in his latest book. See the chapter on 'Nature and Revolution' in *Counter-revolution and Revolt*.

98 Reich's appeal to *both* the politically revolutionary *and* the mystical wings of the youth movement is based on the intimate mixture of political critique, half-developed philosophical criticisms of the conceptions of traditional mind–body dualism, and very complex speculations on a putative 'life energy', the orgone. On his relevance to psychosomatic medicine, see the Translator's Preface (1941) to Wilhelm Reich, *The Function of the Orgasm* (1927) 2nd edn, trans. Theodore P. Wolfe (Panther paperback 1968), pp. 15–24. On the orgone, see Ola Raknes, *Wilhelm Reich and Orgonomy* (St Martin's, 1970; also Penguin Books, Baltimore, Maryland).

99 Marcuse, *Five Lectures*, p. 36.

100 ibid., p. 5.

101 ibid., p. 39.

102 ibid., p. 18.

103 ibid., p. 4. Related arguments in favour of the revolutionary potential of modern technology are presented by Roger Garaudy, *The Turning Point of Socialism* (1969), trans. Peter and Betty Ross (Fontana paperback, 1970), esp. chapter 1 and pp. 237–8; see also Murray Bookchin, *Post-Scarcity Anarchism* (Ramparts paperback, Berkeley 1971). This point of view ignores the problems of imperialism and the third world.

104 Marcuse, *One Dimensional Man*, p. 186.

105 ibid., p. 187; see also Habermas, *Knowledge and Human Interest*, p. 312. It is at this point that non-Marxists tend to shrug and walk away, while orthodox Marxists tend to shout abuse about Hegelian revisionism and idealism. Both reactions could benefit from an extremely careful reading of Marx, which has been made accessible to the uninitiated: Bertell Ollman, *Alienation: Marx's Conception of Man in Capitalist Society* (Cambridge 1971). On the specific issue raised here, see pp. 273 n. 35 and 285 n. 16. On the same theme, Charles Taylor writes: 'One of the

272   *Criticism*

key theses of Marxism is that human nature changes over history, that human motivation is not perennially the same, but that with the growth of consciousness, men seek new ends; their grosser needs become refined'. 'Marxism and Empiricism' in *British Analytical Philosophy*, eds. Bernard Williams and Alan Montefiore (Routledge, 1966), pp. 227–46, esp. p. 235.

106 Marcuse, *One Dimensional Man*, p. 183.

107 I have discussed this episode in the ideological definition of nature in Young, 'Evolutionary Biology and Ideology: Then and Now', *op. cit.* (note 32), at pp. 186–8, where references to the relevant literature are given; a more considered discussion of Lysenkoism will appear in the chapter 'The Ideology of Nature' in my forthcoming book, *Ideology and the Human Sciences* (Allen Lane and Doubleday, New York). The point of the example is that the hegemony of Lysenko's absurd and highly ideologically determined biological theories in Soviet agriculture produced catastrophic crop-failures.

108 Trent Schroyer, 'The Critical Theory of Late Capitalism', in Fisher, *The Revival of American Socialism: Selected Papers of the Socialist Scholars Conference*, ed. George Fisher (Oxford University Press, New York 1971; also paperback), pp. 297–321, esp. p. 297.

109 Habermas, *Knowledge and Human Interests*, p. 4 (see note 15).

110 Schroyer, op. cit., p. 301 (see note 108).

111 ibid., p. 300.

112 ibid., p. 301.

113 ibid., pp. 307–8.

114 Reich, 'What is Class Consciousness?', p. 44 (see note 83).

It has been pointed out to me that – except for one parenthesis – I have not connected the argument of this talk with the Women's Liberation movement. The remark surprised me for two reasons: first, because I had the connection in mind throughout the composition of the talk and, second, because this awareness is not, in fact, manifested in the text. On reflection, I suppose that I did not make it explicit because it has become clear to me in various ways that at the present time – and for perfectly understandable reasons – most women's liberationists are struggling against, rather than in solidarity with, men. A contribution from a man on this theme would therefore be considered male chauvinist, presumptuous and unwelcome. A second issue is that until very recently the Women's Liberation movement has concentrated on consciousness-raising in small groups and has made this approach a priority over relating its struggles to theoretical critiques. Lately, however, efforts have been made to integrate these and other activities with a more general marxist critique, although I have also heard these writers referred to dismissively as 'the theoretical heavies'.

It seems to me that there is a very large gap between the writings of Marx and Engels on the one hand and the existing Women's Lib literature on the other. (An exception is Frederick Engels, *The Origin of the Family, Private Property and the State in the Light of the Researches of*

Lewis H. Morgan, written 1884; 4th edn, 1891, trans. anon., International, New York 1942; also paperback, especially ch. 2, sect. 3.) Similarly, biological arguments have played – and continue to play – an important part in reactionary responses to attempts on the part of women and men to transcend their mutual oppression. I believe that the demystification of the search for the limits of human nature can make a contribution to the demystification of male, female and familial roles and that the arguments of Reich and Marcuse go a long way towards filling the gap mentioned above.

On the relationship between the modern family and the rise of industrial capitalism, see Philippe Ariès, *Centuries of Childhood: A Social History of Family Life*, trans. Robert Baldick (Cape, 1962; also Vintage paperback, New York). For a general discussion of the relationship between sexuality and Marxism, see Reimut Reiche, *Sexuality and Class Struggle*, trans. Susan Bennett and David Fernbach (New Left Books, 1970). Reiche's argument is based on a Marcusan interpretation of psychoanalysis and also draws on a number of Wilhelm Reich's conceptions. His discussions of current issues and practices of New Left libertarians and of 'late capitalist sexual practices' are excellent, particularly his critique of facile and mechanistic attempts to overcome repressive de-sublimation (chs. 5–7).

The literature which I have seen from the Women's Liberation movement does not seem to have drawn significantly on the writings of Reich and Marcuse. In her chapter 'Freudianism: the Misguided Feminism' in *The Dialectic of Sex* (Cape, 1971; also Paladin paperback), Shulamith Firestone praises Reich in passing and mentions Marcuse's concept of repressive de-sublimation but sees psychoanalysis as competing with and suppressing feminism. In her chapters 'The Ideology of the Family' and 'Psychoanalysis and the Family' in *Woman's Estate* (Pelican Books, Harmondsworth 1971), Juliet Mitchell mentions Marcuse and dismisses Reich in an aside which implies a valid criticism of his later writings but not those of the 1930s. She also argues that psychoanalysis – at least potentially – offers much to the cause of women's liberation. She puts the point of my argument very neatly: 'Reactionary ideology always returns us to our biological fate' (p. 171).

Kate Millett's *Sexual Politics* (Rupert Hart-Davis, 1971; also Abacus paperback) offers a well-argued critique of Freud's work and the reactionary role of orthodox psychoanalysis. She is especially incisive about the mixture of biological and social (i.e. conventional) categories under the guise of biology (Abacus edn, pp. 157–233, esp. pp. 180, 187, 190 ff.). However, her use of the ideas of Reich and Marcuse is limited. She draws on Reich primarily for insights into the role of sexual repression in supporting the authoritarianism of German fascism and also uses him as a stick with which to beat Norman Mailer. Marcuse is mentioned in passing as one who, like Reich and Horkheimer, stressed the links between patriarchialism and authoritarian governments.

The Women's Liberation literature on domination and deference fits perfectly with the arguments of Reich and Marcuse given above. Perhaps it is not too soon to suggest that women and men can begin to work together on both the theoretical front and that of praxis, although the rising movement of radical feminism indicates that this suggestion may still be premature. For an introduction to the Women's Liberation literature, see *Sisterhood is Powerful: An Anthology of Writings from the Women's Liberation Movement,* ed. Robin Morgan (Vintage paperback, New York 1970) – which concentrates on the American movement and includes a large bibliography; Michelene Wandor (compiler), *The Body Politic: Writings from the Women's Liberation Movement in Britain, 1969–1972* (Stage 1 paperback, 1972). For a comprehensive bibliography on the relationship between feminism and revolutionary politics, see Sheila Rowbotham, 'Women's Liberation and Revolution: A Bibliography' (Falling Wall Press, 1972, 79 Richmond Rd, Montpelier, Bristol, B56 5EP).

Intellectual production and reproduction are social processes, although individual 'authorship' masks this. In very different ways – and in some cases very indirectly and even unwittingly – the following people contributed to the conception and production of this essay. I want to thank them and to implicate them in the result: Jonathan Treasure, John Fekete, Derek Newton, George Gross, Rudi Dutschke, Jeremy Mulford, Sheila Young, Margot Waddell, Anne Venge, Jonathan Rosenhead, Patrick Bateson, Maureen Fallside, Jeremy Lewis, Jonathan Benthall, Martin Richards, Stephen Guyon, Tamsin Braidwood, Diana Guyon, Heather Glen, Raymond Williams, Pat Reay, Rita van der Straeten.

Index